Decolonising Justice for Aboriginal Youth with Fetal Alcohol Spectrum Disorders

This book reflects multidisciplinary and cross-jurisdictional analysis of issues surrounding Fetal Alcohol Spectrum Disorders (FASD) and the criminal justice system, and the impact on Aboriginal children, young people, and their families.

This book provides the first comprehensive and multidisciplinary account of FASD and its implications for the criminal justice system – from prevalence and diagnosis to sentencing and culturally secure training for custodial officers. Situated within a 'decolonising' approach, the authors explore the potential for increased diversion into Aboriginal community-managed, on-country programmes, enabled through innovation at the point of first contact with the police, and non-adversarial, needs-focussed courts. Bringing together advanced thinking in criminology, Aboriginal justice issues, law, paediatrics, social work, and Indigenous mental health and well-being, the book is grounded in research undertaken in Australia, Canada, and New Zealand. The authors argue for the radical recalibration of both theory and practice around diversion, intervention, and the role of courts to significantly lower rates of incarceration; that Aboriginal communities and families are best placed to construct the social and cultural scaffolding around vulnerable youth that could prevent damaging contact with the mainstream justice system; and that early diagnosis and assessment of FASD may make a crucial difference to the life chances of Aboriginal youth and their families.

Exploring how, far from providing solutions to FASD, the mainstream criminal justice system increases the likelihood of adverse outcomes for children with FASD and their families, this innovative book will be of great value to researchers and students worldwide interested in criminal and social justice, criminology, youth justice, social work, and education.

Harry Blagg is a Professor of Criminology at the University of Western Australia (UWA) Law School and Director of the Aboriginal and Torres Strait Islander Peoples and Community Justice Centre in the Law School.

Tamara Tulich is a Senior Lecturer at the UWA Law School.

Robyn Williams is a Nyoongar woman with extensive experience as a FASD trainer, advocate, and researcher. She works at the Medical School, Faculty of Health Sciences, Curtin University, and the University of Melbourne.

Raewyn Mutch is a Ngāi Tahu woman of New Zealand and Clinical Associate Professor at the University of Western Australia, and Invited Faculty for the Harvard Program for Refugee Trauma, Global Mental Health, Trauma and Recovery (2019–2020).

Suzie Edward May is a Lawyer and Research Officer at the UWA Law School and a member of the Aboriginal and Torres Strait Islander Peoples and Community Justice Centre.

Dorothy Badry is a Professor in the Faculty of Social Work, University of Calgary.

Michelle Stewart is an Associate Professor at the University of Regina on Treaty Four Territory.

Criminology in Focus
Series Editor: Sandra Walklate

This series offers a space for a 'short format' book series which showcases and puts the spotlight on new research in criminology. We are interested in books that fit the 'short-form' model; for example: theoretical think pieces, developments in criminal justice policy, paradigm shifting innovations in the fields, a compelling case study that would be of interest to an international readership. We would like to attract 'big names' as well as up-and-coming scholars; all books should speak and contribute to international criminological debates and conversations.

1 **Decolonising Justice for Aboriginal Youth with Fetal Alcohol Spectrum Disorders**
   Harry Blagg, Tamara Tulich, Robyn Williams, Raewyn Mutch, Suzie Edward May, Dorothy Badry and Michelle Stewart

Decolonising Justice for Aboriginal Youth with Fetal Alcohol Spectrum Disorders

Harry Blagg, Tamara Tulich, Robyn Williams, Raewyn Mutch, Suzie Edward May, Dorothy Badry, and Michelle Stewart

Routledge
Taylor & Francis Group

LONDON AND NEW YORK

First published 2021
by Routledge
2 Park Square, Milton Park, Abingdon, Oxon OX14 4RN

and by Routledge
52 Vanderbilt Avenue, New York, NY 10017

Routledge is an imprint of the Taylor & Francis Group, an informa business

British Library Cataloguing-in-Publication Data
A catalogue record for this book is available from the British Library

Library of Congress Cataloging-in-Publication Data
A catalog record has been requested for this book

ISBN: 978-0-367-35109-0 (hbk)
ISBN: 978-0-429-32552-6 (ebk)

Typeset in Times New Roman
by codeMantra

This book is dedicated to the memory of Ms Clarke.

Contents

Author biographies

Dr Dorothy Badry, PhD, RSW, is a Professor in the Faculty of Social Work, University of Calgary. Her primary research interests focus on FASD and child welfare, women's health and FASD, housing and homelessness, advancing knowledge on FASD, FASD – mental health, suicide and justice, loss and grief issues. She teaches an online course on FASD and child welfare for social work students across the Prairie Provinces in the summer session. Dorothy has been a member of the Canada FASD Research Network Action Team on the Prevention Network Action Team since 2008 and the Child Welfare Research Lead since 2017. She co-chaired the national conference *The Future of Child Welfare*, held in Calgary in 2018 in partnership Prairie Child Welfare Consortium (PCWC); Provincial and Territorial Directors of Child Welfare, and; Faculty of Social Work, University of Calgary. Prior to beginning her work at the University of Calgary in 2002, she worked for 16 years in various positions in child welfare with Alberta Children Services, sparking her interesting in FASD. She was the co-principal investigator on the Brightening Our Home Fires project in the Northwest Territories – a FASD prevention project funded by the First Nations and Inuit Health Branch (2010–2012). She has received numerous research grants on FASD from provincial and national funders, including PolicyWise, the Public Health Agency of Canada and the First Nations, and Inuit Health Branch of Canada, and has many publications on FASD research.

Professor Harry Blagg is a Professor of Criminology at UWA Law School and Director of the Aboriginal and Torres Strait Islander Peoples and Community Justice Centre in the Law School. He has national and international standing as a leading criminologist specialising in Indigenous people and the justice system, and is one of a few scholars currently researching diversionary mechanisms for Aboriginal youth with FASD. He has conducted seminal funded research on Indigenous Night Patrols, the multi-agency approach, policing and Aboriginal communities, local justice partnerships, crime prevention, family violence, restorative justice, court innovations, and youth justice. His work is place-based, participatory, and innovative, with a focus on decolonising relationships and building fresh engagement spaces.

Suzie Edward May is a Lawyer and Research Officer at the UWA Law School and a member of the Centre for Aboriginal and Torres Strait Islander Peoples and Community Justice. She is the co-author of Blagg, H., Tulich, T., Mutch, R., Williams, R., & May, S. (2018) *FASD and the Criminal Justice System: Report to the Australian National Advisory Council on Alcohol and Drugs (ANACAD) Secretariat* and has worked on other large law reform projects in the areas of Aboriginal law and culture, youth diversion, therapeutic justice, and court innovation. Following the completion of her Articles of Clerkship with the WA State Solicitors Office, she joined the Office of the Inspector of Custodial Services, undertaking systemic prison reform, then worked as Legal Consultant to the Law Reform Commission of WA. She also has significant experience as a Non-Executive Director of a large public health authority; a state and national Consumer Advocate in chronic disease; a Consumer Advisor in medical research; and a Tertiary Lecturer in medical and allied health faculties.

Dr Raewyn Mutch is a Ngāi Tahu woman of New Zealand and Clinical Associate Professor at the University of Western Australia, and Invited Faculty for the Harvard Program for Refugee Trauma, Global Mental Health, Trauma and Recovery (2019–2020). Raewyn is a triple-qualified specialist paediatrician in (i) General Paediatrics, (ii) Community Paediatrics, and (iii) Respiratory Medicine, appointed to Perth Children's Hospital in Western Australia. Raewyn has collaborated in research, co-design, and the use of Indigenous methods with service recipients; government and non-government providers; and stakeholders at a local, state and national level: measuring Knowledge Attitudes and Practices among professionals across statutory systems of care; developing the Australian FASD Diagnostic Tool; developing the Western Australian FASD Model of Care; as an Associate Investigator on the Fitzroy Valley FASD study; and, Chief Investigator on the Western Australian Banksia Hill study.

Dr Michelle Stewart is an Associate Professor at the University of Regina on Treaty Four Territory. Michelle is an interdisciplinary and community-based researcher. Her applied research and policy work comes together at the intersection of disability, systemic racism, settler colonialism, and gender. Her projects include a focus on complex cognitive disabilities, mental health, and addictions as well as racialised inequalities in the justice system(s). Michelle has held individual and team grants, including funding from the Social Sciences and Humanities Research Council, Canadian Institutes for Health Research, as well as the National Science Foundation. Michelle has authored/co-authored numerous articles and book chapters as well as policy documents, including the Truth and Reconciliation Call to Action #34: A Framework for Action. She is currently the Project Lead for the Integrated Justice Program, which holds multi-year funding, including funding from Public Safety Canada.

Dr Tamara Tulich is a Senior Lecturer at UWA Law School. Tamara researches and publishes in the areas of preventive justice, anti-terror lawmaking, and indefinite detention regimes, and is a co-editor of the collection *Regulating Preventive Justice* (Routledge, 2017). Tamara's recent research projects focus on expanding diversionary alternatives for Aboriginal youth with FASD, understanding the role of law and culture in Aboriginal and Torres Strait Islander communities in responding to and preventing family violence, and reform to Australian proceeds of crime legislation.

Dr Robyn Williams is a Nyoongar woman with extensive experience as a FASD trainer, advocate, and researcher. This expertise includes international FASD training in North America/Canada and many years' experience working with families. Since 2008, Robyn has worked in an advocacy role supporting families caring for children with FASD. In 2014 and 2018, she presented at international conferences on FASD in Canada. This trip also included an intensive five-week study tour during which she was trained, and she continues to be mentored by leading international experts in FASD. Robyn completed her PhD on FASD in the South West region of WA and has developed an FASD training package for professional development and families caring for children with FASD. This study included engaging and consulting with 180 Aboriginal people on FASD to inform culturally secure practice. Robyn's professional roles have included working at various health agencies, among them Derbarl Yerrigan Health Service, Aboriginal Alcohol and Drug Service, Edith Cowan University, and the Office of Aboriginal Health (Western Australia). She currently works at the Medical School, Faculty of Health Sciences, Curtin University, and the University of Melbourne.

Foreword

At the time of writing, the killing of George Floyd in Minneapolis in the United States has been the catalyst for thousands of people to march in support of the *Aboriginal Lives Matter* movement in the streets of Australia's capital cities, despite COVID-19. Led by Aboriginal people around the nation, many thousands gathered and marched, Aboriginal and non-Aboriginal side by side, seeking to end Aboriginal deaths in custody and institutional racism.

Despite this national outrage governments continue to enact statutes likely to have a disproportionate impact on Aboriginal people. In Western Australia, the *High Risk Serious Offenders Bill 2019 (WA)* was passed by the Parliament and commenced operation in August 2020 (except Sch 1, Div 2, Subdiv 1). It introduces a scheme for continuing incarceration or supervision of violent offenders, beyond the completion of their sentence, when they are deemed to pose an unacceptable risk to the community. It applies to youth from 16 years of age as well as adults. In a similar vein, the *Criminal Law (Mentally Impaired Accused) Act 1996 (WA)*, which deals with an accused person who is unfit to stand trial or found not guilty by reason of insanity, has had a disproportionate impact on Aboriginal people. The operation of the latter Act is analysed in Chapter 4.

Since 2009 over 13 separate Senate and Commonwealth inquiries have been conducted,[1] examining the various factors that have contributed, and still contribute, to the high rates of Aboriginal incarceration in Australia, particularly in Western Australia. This is some acknowledgement that colonisation, dispossession, and systemic discrimination underpin the current rates of incarceration. While findings about the correlation between FASD and contact with the criminal justice system are inconclusive, the research in this book demonstrates that FASD should be considered at every stage of the criminal justice system. As succinctly observed by Justice Cozens:

The problematic consumption of alcohol that has resulted in children being born suffering from the permanent effects of FASD often finds its roots in the systemic discrimination of First Nations peoples, and resultant alienation they experience from their ancestry, culture and their families.

R v Quash [2009] YKTC 54, [62]

Whatever the reader's knowledge, experience, or role, this book has much to offer in terms of elucidation of the lifelong condition of FASD, the nature of the brain damage it causes, its impact on the individual, and its prevalence. The book examines the ways in which cognitive impairments associated with FASD clash with underlying assumptions about the individual which underpin the criminal justice system and in some cases expose the individual to indefinite detention on the basis that they are not fit to stand trial. The reader will learn that there is no systematic screening or assessment of children or young people entering the criminal justice system to identify neurodevelopmental disability. In many cases, a neurodevelopmentally compromised individual, who may suffer undiagnosed impairments in memory, executive function, and language, for example, will be sentenced as if they were neurodevelopmentally typical. That has adverse consequences for the individual, their family, and the society as the legal system fails to recognise the brain damage and resultant impact on behaviour and capacity. By doing so the community is likely to suffer the repetition, and indeed escalation, of the offending behaviour, with all the associated costs, including harm to others and incarceration.

One of the key narratives of this book is that FASD among Aboriginal people has to be seen in the context of the colonial project by which First Nations societies were dispossessed; their sovereignty extinguished; and their law, culture, and languages destroyed in the service of establishing the settler society, the effects of which have included intergenerational trauma. The book explores the connection between colonization and the high rate of FASD among Aboriginal youth.

It is important to emphasise that FASD is not confined to Aboriginal people or their communities. As the 2018–2028 National FASD Action Plan expressly states, 'FASD affects many communities – it is not isolated to a specific country, region or population group.' It is simply that the 'prevalence of FASD in vulnerable populations is higher.'[2] And this brings to the forefront the specific factors that have made and continue to make Aboriginal people and communities 'vulnerable' to injustice.

How is 'justice' to be achieved for Aboriginal youth with FASD in Australia? What is the alternative to criminalising neurodevelopmentally compromised youth and condemning them to a lifetime of incarceration? The authors propose a strategic framework for supporting and managing youth, across their life-spans, which puts Aboriginal-led, culturally appropriate, and innovative solutions at the centre. Implementation is urgent. It starts with educating families, carers, communities, policy-makers, professionals, politicians. This book shows the way forward.

Catherine Crawford[3] & Robyn Williams
July 2020

Notes

1 2009 Senate access to justice inquiry (31 recommendations); 2010 Australian Law Reform Commission inquiries into family violence and family violence and commonwealth laws; 2011 Lower house inquiry into Indigenous youth experiences with the criminal justice system (40 recommendations); 2012 Lower house inquiry into the prevention and diagnosis of foetal alcohol spectrum disorders (19 recommendations); 2013 Senate inquiry into justice reinvestment (Nine recommendations);

2014 Productivity Commission report on access to justice (83 recommendations); 2015 Senate Standing Committee on Indigenous Affairs inquiry into Harmful Use of Alcohol in Aboriginal and Torres Strait Islander Communities; 2016

Senate Standing Committee on Finance and Public Administration inquiry into Aboriginal and Torres Strait Islander Experience of Law Enforcement and Justice Services; 2016 Senate Standing Committee on Community Affairs inquiry into Indefinite Detention of People with Cognitive and Psychiatric Impairment in Australia; 2017 The Royal Commission into the Protection and Detention of Children in the Northern Territory(227 recommendations); 2018 Australian Law Reform Commission's Pathways to Justice; 1994 – 2019 Reports of the Aboriginal and Torres Strait Islander Social Justice Commissioner; 2010 – 2022 The National Plan to Reduce Violence against Women and their Children.

2 https://www.health.gov.au/sites/default/files/national-fasd-strategic-action-plan-2018-2028.pdf

3 B. Juris., LL.B., (University of WA), LL.M. (International Human Rights) (University of Essex) & Magistrate, Children's Court of Western Australia, from 2011 to date.

Acknowledgements

The idea for this book arose out of research that Harry, Tamara, Raewyn, Robyn, and Suzie completed for the Australian National Advisory Council on Alcohol and Drugs (ANACAD) Secretariat on FASD and the criminal justice system, and we acknowledge the support provided by ANACAD.

This book has been a genuinely collective project – built on conversations and research collaborations, some new and many old, and drawing on the knowledges, perspectives, and scholarship of a multidisciplinary team. It would not have been possible without the wisdom and energy of all authors and Suzie's erudite editorial assistance and coordination. We thank the editorial team at Routledge, who provided us with invaluable support and guidance throughout the project.

Harry and *Tamara* would like to thank everyone involved in our research in the Kimberley region, to develop culturally secure diversionary alternatives to the criminal justice system for Aboriginal youth with FASD. We are extremely grateful to Cherie Sibosado, Jeanie Roberts, and Maureen Carter from our three partner organisations – Life Without Barriers (Broome), Garl Garl Walbu Aboriginal Corporation Derby Sobering Up Shelter (Derby), and Nindilingarri Cultural Health Service (Fitzroy Crossing). Thanks are also due to June Oscar, Emily Carter, and Jane Pedersen from Marninwarntikura Women's Resource Centre in Fitzroy Crossing. The West Australian Police were extremely helpful and always willing to assist in our field work; special thanks to Sergeant Neville Ripp, Inspector Brett Baddock, and Deputy Commissioner Gary Dreibergs. We are very grateful for the support of Magistrate Steve Sharratt in Broome, for his kindness and hospitality, and for allowing researchers access to court proceedings. Our thanks are owed to the lawyers from Legal Aid and the Aboriginal Legal Service of Western Australia for raising issues about FASD and fitness to stand trial, which sparked our research. We acknowledge the funding contribution of the Australian Institute of Criminology through the Criminology Research Grants programme. Thanks to Zoe Bush for her outstanding contribution as Research Assistant. Harry would also like to thank Professor Thalia Anthony for her helpful comments on our research reports and for her contribution to our ideas about decolonisation. Our greatest thanks go to the Aboriginal people who participated in the research and shared their knowledge and experiences.

We are indebted to members of the Research Reference Group of the Aboriginal and Torres Islander Peoples and Community Justice Centre, School of Law, University of Western Australia, for their invaluable support, guidance, and advice. We owe particular thanks to Daryl Kickett, Donna Nelson, Justine Bennell, Professor Vickie Hovane, and Donella Raye for their steadfast support and guidance. We would also like to thank Tarryn Harvey and Peter Collins for their support and strong advocacy for Aboriginal young people with FASD in Western Australia.

Tamara also wishes to thank Vickie Hovane, Ambelin Kywamullina, Raewyn Mutch, Donella Raye, and Robyn Williams for their friendship, wisdom, and generosity in sharing their knowledge. Our conversations continually teach, inspire and challenge me. Tamara is indebted to Sarah Murray for her friendship, advice and support.

Finally, none of this would be possible without Ali, Ayla, and Gilly, and their love, kindness, and unwavering support.

Suzie would like to thank Chris, Oscar, and Olive for their unconditional love and support.

Robyn and *Dorothy* acknowledge some of our first advocates in this space, Dr Jan Hammill, Dr Lorian Hayes, and Dr Vicki Russell, for laying the foundation for the next generation of advocacy for protecting and supporting the most vulnerable in our community. We acknowledge and thank the Aboriginal community and Aboriginal community-based organisations for working tirelessly with our families, in particular, Derbarl Yerrigan Health Service, South West Aboriginal Medical Service, Wadjak Northside Aboriginal Corporation, and the Aboriginal Legal Service. We acknowledge the tireless work by many on the 'frontline' and all of those that go the extra mile as well as our families and kinship carers for raising children with FASD. International acknowledgement and thanks to Audrey McFarlane, Executive Director, and the Board of Directors of the Canada FASD Research Network for supporting our ongoing international research collaboration and working partnership between Australia and Canada.

'E hara taku toa I te toa takitahi he toa takitini': 'My strength is not as an individual, but as a collective.'

Raewyn would like to thank Professor Carol Bower and Dr Jan Payne for first asking me to work with you on the prevention and diagnosis of FASD. I thank and am deeply grateful to Professor Harry Blagg and Dr Tamara Tulich for our collaboration and friendship. Thank you for sharing your erudite and diligent minds, your practice of respectful inclusivity, and your iterative commitment to First Nation's people and their wisdom. Thank you for inviting me to walk with you; you have nurtured my hope. Thank you to Suzie Edward May for precisely honing our cohesive narrative with patience and humour. To my mooditj yorta, Dr Robyn Williams, you inspire endurance and lead and mentor by dignified example. To Dr Dorothy Badry, thank you for your unconditional sharing of knowledge and kindness. Dr Michelle Stewart, thank you for bravely exposing duplicity and systemic failures. To the children and adolescents still waiting for the equitable provision of culturally nuanced services to their family and place, to nourish their development, their health and well-being, I hope this book may be a catalyst for change so you can expect your best life, know freedom, and live with dignity. Dear George and Irene, thank you for sacrificing so much so I could learn. To Peter and Lucie, thank you for my best life, our adventures, and our love; Ka nui toku aroha ki a koe. And to Lucie, 'Ko te pae tawhiti, whaia kia tata; ko te pae tata, whakamatua kia tina': 'Seek out distant horizons and cherish those you attain.'

Michelle would like to thank Robyn Pitawanakwat for insights not only on my chapter but also on my projects and collaborations, more broadly, as the aims of decolonising one's work and practices can often come about through the careful labour of others, whose attention to our actions and language help bring about transformative change and yet often go unrecognised. Thanks also to Chris Kortright and Krystal Glowatski for comments on Chapter 8. Thank you to Myles Himmelreich for pushing me to think differently. Thank you to the editors of *Settler City Limits: Indigenous Resurgence and Colonial Violence in the Urban Prairie West* and, in particular, Robert Henry and David Hugill for the discussion about specificity in the language we choose. Thank you to the editors and authors of this book as our conversations in recent years have helped to shape and reshape my own conceptual frameworks and understandings. I hope it serves to further our own discussions and helps to foster others.

Finally, we would like to acknowledge that this work is going to press during the COVID-19 pandemic, which has only enhanced the experiences of loneliness, separation, and disenfranchisement through no or limited access to services for those in prison or on remand.

1 Introduction

Tamara Tulich, Harry Blagg, Robyn Williams, Dorothy Badry, Michelle Stewart, Raewyn Mutch, and Suzie Edward May

Introduction

Aboriginal youth with Fetal Alcohol Spectrum Disorders (FASD) are worryingly overrepresented in the criminal justice system in Australia, mirroring the experience in other settler states including Canada, New Zealand, and the United States. FASD results from exposure to alcohol in utero, leading to cognitive, social, and behavioural difficulties, including difficulties with language, memory, impulse control, and linking actions to consequences (Douglas, 2010). American research suggests that over half of persons with FASD will interact with the criminal justice system: around 60% will be arrested, charged, or convicted of a criminal offence, and about half will have spent time in juvenile detention, prison, inpatient treatment, or mental health detention (Streissguth, Barr, Kogan & Bookstein, 1997; Streissguth, Bookstein & Barr, 2004). Canadian research indicates that young people with FASD are 19 times more likely to be arrested than their peers (Popova, Lange, Bekmuradov, Mihic & Rehm, 2011). A recent study undertaken in Western Australia's juvenile detention centre found that 36 out of 100 youth detainees had FASD, with 34 of the 36 identifying as Aboriginal. This is 'the highest reported prevalence of FASD in a youth setting worldwide' (Bower et al., 2018, p. 7). Repeated contact with the criminal justice system compounds the condition and causes contributory outcomes, such as psychiatric disorders (O'Malley, 2007), reinforcing the vulnerability of a person with FASD to contact with the criminal justice system (as victims and offenders) (Blagg & Tulich, 2018; Blagg, Tulich & Bush, 2016, 2017; Koren, 2004). At the same time, there is a growing collection of parliamentary reports, case law, and commentary highlighting the inadequate accommodation of FASD-associated impairments within the criminal justice system in Australia, particularly for Aboriginal youth.

The aim of this book is to provide a multidisciplinary and cross-jurisdictional analysis of issues surrounding FASD and the criminal justice system, and its impact on Aboriginal children, young people, and their families. It is largely based on research in Australia and Canada; however, it also makes reference to the experience in the USA and New Zealand, especially the latter, due to its commitment to legislative reform and Indigenous empowerment. One of the key themes through the text is that, far from providing solutions to FASD, the mainstream criminal justice system increases the likelihood of adverse outcomes for children with FASD and their families. Over the last few decades youth justice systems in many Western societies have been increasingly modelled on the adult criminal justice system, as part of a US-initiated 'punitive turn' in sentencing (Simon, 2007). There is a much greater focus than hitherto on risk management, punishment, and offender accountability, eclipsing the previous interest in child welfare and development. What John Muncie (2008) calls a populist 'resurgent authoritarianism' in criminal justice policy, is dissolving the difference between the adult and the youth justice systems in some jurisdictions. However, this is not a uniform process, and not every element of the US punitive populist agenda has been copied by other jurisdictions. New Zealand, in particular, has maintained a commitment to a child-centred approach, coupled with a commitment to involving family (whānau) in decision making at every stage of contact with the criminal justice system. There are also differences in the approach taken in different Australian states, and territories in Canada, regarding youth justice. In Australia, the state of Victoria has had a relatively low rate of imprisonment for young people, while the Northern Territory and Western Australia have relatively high rates of detention: they also have the highest rate of Indigenous youth incarceration in Australia. This is not surprising since issues of race have fuelled the punitive turn in sentencing according to criminologists (Cunneen 2006, 2018; Simon, 2007; Wacquant 2010, 2014).

The over-representation of Indigenous youth with FASD in the justice systems in settler states is about intersecting forms of oppression that are founded in, and sustained by, settler colonialism. High rates of FASD in Aboriginal communities in Australia are the consequence of unhealed intergenerational and transgenerational trauma linked to colonial violence and dispossession and its pervasive impact on social, emotional, and cultural well-being of individuals, families, and communities (Blagg & Tulich, 2018; Blagg et al., 2016, 2017; Dudgeon, Milroy & Walker, 2014; Williams, 2018). Intergenerational and transgenerational trauma convey the extent to which the pain and trauma associated with colonial dispossession and colonial practices are transmitted from one generation to the next generation and across generations (Atkinson, Nelson, Brooks, Atkinson & Ryan, 2014). The 'founding violence' of colonisation has cascaded through time leaving destruction in its wake, and in the words of Professor Judy Atkinson, of the Jiman and Bundjalung peoples, 'trauma trails' that 'run across country and generations' (Atkinson, 2002, p. 88). The transgenerational impacts of colonisation and colonial trauma were amplified when generations of Aboriginal and Torres Strait Islander children were stolen from their parents and assimilated into statutory systems (Atkinson, 2002). The colonial-trauma is iterative across statutory systems and the impacts are intergenerational and intracellular.

Intergenerational and transgenerational trauma involve many coping mechanisms including alcohol consumption. Maria Yellow Horse Brave Heart (2011) (Hunkpapa and Oglala Lakota) discusses the cumulative impacts of trauma across the life of an individual and across generations, which can result in self-medicating with substances to avoid these painful memories or experiences. Emily Carter (2017, Weston & Thomas, 2018, p. 4), a Gooniyandi Kija woman from the central Kimberley, and CEO of Marninwarntikura Women's Resource Centre in Fitzroy Crossing, explains:

> We can't understand anything about FASD without understanding trauma. Many in the Fitzroy Valley drink so they don't have to feel the overwhelming emotions triggered by trauma. Instead of judging people for the outcome of their actions we must start asking what has happened. As soon as we look beyond the judgement, we can start changing the outcome and create better futures.

This requires us to decolonise FASD as a disability: to recognise the connection between FASD and inherited disparity as a consequence of colonisation, and the role of colonisation in the *production* of impairment and disability (Chisholm, Tulich & Blagg, 2017; Grech & Soldatic, 2015; Hollingsworth, 2013; Jaffee, 2016; Meekosha, 2011; Soldatic, 2013, 2015). Disability compounds the disparities confronting Indigenous populations, and racism further contributes to the disproportionate social, health, and economic disadvantages (Green et al., 2018; see also Macedo, Smithers, Roberts, Paradies & Jamieson, 2019). This continues to be reflected in the higher prevalence rate of disability amongst Indigenous populations than the settler mainstream in Australia, Canada, and the United States (Fitts & Soldatic, 2020), and the higher prevalence rate of First Nations peoples with disability in the criminal justice systems in settler states (Australian Law Reform Commission [ALRC], 2018; Australian Institute of Health and Welfare [AIHW], 2018). The over-representation of impairment amongst Aboriginal peoples in Australian is both a product of, and continuously produced by, the settler state. Soldatic (2015, p. 64) explains:

> It has been suggested that the over-representation of impairment is a reflection of Aboriginal Australians' dispossession, or to use a term from Deborah Rose (2006), a 'double death' – the interstice of white-settler disabling societies and colonizing violence and dispossession – producing impairment *and* disablement.

Increasingly Indigenous peoples in settler colonial societies maintain that meaningful change requires a process of *decolonisation,* rather than the reform, of the criminal justice process (Agozino, 2004; Anthony, 2013; Cunneen & Tauri, 2017, 2019; Jackson, 1987; Park, 2015; Tauri, 2016a, b). In opposition to the 'correctionalisation' of youth justice, we advocate for an approach that recognises the unique needs of children and young people, and strengths of First Nations communities, and that is situated in a decolonising perspective. Dr Ambelin Kwaymullina (2020, pp. 62–63), of the Palyku people of the Pilbara region in Western Australia, explains a strengths-based approach:

> A strengths-based approach
> recognises
> the great gifts
> resilience
> knowledges
> of Indigenous peoples
> And seeks to build upon
> celebrate
> utilise
> these strengths
> A strengths-based approach
> recognises
> that the cause of Indigenous disadvantage
> is dispossession
> and all that was done
> to achieve it
> sustain it
> justify it
> We are not a problem to be solved

we are partners on pathways
to all the knowledges
inventions
joys
wonders
that will come out of respectful relationships

We argue for a strategic framework for the management of FASD that is multidisciplinary and community-focussed, prioritising diversion from the criminal justice system into community-owned networks of care and support. It is not enough to develop multidisciplinary approaches and multi-disciplinary teamwork if Indigenous knowledges are excluded from the process. Initiatives on a local level must be initiated from the bottom up, not the top down, be led by Aboriginal and Torres Strait Islander peoples and centre Aboriginal and Torres Strait Islander Law and Culture. The empowerment of Aboriginal communities as a necessary prerequisite for meaningful reform – that is, reform that contributes to healing, to overcoming trauma (Dudgeon, Holland & Walker, 2019). This is also in line with the work by the First Nations Disability Network to shift the focus away from deficit language around 'disability' towards 'inclusion' in line with Aboriginal cultural values (Avery, 2018; First Peoples Disability Network [FPDN], 2019). We assert that reforms to domestic laws and policies that impact Aboriginal peoples with FASD should be centred around Aboriginal 'place' (or 'country'); support Aboriginal knowledges, Aboriginal-led solutions and community-based services; and provide what we describe as culturally appropriate 'external scaffolding' or circle of care around Aboriginal youths with FASD and their families.

Our decolonising approach is grounded in three contemporary theoretical frameworks: postcolonial theory, settler colonial theory, and decolonising theory. Post-colonial theories, associated with the work of Edward Said (1978), stress the degree to which colonial relationships of dominance and subordination continue in the present. The prefix 'post' is frequently misunderstood as meaning *after* colonialism, when in fact it describes the degree to which the world has been transformed by colonial power (Bhambra, 2007; Blagg & Anthony, 2019). It also stresses that colonised peoples engage in and create constant cultural contestation, which often takes place in the 'interstitial spaces' (Bhabha, 1994; Waters, 2001) between the settler mainstream and Indigenous peoples. These interstitial spaces are sites of ambivalence, hybridity, compromise, resistance, and contestation, and move us beyond the focus on entrenched, binary opposition between coloniser and colonised, creating possibilities for fresh narratives to emerge within 'in-between' (Bhabha, 1994) spaces. It opens space for a pluralist alternative where settler law increasingly cedes sovereign power to Indigenous Law and Culture, allowing what Fitzgerald (2001, p. 41) calls a 'vibrant and decentered' justice system to flourish that respects Indigenous Law and Culture. Our approach is intended to heal, rather than perpetuate, colonial binaries. We have also been influenced by the work of Patrick Wolfe (2006), who argued that settler colonisation remains a structure rather than an event. Settler colonisation is not something we can consign to the distant past but continues to shape relationships in the present. Decolonisation of relationships between the mainstream and Indigenous peoples must take precedence over other justice 'reforms' that may be a priority for non-Indigenous activists (Blagg & Anthony, 2019).

Our work has also been strongly influenced by the decolonising framework set out by Māori scholar Linda Tuhiwai Smith (Ngāti Awa and Ngāti Pouro) (1999) in her foundational text on the way Western knowledge systems have deployed notions of scientific rigour, evidence, and neutrality to suborn Indigenous knowledges and naturalise the occupation and exploitation of Indigenous lands. We view Aboriginal and Torres Strait Islander communities as places of knowledge production, rather than simply 'raw material' to be refined by Western sites of knowledge production, such as universities, think tanks, and government departments (see Comaroff & Comaroff, 2012).

The Authors

A discussion about FASD requires an equally complex discussion about context: settler colonialism. We must carefully and thoughtfully consider the ongoing impacts of settler colonialism, the role of intergenerational and transgenerational trauma, and systemic racism. As authors we must consider our own positionality, just as the reader is invited to consider theirs.

Individually and collectively, naming colonial practices and structures, and considering how we can work towards transformational change is the first step towards decolonisation. Colonial structures are immense, interlocking, and rely on compliance and complacency as much as ideology and violence. These structures are upheld by bureaucracies that are operationalised by individuals. Therefore, to decolonise FASD is to decolonise systems – at all levels – to reimagine and reconfigure who we are, what we do, and to consider the ways that we can positively contribute to change in oppressive structures.

Kwaymullina (2020, pp. 15–16) (Palyku) makes a powerful call to settlers in Australia:

Decolonisation
Settler-colonial lands
will only be decolonised
when the structures of settler-colonialism
have been replaced
by structures grown out of respectful relationships
with Indigenous sovereignties
The structures of settler-colonialism
are everywhere
in governments
corporations
educational institutions
in every place
where something was founded
developed
sustained
in the absence of respect
for Indigenous sovereignties
These structures also exist
within Settlers
in the form
of patterns of thought
and behaviour
Decolonisation requires
that Settlers
continually identify
challenge
disrupt
the structures of settler-colonialism
including those patterns embedded
in minds and hearts
and in ways of relating
to Indigenous peoples
Decolonisation
is processes
It is journeys
not destinations
A series of transformations
which can only be born out of

and be answerable to
locally based relationships
with the sovereign Indigenous peoples
in whose homelands
Settlers live
Work
Play

As researchers/workers we must *position ourselves* in the work we do. If the ultimate goal is to decolonise justice practices, policies, and FASD, this requires clarity around the type of colonisation being addressed, and *what* exactly is colonial about the practice or policy. Ultimately, the process of identifying colonial structures can help to denaturalise that which appears logical, and to then challenge and dismantle that which is unjust. However, this is a path that is fraught with discomfort and, as Michelle Stewart develops in Chapter 8, dis-ease as it challenges many to think differently about their own practices as well as the ongoing impacts of settler colonialism.

The authors of this book are Indigenous and non-Indigenous scholars and practitioners from a range of legal, criminological, and health backgrounds who work in the FASD space.

Indigenous protocols require that our First Nations authors introduce themselves and their family line (Ardill, 2013; Kickett, 2011; Wilson, 2008). Dr Robyn Williams is a Nyoongar woman, and a descendant of Nyoongar and Yamatji people from Western Australia. Nyoongar country consists of 14 clans and includes Nganda, Amangu, Yuat, Balardong, Whadjuk, Pindjarup, Wardandi, Biblelmen, Minang, Kaneang, Wilman, Nadji Nadji, Wudjari, and Njunga. These clans co-existed for many thousands of years and were governed by their own lores and protocols. Dr Raewyn Mutch is a Ngāi Tahu woman of New Zealand. This is her whakapapa:

ko Tahu Potiki te Tangata, ko Ngai Tahu te iwi,
ko Ngai Te Atawhiua te hapu,
ko Waihopai raua ko Awarua aku marae.
Ko Aoraki te maunga, ko Waitaki te awa,
ko George Newton taku tupuna matua,
ko Wharetutu taku tupuna whaea,
ko George Mutch taku papa, ko Irene Mutch taku mama,
ko Peter O'Sullivan taku tane, ko Lucie O'Sullivan taku tamahine
ko Raewyn Mutch tenei
no reira e aku hoamahi koutou.

Dr Michelle Stewart was raised as a settler and lived most of her youth on unceded Coast Salish Territory in British Columbia Canada. Her family on her father's side has a complex relationship to the Indian Act with roots in New Brunswick, and she is a second-generation immigrant on her mother's side. She currently lives and works on Treaty 4 Territory in Saskatchewan Canada.

Prof Dorothy Badry is a non-Indigenous researcher from Calgary, Alberta, Canada who lives in Treaty 7 Territory – home of the Stoney Nakoda, Kainai, Piikani, Siksika, and Tsuut'ina First Nations. This land is home to many people of the Me'tis Nation of Alberta. The University of Calgary Indigenous Strategy – ii' taa' poh' to' pi highlights the value of walking parallel paths together in a good way.

Prof Harry Blagg, Dr Tamara Tulich, and Mrs Suzie Edward May are non-Indigenous researchers based in Perth, Western Australia and work on Noongar Boodjar, the land of Whadjuk people of the Noongar nation. We acknowledge the traditional custodians of the land on which we live and work, and recognise the strength, resilience, capacity, and continuing culture and contribution of the Noongar peoples (South West Aboriginal Land and Sea Council, n.d.).

As white researchers our standpoint is framed by our experiences of privilege, by our cultural, racial, class, and gender positions, and by living within the dominant worldview of the coloniser (Walter, 2016). Unacknowledged and unproblematised, our standpoints bind and limit us: blocking alternative narratives, experiences, and understandings (Walter, 2016) – and worse, contribute to White erasure (Bruce, 2020). Throughout this book, we have sought to give prominence to Indigenous voices (Evans, Hole, Berg, Hutchinson & Sookraj, 2009, p. 894), and to engage in respectful relationships with Indigenous peoples and knowledges. Kwaymullina (2018, pp. 201–202) (Palyku) writes of enacting respect through listening, a process that involves, among other things, not speaking for but prioritising Indigenous voices 'as the primary and most authentic sources of our own realities.'

We are conscious of about what and for whom we may speak. As white lawyers and criminologists, we can name the colonial practices perpetuated through the law and justice systems; the complicity of the law in racial oppression and in the reproduction of inequality in the face of ongoing resistance and contestation by First Nations peoples. We seek to highlight the *potential for* decolonised diversionary processes to promote Aboriginal-led, community- and strengths-based alternatives for Aboriginal peoples with FASD subject to the criminal law.

We recognise, at the same time, what Allie Jane Bruce (2020) describes as 'an inescapable truth,' that we, as white researchers, bring our 'own Whiteness and ...racism into anti-racist spaces' and 'will often reproduce racism in those spaces.' Bruce (2020) explains:

> I can always work to do better, but part of doing better is accepting and sitting with the inherent contradiction of my being in these spaces at all, trying to do anti-racist work while not denying the fact that I am racist.

We are conscious too of the colonising tendencies of concepts such as 'white fragility' (DiAngelo, 2011) as Alison Whittaker (2020) a Gomeroi poet and researcher, has demonstrated:

> Making whiteness visible by naming it is, of course, important, but in its new visibility we cannot let it take the centre of a movement, much less without understanding the conditions that create, define and express its power.

We recognise the deeply uncomfortable and inescapable truth that we, as White researchers, profit from being in the space. White careers are made and maintained. White names are known. White voices are heard. In sitting with the discomfort and inherent contradiction of working in this space, we have been particularly influenced by Tuck and Yang's (2012) work on decolonisation and 'settler moves to innocence', Kwaymullina's (Palyku) work on listening (2018, 2020) and alliances (2020), Barker (2010) on alliances, and Regan's work (2006, 2010) on forging authentic alliances through an ethics of recognition, 'unsettling the settler within' by confronting our role and identity as settlers. Ceding power starts with each of us: our words, our actions, and our lives. It involves guarding against inadvertent complicity in the colonial project and the well-meaning, but pernicious, colonising projects and relationships that may form through alliances. We thank our Aboriginal colleagues, friends, scholars for standing beside us and supporting us to learn, and continue to learn, to be allies: to stand with Indigenous peoples, as they lead.

Overview of the book

We begin, in Chapter 2, by outlining the history of FASD, and how the impairments associated with FASD are relevant to each stage of the criminal justice process – from arrest, bail, and parole, to participating in police interviews and instructing lawyers, to understanding the court process, the availability of certain defences, sentencing, complying with court orders, accessing appropriate treatment and management if imprisoned. We include two case studies which ground and contextualise the critical need for FASD screening and assessment in the youth justice system.

In Chapter 3, we outline existing research on the prevalence of FASD, including two leading Australian studies: the Lililwan project and the Banksia Hill study. We examine best practice in diagnosis and management, including current diagnostic assessments used by a multidisciplinary diagnostic team, and explore the problems of undiagnosed FASD, access to diagnosis and trauma in Aboriginal communities.

In Chapters 4 and 5, we explore two key junctures in the criminal justice process that highlight the inadequate accommodation of Aboriginal youth with FASD: legislative regimes for fitness to stand trial and sentencing. Drawing on international best practice examples, we canvas decolonising reform options to improve outcomes for unfit accused with FASD, and reform options to improve sentencing outcomes for Aboriginal youth with FASD by maximising therapeutic outcomes with community-based alternatives.

Chapter 6 highlights the linkages between the child welfare system and engagement in the youth justice system. We examine the challenges people with FASD encounter in correctional settings from a decolonising lens, identifying concerns regarding the need for training on FASD for correctional staff and provide guidance on delivering culturally secure training. Intensive, formalised education and training on FASD in the youth justice system from first contact with the law, in community-based prevention programmes and institutional care is an ethical imperative.

In Chapter 7, we argue for a radical recalibration of theory and practice around diversion. Adopting a decolonising approach, we argue for reform to primary diversion (police cautioning) and secondary diversion (family conferencing models) to better respond to the needs, including cultural needs, of people with FASD.

In Chapter 8, Michelle Stewart examines the role of settler colonialism and FASD through an exploration of contemporary justice issues in Canada. She investigates the role of settler discomfort and a particular type of 'dis-ease' that can surround the complexities of FASD – and the ways in which settler colonialism can be bracketed out as part of those complexities.

A note on terminology

Throughout this book, we use the term 'Indigenous peoples' to collectively refer to First Peoples across the globe who practice unique traditions, and 'retain social, cultural, economic and political characteristics that are distinct from the dominant societies in which they live' (UN Permanent Forum on Indigenous Issues, n.d.). In so doing, we acknowledge that the term Indigenous is a colonial term, and 'used in the international and United Nations context to define peoples in relation to their colonizers' (Monchalin, 2016, p. 2). When collectively referring to First Peoples of Australia, we use Aboriginal and Torres Strait Islander peoples. This is the preferred terminology of many Aboriginal and Torres Strait Islander people, some of whom reject the term 'Indigenous' as too generic and failing 'to respect their identity and preferences' (Australian Institute of Aboriginal and Torres Strait Islander Studies [AIATSIS], 2018; UWA Law School, 2020). Where appropriate, we use the inclusive terms 'Aboriginal peoples' and 'Torres Strait Islander peoples' to distinguish between Aboriginal and Torres Strait Islander peoples. In adopting the plural form 'peoples' and 'communities' we acknowledge the diversity of communities, cultures, laws, languages, kinship structures, and histories of over 250 groups that make up First Nations people in Australia, and the heterogeneity of Aboriginal worldviews (Kwaymullina, Kwaymullina & Butterly, 2013).

We also acknowledge the preference of Aboriginal people to identify themselves by their language group and nation, and Torres Strait Islander people by their home island (AIATSIS, 2018; UWA Law School, 2020). Where appropriate, we refer to a particular language group and nation for Aboriginal peoples, and island home for Torres Strait Islander peoples. In Chapter 8, in relation to Canadian context, we use the term 'Indigenous Peoples' to refer to the over 50 different Indigenous Nations in Canada. We acknowledge the preference of many Indigenous people in Canada to be identified as they describe themselves, according to their nation, treaty, or ancestral background, and where possible we do so (Monchalin, 2016, pp. 3–4).

References

Agozino, B. (2004). Imperialism, crime and criminology: Towards the decolonisation of criminology. *Crime, Law and Social Change*, 41, 343–358.

Anthony, T. (2013). *Indigenous people, crime and punishment*. Oxon, UK: Routledge.

Ardill, A. (2013). Australian sovereignty, indigenous standpoint theory and feminist standpoint theory first peoples' sovereignties matters. *Griffith Law Review, 22*(2), 315–343.

Atkinson, J. (2002). *Trauma trails, recreating song lines: The transgenerational effects of trauma in Indigenous Australia*. Melbourne, Australia: Spinifex Press.

Atkinson, J., Nelson, J., Brooks, R., Atkinson, C., & Ryan, K. (2014). Addressing individual and community transgenerational trauma. In P. Dudgeon, H. Milroy, & R. Walker (Eds.), *Working together: Aboriginal and Torres Strait Islander mental health and wellbeing principles and practice* (2nd ed., pp. 289–307). Canberra, Australia: Commonwealth of Australia.

Australian Institute of Aboriginal and Torres Strait Islander Studies. (2018). Indigenous Australians: Aboriginal and Torres Strait Islander people. Retrieved from https://aiatsis.gov.au/explore/articles/indigenous-australians-aboriginal-and-torres-strait-islander-people

Australian Institute of Health and Welfare. (2019). *The health of Australia's prisoners 2018*. Canberra, Australia: AIHW. Retrieved from https://www.aihw.gov.au/reports/prisoners/health-australia-prisoners-2018/contents/table-of-contents

Australian Law Reform Commission. (2018). *Pathways to justice—Inquiry into the incarceration rate of Aboriginal and Torres Strait Islander peoples* (Report no. 133). Canberra, Australia: ALRC.

Avery, S. (2018). *Culture is Inclusion: A narrative of Aboriginal and Torres Strait Islander people with disability*. Sydney, Australia: First Peoples Disability Network.

Barker, A. J. (2010). From adversaries to allies: Forging respectful alliances between Indigenous and settler peoples. In L. Davis (Ed.), *Alliances: Re/envisioning Indigenous–non-Indigenous relationships* (pp. 316–333). Toronto, Canada: University of Toronto Press.

Bhabha H. K. (1994). *The location of culture*. London, UK: Routledge.

Bhambra, G. K. (2007). Sociology and postcolonialism: Another "missing" revolution? *Sociology, 41*(5), 871–884.

Blagg, H., & Anthony, T. (2019). *Decolonising criminology: Imagining justice in a postcolonial world*. Basingstoke, UK: Palgrave Macmillan.

Blagg, H., & Tulich, T. (2018). Diversionary pathways for Aboriginal youth with fetal alcohol spectrum disorder. *Trends & issues in crime and criminal justice* No. 557. Canberra, Australia: Australian Institute of Criminology.

Blagg, H., Tulich, T., & Bush, Z. (2016). Placing country at the centre: Decolonising justice for indigenous young people with foetal alcohol spectrum disorders (FASD). *The Indigenous Law Review, 19*(2), 4–16.

Blagg, H., Tulich, T., & Bush, Z. (2017). Indefinite detention meets colonial dispossession: Indigenous youths with foetal alcohol spectrum disorders in a white settler justice system. *Social and Legal Studies, 26*(3), 333–358.

Bower, C., Watkins, R. E., Mutch, R. C., Marriott, R., Freeman, J., Kippin, N. R., Safe, B., Pestell, C., Cheung, C. S., Shield, H., & Tarratt, L. (2018). Fetal alcohol spectrum disorder and youth justice: A prevalence study among young people sentenced to detention in Western Australia. *BMJ open, 8*(2), 1–10.

Bruce, A. J. (2020, May 21). White erasure of BIPOC people and work [blog post]. Retrieved from http://readingwhilewhite.blogspot.com/2020/05/white-erasure-of-bipoc-people-and-work.html

Carter, E. (2017) Breakfast speech, Melbourne, September 2017.

Chisholm, R. L., Tulich, T., & Blagg, H. (2017). Indigenous young people with foetal alcohol spectrum disorders: The convention on the rights of persons with disabilities and reform to the law governing fitness to stand trial in Western Australia. *Law in Context, 35*(2), 85–107.

Comaroff, J., & Comaroff, J. L. (2012). Theory from the south: Or, how Euro-America is evolving toward Africa. *Anthropological Forum, 22*(2), 113–131.

Cunneen, C. (2006). Racism, discrimination and the over-representation of indigenous people in the criminal justice system: Some conceptual and explanatory issues. *Current Issues in Criminal Justice, 17*(3), 329–346.

Cunneen, C. (2018). Sentencing, punishment and indigenous people in Australia. *Journal of Global Indigeneity, 3*(1), 1–22.

Cunneen, C., & Tauri, J. M. (2016). *Indigenous criminology.* Bristol, UK: Policy Press.

Cunneen, C., & Tauri, J. M. (2019). Indigenous peoples, criminology, and criminal justice. *Annual Review of Criminology, 2*, 359–381.

DiAngelo, R. (2011). White fragility. *International Journal of Critical Pedagogy, 3*(3), 54–70.

Douglas, H. (2010). The sentencing response to defendants with foetal alcohol spectrum disorder. *Criminal Law Journal, 34*(4), 221–239.

Dudgeon, P., Holland, C., & Walker, R. (2019). *Fact sheet 4 transgenerational trauma and suicide.* Centre of Best Practice in Aboriginal and Torres Strait Islander Suicide Prevention (CBPATSISP); Poche Centre for Indigenous Health, School of Indigenous Studies, University of Western Australia.

Dudgeon, P., Milroy, H., & Walker, R. (Eds.) (2014). *Working together: Aboriginal and Torres Strait Islander mental health and wellbeing principles and practice* (2nd ed.). Canberra, Australia: Commonwealth of Australia.

Evans, M., Hole, R., Berg, L. D., Hutchinson, P., & Sookraj, D. (2009). Common insights, differing methodologies: Toward a fusion of Indigenous methodologies, participatory action research, and white studies in an urban Aboriginal research project. *Qualitative Inquiry, 15*(5), 893–910.

First Peoples Disability Network Australia. (2019). Annual report 2019. Retrieved from https://fpdn.org.au/wp-content/uploads/2019/11/FPDN_ANNUAL-REPORT-2019.pdf

Fitts, M. S., & Soldatic, K. (2020). Who's caring for whom? Disabled Indigenous carers experiences of Australia's infrastructures of social protection. *Journal of Family Studies*, 1–16, doi:10.1080/13229400.2020.1734478.

Fitzgerald, T. (2001). *The Cape York justice study.* Brisbane, Australia: Department of the Premier and Cabinet.

Grech, S., & Soldatic, K. (2015). Disability and colonialism: (Dis)encounters and anxious intersectionalities. *Social Identities, 21*(1), 1–5.

Green, A., Abbott, P., Davidson, P. M., Delaney, P., Delaney, J., Patradoon-Ho, P., & DiGiacomo, M. (2018). Interacting with providers: An intersectional exploration of the experiences of carers of Aboriginal children with a disability. *Qualitative Health Research, 28*(12), 1923–1932.

Hollinsworth, D. (2013). Decolonizing Indigenous disability in Australia. *Disability & Society, 28*(5), 601–615.

Jaffee, L. J. (2016). Disrupting global disability frameworks: Settler-colonialism and the geopolitics of disability in Palestine/Israel. *Disability & Society, 31*(1), 116–130.

Kickett, M. (2011). *Examination of how a culturally-appropriate definition of resilience affects the physical and mental health of Aboriginal people.* Unpublished doctoral dissertation. University of Western Australia.

Koren, G. (2004). Hypothetical framework: FASD and criminality – Causation or association? The limits of evidence based knowledge. *Journal of FAS International, 2*(2), 1–5.

Kwaymullina, A. (2018). You are on Indigenous land: Ecofeminism, Indigenous peoples and land justice. In L. Stevens, P. Tait, & D. Varney (Eds.), *Feminist ecologies: Changing environments in the anthropocene* (pp. 193–208). Cham, Switzerland: Palgrave Macmillan.

Kwaymullina, A. (2020). *Living on stolen land.* Broome, Australia: Magabala Books.

Kwaymullina, A., Kwaymullina, B., & Butterly, L. (2013). Living texts: A perspective on published sources, Indigenous research methodologies and Indigenous worldviews. *International Journal of Critical Indigenous Studies, 6*(1), 1–13.

Macedo, D. M., Smithers, L. G., Roberts, R. M., Paradies, Y., & Jamieson, M. (2019). Effects of racism on the socio-emotional wellbeing of Aboriginal Australian children. *International Journal for Equity in Health, 18*(132), 1–10.

Maria Yellow Horse Brave Heart. (2011). The historical trauma response among natives and its relationship with substance abuse: A Lakota illustration, *Journal of Psychoactive Drugs, 35*(1), 7–13.

Meekosha, H. (2011). Decolonising disability: Thinking and acting globally. *Disability & Society, 26*(6), 667–682.

Monchalin, L. (2016). *The colonial problem: An indigenous perspective on crime and injustice in Canada.* Toronto, Canada: University of Toronto Press.

Muncie, J. (2008). The 'punitive' turn in juvenile justice: Cultures of control and rights compliance in western Europe and the USA. *Youth Justice, 8*(2), 107–121.

O'Malley, K. D. (2007). Fetal alcohol spectrum disorders: An overview. In K. D. O'Malley (Ed.), *ADHD and fetal alcohol spectrum disorders* (pp. 1–24). New York: Nova Science Publishing.

Park, A. S. J. (2015). Settler colonialism and the politics of grief: Theorising a decolonising transitional justice for Indian residential schools. *Human Rights Review, 16*(3), 273–293.

Popova, S., Lange, S., Bekmuradov, D., Mihic, A., & Rehm, J. (2011). Fetal alcohol spectrum disorder prevalence estimates in correctional systems: A systematic literature review. *Canadian Journal of Public Health, 102*, 336–340.

Regan, P. (2006). *Unsettling the settler within: Canada's peacemaker myth, reconciliation, and transformative pathways to decolonization.* Doctoral dissertation. Retrieved from http://hdl.handle.net/1828/1941

Regan, P. (2010). *Unsettling the settler within: Indian residential schools, truth telling, and reconciliation in Canada.* Vancouver, Canada: UBC Press.

Said, E. W. (1978). *Orientalism.* London, UK: Routledge.

Simon, J. (2007). *Governing through crime: How the war on crime transformed American democracy and created a culture of fear.* New York: Oxford University Press.

Smith, L. T. (1999). *Decolonizing methodologies: Research and Indigenous peoples.* New York: Zed Books.

Soldatic, K. (2013). The transnational sphere of justice: Disability praxis and the politics of impairment. *Disability & Society, 28*(6), 744–755.

Soldatic, K. (2015). Postcolonial reproductions: Disability, indigeneity and the formation of the white masculine settler state of Australia. *Social Identities, 21*(1), 53–68.

South West Aboriginal Land and Sea Council. (n.d.). *Living culture – Living land and its people; Noongar protocols: Welcome to country.* Retrieved from http://www.noongar.org.au/noongar-protocols/

Streissguth, A., Barr, H., Kogan, J., & Bookstein, F. (1997). Primary and secondary disabilities in fetal alcohol syndrome. In M. Lowry, M. Dorris, A. Streissguth, & J. Kanter (Eds.), *The challenge of fetal alcohol syndrome: Overcoming secondary disabilities* (pp. 25–39). Seattle: University of Washington Press.

Streissguth, A. P., Bookstein, F., Barr, H., Sampson, P. D., O'Malley, K., & Kogan Young, J. (2004) Risk factors for adverse life outcomes in fetal alcohol syndrome and fetal alcohol effects. *Journal of Developmental and Behavioural Pediatrics, 25*(4), 228–238.

Tauri, J. (2016a). *The state, the academy and Indigenous justice: A counter-colonial critique.* Doctoral dissertation. University of Wollongong.

Tauri, J. (2016b). Indigenous peoples and the globalization of restorative justice. *Social Justice, 43*(3), 46–67.

Tuck, E., & Yang, K. W. (2012). Decolonization is not a metaphor. *Indigeneity, Education & Society, 1*(1), 1–40.

United Nations Permanent Forum on Indigenous Issues. (n.d.). *Who are Indigenous peoples?* Retrieved from http://www.un.org/esa/socdev/unpfii/documents/5session_factsheet1.pdf

UWA Law School. (2020). *Danjoo Waarnkiny (Talking together): Indigenous terminology guide.* Perth, Australia: UWA Law School.

Wacquant, L. (2010) Class, race & hyperincarceration in revanchist America. *Dædalus, 139*(3), 74–90.

Wacquant, L. (2014). Marginality, ethnicity and penality in the neo-liberal city: An analytic cartography. *Ethnic and Racial Studies, 37*(10), 1687–1711.

Walter, M. (2016). Indigenous peoples, research and ethics. In M. Adorjan & R. Ricciardelli (Eds.), *Engaging with ethics in international criminological research* (pp. 87–105). Abingdon, UK: Routledge.

Waters, A. (2001). Ontology of identity and interstitial being. *Newsletter on American Indians and Philosophy, 00*(2), 9–17.

Weston, J., & Thomas, S. (2018). *Fetal alcohol spectrum disorders (FASD) and complex trauma: A resource for educators.* Fitzroy Crossing, WA: Marninwarntikura

Women's Resource Centre. Retrieved from https://mwrc.com.au/blogs/news/ fasd-and-complex-trauma-a-resource-for-educators-2nd-edition

Whittaker, A. (2020). So white. So what. *Meanjin, 79*(1). Retrieved from https://meanjin.com.au/essays/so-white-so-what/

Williams, R. (2018). *Understanding fetal alcohol spectrum disorder through the stories of Nyoongar families and how may this inform policy and service delivery.* Unpublished doctoral dissertation. Health Sciences, Curtin University.

Wilson, S. (2008). *Research is ceremony: Indigenous research methods.* Black Point, Canada: Fernwood Publishing.

2 Children, adolescents, and FASD in the criminal justice system

Raewyn Mutch, Dorothy Badry, Robyn Williams, and Tamara Tulich

Introduction

This chapter introduces FASD, including the history of FASD and its emergence in Australia and other settler states such as New Zealand, Canada, and the US ('CANZUS societies'), and the primary and contributory outcomes of FASD. This chapter outlines research on the susceptibility of people with FASD to the criminal justice system and, using case examples, examines how the impairments associated with FASD are relevant to each stage of the criminal justice process – from arrest, bail, and parole, to participating in police interviews and instructing lawyers, to understanding the court process, the availability of certain defences, sentencing, complying with court orders, accessing appropriate treatment and management if imprisoned. In doing so, this chapter highlights the oral language difficulties experienced by people with FASD that create particular vulnerabilities throughout the legal process. The chapters that follow provide an in-depth account of the key sites where people with FASD are inadequately accommodated in the criminal justice system: diagnosis and assessment, communication, fitness to stand trial, sentencing and custodial care.

Fetal alcohol spectrum disorder

FASD was first identified in the 1950s and 60s in France in the respective works of a doctoral researcher, Jaqueline Roquette, and French paediatrician, Professor Lemoine (Lowenfels & Tuyns, 1994). In the 1960s, Lemoine, Harrouseau, Borteyru, and Menoet (1968, 2003) conducted a study of 127 cases examining the impact of maternal alcohol consumption during pregnancy and publishing the first article on the subject in 1968 (Koren & Navioz, 2003; Williams, 2018).

In 1973, North Americans, Jones and Smith, published eight cases with the same conclusions as the French team and coined the term Fetal Alcohol Syndrome (FAS) (Jones et al., 1973; Jones & Smith, 1973; Koran & Navioz, 2003).

Jones and Smith (1973) used FAS to describe a group of children born to women with substance-dependency and a shared history of chronic consumption of alcohol throughout their pregnancies. Their newborn infants were growth restricted and possessed similar dysmorphic facial features. While some infants with prenatal alcohol exposure (PAE) also had microcephaly and other birth defects (Jones et al., 1973), all infants had developmental difficulties (Jones et al., 1973). Drinking alcohol during pregnancy alters DNA methylation and histone codification of many biologically relevant genes at the fetal stages. These changes may persist into later life and influence gene transcription and lifetime health outcomes (Resendiz et al., 2013).

Physical growth, as well as brain growth and brain development, continue throughout pregnancy. The timing, frequency, and quantity of PAE are linked to adverse cognitive, behavioural, and neurodevelopmental outcomes (O'Leary, 2004; O'Leary & Bower, 2009; O'Leary, Nassar, Kurinczuk, & Bower, 2009; O'Leary et al., 2010; O'Leary et al., 2010). The variation in timing, quantity and frequency of PAE is associated with variation in type and severity of developmental differences (O'Leary et al., 2010), although no exact dose-relationship of PAE is understood (Astley, 2011; Feldman et al., 2012; O'Leary & Bower, 2012). Inherent maternal and fetal characteristics may be protective against or synergistic with the harmful and teratogenic effects of PAE.

By 2000, there was global agreement that PAE was reliably associated with the risk of neurodevelopmental impairment for the developing fetus and that FASD is one of the most common preventable causes of developmental disability (Mattson, Bernes & Doyle, 2019; Rasmussen et al., 2008). Alcohol is a teratogen (Mattson, Schoenfeld & and Riley, 2001), or a substance identified as crossing the placenta and causing structural damage to a developing infant (Chudley, 2008). There is universal agreement that (i) PAE is associated with a risk and range of lifelong physical, cognitive (Larroque et al., 2000), behavioural (Kodituwakku, 2007) and neurodevelopmental impairments (Mattson & Riley, 1998; (ii) the neurodevelopmental damage from PAE is an acquired brain injury (ABI) (Mattson & Riley, 1999, 2000; Mattson et al., 2010); and (iii) most infants with PAE do not exhibit dysmorphic features.

Initially, FASD was used as an overarching term to include any individual with developmental differences associated with PAE, with or without dysmorphic features. The diagnostic terms of FAS, Partial FAS, Alcohol-Related Neurodevelopmental Disorder (ARND), and Alcohol-Related Birth Defects were included under FASD (Sokol, Delaney-Black & Nordstrom, 2003). The three dysmorphic facial features associated with PAE are known as sentinel facial features and include: (i) a shortened eye-opening length (the palpebral fissure length); (ii) an elongated and flattened upper-lip philtrum (the space between the base of the nose and the upper lip); and (iii) a thin upper-lip volume. Despite international diagnostic guidelines for FASD being developed, recognising the physical, cognitive, behavioural, and neurodevelopmental difficulties associated with PAE, there is no consensus (Mutch et al., 2009). Differences between guidelines include the diagnostic terms, the attribution of PAE, and the methods for determining and assigning neurodevelopmental impairment (Astley, 2004, 2006; Astley & Clarren, 1999; Astley et al., 2000; Chudley et al., 2005; Hoyme et al., 2005; Landgraf, Nothacker & Heinen, 2013; Stratton, Howe & Battaglia, 1996).

In 2016, Australia adopted the Canadian concept (Cook et al., 2016) of FASD being used as a diagnostic term rather than an overarching term. The appellation of FASD replaced all prior diagnostic terms including FAS. Consequently, for a diagnosis of FASD in Australia, an individual must have both (i) proven PAE and (ii) severe neurodevelopmental impairment in at least three of ten specified domains of central nervous system structure or function (Bower & Elliott, 2016). The term FASD is then subdivided further into two categories: (i) FASD with three sentinel facial features (similar to the previous diagnostic category of FAS); and (ii) FASD with less than three sentinel facial features (which encompasses the previous diagnostic categories of partial FAS, ARND, and Neurodevelopmental Disorder-Alcohol Exposed). The diagnosis of FASD with three sentinel facial features can be made when PAE is unknown, provided there is severe neurodevelopmental impairment and other reasons for the facial dysmorphisms and impairment have been excluded.

FASD in the juvenile justice system

The association between exposure to childhood trauma and negative outcomes in adolescence is well established, particularly regarding risk and cause for early involvement in the juvenile justice system (Felske et al., 2012; Hazel et al., 2008; Kerig, 2019). Young people with FASD experience higher rates of lifetime adversity, and elevated risk of early and repeat contact with statutory systems such as early-life and iterative placement into out-of-home care and justice settings (Adelson, 2005; American Psychiatric, 2013; Fast & Conroy, 2009; Hughes et al., 2016; McLachlan, 2017). Individuals with FASD can become involved in the juvenile justice system as victims, witnesses or accused persons (Fast & Conroy, 2009; Wyper & Pei, 2015). For equality before the law and across all stages of the legal process, their lived experiences need consideration together with a comprehensive assessment of their neurodevelopmental strengths and difficulties (Hamilton, 2020; Kippin et al., 2018; Mutch, 2009, 2016a). Evidence globally and across Australia confirms that children and adolescents with FASD are more likely to engage with juvenile justice services and statutory systems from a young age. Yet even with repeat proof of negative legal consequence for individuals with neurodevelopmental impairment and FASD, no jurisdiction provides routine comprehensive assessment to determine the presence of neurodevelopmental impairment, strengths, and difficulties, and FASD. The Banksia Hill FASD prevalence study in Western Australia, discussed in greater detail in Chapter 3, found that none of the participating children and adolescents, representative of all sentenced youth, had ever been afforded a comprehensive health and neurodevelopmental assessment during their repeated and prior engagement with statutory services (Bower et al., 2018).

Compounding this is a fundamental inadequacy of criminal justice processes to accommodate FASD-associated impairments. It is well recognised that the impairments associated with FASD, and particularly language difficulties (Hand, Pickering, Kedge & McCann, 2016; Kippin et al., 2018; Reid, Moritz & Akison, 2019) are relevant to each stage of the criminal justice process – from participating in police interviews, to arrest and bail processes, instructing lawyers, understanding the court process, the availability of certain defences, sentencing, complying with court orders, accessing appropriate treatment and management if imprisoned and complying with parole conditions. The fundamental challenges for young people with FASD in the criminal justice process include the following:

The assumptions of free will and individual responsibility that underpin Australian criminal law are largely incompatible with the impairments associated with FASD (Roach & Bailey 2009, p. 3).

Poor identification (and therefore specialist assessment) of individuals with FASD and referral for specialist assessment (Mutch et al., 2013).

A lack of awareness by police, prosecutory authorities, lawyers, and justice professionals of FASD (Douglas et al., 2012; Mutch et al., 2013).

The suggestibility that a person with FASD may experience means they are more likely to gratuitously concur with propositions put to them by police in interviews (Parliament of Western Australia, 2012, p. 75; Parliament of Australia, 2017).

Difficulties with memory may place persons with FASD at a disadvantage when trying to explain behaviour, give instructions to lawyers, or give evidence (Parliament of Western Australia, 2012, p. 75; Parliament of Australia, p. 2017). Difficulties with memory can also trigger confabulation – 'the subconscious creation of unintentional false memories used to compensate for gaps in memory' – creating specific challenges for people with FASD in police interviews, and court processes (Leveque & Badry, forthcoming).

Specific difficulties with oral language and communication, in particular higher-level language skills, may mean a person with FASD is unable to adequately understand and participate in police interviews and court processes even where they appear, superficially, to have verbal capacity (Brown, Carter, Haun, Wartnik & Zapf, 2019; Hand et al., 2016; Kippin et al., 2018; Reid, Kippin, Passmore & Finlay-Jones, 2020).

The legislative regimes for fitness to stand trial, as they apply to persons with FASD, are unsatisfactory, in particular the West Australian regime (Blagg, Tulich & Bush, 2016, 2017; Crawford, 2010, 2014; Martin, 2015; Parliament of Western Australia, 2012; *State of Western Australia v BB (a Child)* [2015]; *State of Western Australia v Tax* [2010]), including for the absence of appropriate accommodations (Arstein-Kerslake, Gooding, Andrews & McSherry, 2017; Gooding, McSherry, Arstein-Kerslake & Andrews, 2017; Parliament of Australia, 2017).

The absence of appropriate diversionary alternatives, and in particular place-based 'on country' therapeutic diversionary alternatives for Aboriginal youth with FASD (Blagg & Tulich, 2018; Blagg, Tulich & Bush, 2016, 2017; Parliament of Australia, 2017).

Sentencing responses to FASD have been criticised as inadequate and likely to be the cause of deeper enmeshment in the justice system (Chartrand & Forbes-Chilibeck, 2003; *Churnside v the State of Western Australia* [2016]; Crawford, 2015; Freckelton, 2016; Milward, 2014; Douglas, 2010).

Unrealistic diversionary options as persons with FASD may have difficulties with memory and linking actions with consequences, rendering alternatives to prison such as fines, community-based orders, and good behaviour bonds, futile (Douglas, 2010, p. 228). The imposition of community-based orders on persons likely affected by FASD was recently criticised as 'unrealistic' by the Court of Appeal of the Supreme Court of Western Australia in the case of *AH v Western Australia* [2014]. A person with FASD may be unable, rather than wilfully unwilling, to comply with court orders.

Challenges to the effective management of people with FASD in the justice system, including lack of appropriate treatment programmes (*AH v Western Australia*, 2014; *Churnside v the State of Western Australia*, 2016; Mutch et al., 2013; Freckelton, 2016).

Unlikely ability for people with FASD to comply with prison rules due to difficulties with memory and linking actions with consequences, also leaving people with FASD open to being victimised, exploited, and manipulated in prison due to their suggestibility (Chudley, Kilgour, Cranston & Edwards, 2007, p. 269; Douglas, 2010, p. 228; Fast & Conroy, 2009, p. 252; Institute of Health Economics, 2013, p. 25).

Incarceration in prison can worsen or exacerbate the condition of an offender with FASD (*AH v The State of Western Australia*, 2014).

FASD is an unrecognised disability in the justice sector

Baldry, Briggs, Golson, & Russell identify the need to address the intersection of 'socio-economic disadvantage, mental health disorders, cognitive disabilities, complex support needs and processes of criminalisation' (2018, p. 638) in the youth justice system and have undertaken this research in the *Comparative Youth Penalty Project*. From a critical disability studies lens, Baldry et al. note that the youth justice system has overlooked disability, while from a critical criminology lens, 'the criminalisation of disability' (2018, p. 639) has contributed to disadvantaged youth being placed in justice institutions, in the absence of other alternatives. The criminalisation of behavioural problems is not uncommon for individuals with FASD and others with cognitive disabilities, and the involvement with youth justice systems creates a pathway to involvement in the adult justice system as noted by Baldry (2014). It is important to recognise that early life experiences including trauma, abuse, being placed in out of home care, involvement with youth justice and early contact with police, are all risk factors for individuals with cognitive disabilities and mental health problems to be involved with the adult criminal justice system (Baldry, Clarence, Dowse, & Trollor, 2013).

As a disability, FASD has been excluded from many mainstream service delivery systems. A system of care for individuals with FASD is not well established and infrastructure in responding to this disability remains sparse. Youth with FASD who have never been assessed or diagnosed are at high risk in the youth justice system due to the vulnerabilities associated with FASD. FASD has been identified as a neurocognitive disability (Wyper & Pei, 2016). Youth with FASD are vulnerable to peers that will take advantage of them and at increased risk of harm in custody when professionals have no knowledge of FASD.

Youth with FASD experience multiple challenges not experienced by their peers; including unstable home life, challenges at school, physical and sexual abuse, victimisation, mental health issues, and negative peer influences (Peled et al., 2014). For many, unstable beginnings, compounded by multiple placements, leads to a lack of trust in foster carers and case managers. In one study, 43% of youth with FASD had moved homes in the past year compared to 22% of their peers in care without FASD (Fuchs, Burnside, Reinink, & Marchenski, 2010). Youth with disabilities including FASD are faced with a double set of risks for negative outcomes (Fuchs et al., 2010). Female youth with FASD often have babies younger, and in one study, six out of ten females with FASD had experienced teenage pregnancy and became young mothers, whilst in care. All infants were removed except for one who remained with their mother (Fuchs et al., 2010). Chasnoff, Wells, and King (2015) in their study of adopted and foster children, found the majority (86.5%) had never been previously diagnosed with FASD or had been misdiagnosed. FASD is a disability that seriously affects the life trajectory of individuals and has a range of physical, neurological, cognitive, socio-emotional, and behavioural impairments (Chudley et al., 2005) that contribute to 'lifelong environmental adversity' (Wyper & Pei, 2016, p. 101). The distinct needs of individuals with FASD often go unrecognised in the justice system, mental health system, in alcohol or drug programmes and in the child welfare system, due to a lack of knowledge and training.

Australian research by Elliot & Bower (2004), found that the majority of children who were diagnosed with FASD in Australia were not living with their biological parents, and were instead living in foster care. Further, the mothers were also found to have more than one child with FASD. Later research by Elliot, Payne, Morris, Haan, & Bower (2008) surveying Paediatricians in Australia, found that 49% of children in care had been assessed for FASD. Another

12% were strongly suspected by specialists of having FASD; however, paediatricians believed that a diagnosis would stigmatise the child. Whilst Australian government reports and research conclude that children in care with FASD are overrepresented, there appears to be little to no strategic planning in addressing the issue (McLean & McDougall, 2014).

Peled et al., (2014) reported on a profile of 260 youth with FASD in British Columbia, Canada, aged between 12 and 19 years of age, including youth who had recently been in detention. In comparison with their peers, youth with FASD were more likely to disengage with education, and reportedly coped better in education support centres where they were able to work at their own pace. They found that 48% of youth had received a mental health diagnosis such as ADHD, depression, or bipolar disorder, as well as anger management problems. The study also found higher rates of self-harm and attempted suicide amongst both male and female youth with FASD. In the same study, psychiatrists and counsellors acknowledged their lack of understanding of FASD, and that common therapeutic techniques such as talk therapy and confronting past trauma, were not viable treatment options for youth with FASD. This research concludes that factors precipitating youth involvement with the justice system included an unstable home life; involvement in out of home care (including foster care and group homes); parents with alcohol or drug problems (46%); school absences; mental health problems including depression, anxiety and Post Traumatic Stress Disorder; experiences with victimization and bullying; susceptibility to negative peer influences; and substance use. In terms of victimisation, youth with FASD were more likely to have been sexually or physically abused; were at higher risk of sexual exploitation by adults; and, in mainstream schools, were more likely to have a boyfriend/girlfriend and have been a victim of physical violence in the relationship. In terms of negative peer influences, youth with FASD were easily influenced into taking responsibility for the criminal activity of their peers. Particular challenges were noted in youth contact with the justice system, including poor understanding of probation and conditions which often led to the young person being placed back in custody. While the research by Peled and colleagues notes many risk factors for youth with FASD, it also highlights the potential of protective factors that can reduce these challenges, such as a strengths-based approach, the use of positive peer mentors, life and work skills development, cultural engagement and connectedness, and involvement with physical activity.

Case studies

Case studies offer a deeper look into the lives of young people and are identified in order to illuminate the challenges faced by youth with FASD who come into contact with the law, offering insight into their complex circumstances.

Case 1 – Ella

Ella is an 18-year Indigenous female who is the youngest of seven children. All her siblings are suspected to have FASD with the younger children being more severely affected but no assessments have been undertaken. Ella can barely read or write and has been in out-of-home care (OOHC) for the past six years. She is eight months pregnant and in custody charged with armed robbery. She is actively using alcohol. Ella has already been advised that her baby will be removed from her care once born and her future remains uncertain.

Case 2 – LCM

"At the age of 15 years and 10 months LCM violently assaulted his newborn son in a room at the Bunbury Regional Hospital with two blows to the right and left side of his head, fracturing his skull and causing severe injuries. The assault caused the baby's death. LCM was charged with murder but was not prepared to plead guilty" (Freckelton, 2017, p. 486).

The challenges in these two case studies present the basic question – where to begin? We see two youth committing serious crimes whose disabilities have been undiagnosed and likely unrecognised until the time they have come into contact with the law under serious circumstances. One has to consider the life history that unfolded for these two young people before they landed in the justice system. In Ella's case, the outcome is unknown and earlier intervention may have supported a different pathway in her life. Ella has been in out-of-home care and the information regarding her case suggests evidence of FASD, although this was never identified. It is clear she has had lengthy involvement with the child protection system. Ella's case is not unique in Australia and female youth with FASD routinely have babies younger. She does not have a FASD diagnosis, despite evidence to suggest that it would be beneficial to refer her for assessment. Poole, Schmidt, Green, & Hemsing (2016) identify the reluctance of women to seek help due to fears of child apprehension and a lack of trust in the social service system. In one study, six out of 10 females with FASD had experienced teenage pregnancy and became young mothers, whilst in care. All the infants were removed except for one who remained with their mother, requiring intensive supports (Fuchs et al., 2010). If no training on FASD is provided for justice and social service professionals, how does one know what case practice should be prioritised and applied for young women, when providing services for her and her family?

There is mounting evidence that a FASD diagnosis is a credible factor in criminal cases to mitigate sentencing outcomes for Indigenous youth. For example, a critical case commentary by Ian Freckelton (2017) highlighted the issue of FASD and its relationship to sentencing in youth criminal justice. The case involved a young Aboriginal father who was convicted of murder following the death of his child. A court report prepared by a psychiatrist and psychologist on the youth's background, noted he came from a 'large, fragmented family system... characterized by domestic abuse, neglect, abandonment, disrupted attachment relationships, parental substance misuse and involvement in the criminal justice system' (Freckelton, 2017, p. 486). He left school at year eight and was subsequently charged with several crimes. He was in an intimate relationship with the mother of his child since the age of 12. The expert report noted that 'there was no evidence of a major, or even transient, psychiatric disorder that could explain LCM's violent behaviour towards his son' (Freckelton, 2017, p. 486). The youth plead guilty and received a sentence of ten years for manslaughter. Despite his family history, LCM was not assessed for FASD, although he was subsequently diagnosed with FASD which became a mitigating factor in a sentence reduction on appeal (*LCM v The State of Western Australia*, 2016).

A review of the LCM case indicates that advocacy through the youths' lawyer played a critical role in his referral to the FASD diagnostic team at the Telethon Kids Institute (Western Australia), noting 'The diagnosis of FASD and recognition of [LCM's] vulnerabilities arising from his many domains of significant impairment should be considered by the courts. Tragically, if a detailed nature of [LCM's] impairment had been understood and provided with some intervention early in his life, some of his and his loved ones' trauma may have been prevented' (Freckelton, 2017, p. 489). Freckelton identified that LCM had a traumatic upbringing and had been brought into care due to documented substantial substance abuse in the family. Then Chief Justice of Western Australia, Martin CJ noted, 'it is remarkable that those responsible for his care and protection did not initiate an assessment of whether or not he was affected by FASD' (*LCM v The State of Western Australia*, 2016, para 4, extracted in Freckelton, 2017,

p. 491). Freckelton (2017, p. 493) stresses that the case highlights '…the need for further education of both the forensic mental health and legal professions about the disorder and its forensic analysis' as well as the crucial need for training within the child protection system, as noted by Martin CJ in *LCM v The State of Western Australia* [2016] at paras 4–5. This will be further explored in Chapter 6.

Standard juvenile justice services

Globally, standard out-of-home care and juvenile justice services are not yet routinely designed to accommodate individual neurodevelopmental disabilities and vulnerabilities, and least able to manage the difficulties common among young people with FASD (Novick Brown, Connor & Adler, 2012). Application of remand and detention orders on children and adolescents, essentially assigns punishment as a consequence for disruptive behaviours and impaired affect regulation. Punishment and detention are invoked with an expectation the child and adolescent will understand consequence and in turn learn and do differently in the future. Expecting learning and behaviour change as a consequence of punishment, is essentially a developmentally incongruous idea, even for the typically developing child and adolescent brain. Detention and punitive measures are even less likely to teach or modify disruptive behaviours and impaired affect regulation for the non-typically developing child and adolescent. Typically developing children and adolescents are neurocognitively wired at this chronological age to be less receptive to punitive consequences. Rather, their typically developing brain is wired to be receptive to reward, especially when it is immediate. However, the child and adolescent with FASD are not typically developing. Most often they have impairments of executive function, attention, memory, communication, and language plus sensory difficulties. By late childhood, the child and adolescent with FASD has developed and experienced real-life consequences often associated with a neurodevelopmental disability including, for example, academic failure, low self-esteem, self-harm and mental health disorders, high-risk choices, and substance use. Together, these common occurring primary and secondary neurodevelopmental impairments engendered by PAE, corrupts typical learning, severely limits, or entirely removes the ability to consider cause and effect, impairs the ability to encode, remember and recall, and makes affect regulation and containing impulsivity highly unlikely. The common vulnerabilities of any child and adolescent with FASD, with or without normal IQ, makes the application of detention and punitive consequences highly unlikely to provide positive learning experiences to promote changes in behaviour. Individualised therapeutic services necessary for rehabilitation and healing are far more effective than punitive consequences for children and adolescents with FASD. Furthermore, current juvenile justice facilities in Australia do not provide the necessary multidisciplinary health teams to routinely determine every child and adolescent's neurodevelopmental strengths and difficulties. If this was present, individualised rehabilitation plans could be designed and culturally safe and trauma-informed therapeutic services could be provided, responsive to the changing needs of individuals.

Essential multidisciplinary health teams (MDT) in juvenile justice

The common risk factors for early engagement in juvenile justice include social inequality and adversity, early, and iterative episodes of trauma, and co-morbid unmitigated neurodevelopmental vulnerabilities. Diagnosis of the social and psychological needs of the child and adolescent with mandated consideration of their individual neurodevelopmental strengths and vulnerabilities by a MDT is essential. The outcome of such a comprehensive MDT assessment can best inform immediate and long term therapeutic and restorative programmes, to mutual advantage. This is in contrast to traditional behaviour modification in detention settings, predicated on the participant possessing typical communication and executive function abilities. Furthermore, the routine and schedule imposed on the child and adolescent in out-of-home care and secure settings can hide adaptive impairment. Specific accommodation of any rehabilitation and therapeutic programmes to be intentionally scaffolded on an individual's measured vulnerabilities and relative strengths can increase the likelihood of personal and programme success. Increasing the likelihood of personal and programme success is possible when an individuals' vulnerabilities are understood and their specific accommodations are implemented by their circle of care including parents, foster parents, community case-workers, social workers, probation workers, custodial staff, through-care workers, allied health therapists, and teachers. An individual's comprehensive MDT neurodevelopmental assessment informs the necessary and specific accommodation required for optimal rehabilitation and their future success. Uniform provision of the accommodation needs by the circle of care supports learning, amplifies opportunity for personal and programme success and if provided to through-care workers, can reduce recidivism and later-entry into adult correctional facilities

(Boland, 2002; Bower et al., 2018; Famy et al., 1998; Hughes, 2015; Kinner, Lennox & Taylor, 2009; Kinner et al., 2014; Streissguth et al., 1991, 1997, 1994). The adaptation of models of care is routine when an individual is identified as having an intellectual disability, triggering funding to provide person-to-person support. The child or adolescent with FASD without an intellectual disability, but with the same complexity of neurodevelopmental impairment, is equally deserving of funding to provide person-to-person support as the person with an intellectual disability (Kinner, Lennox & Taylor, 2009; Kinner & Milloy, 2011; Kinner et al., 2015; van Dooren et al., 2010).

The importance of communication and language support

Communication and language abilities are integral to the notion of equality before all legal proceedings, such as comprehension of verbal instruction in court, providing verbal assistance to counsel, answering questions, describing events, and more. In addition, communication and language are key abilities to provide understanding and support compliance with instructions during apprehension and police interviews. Deficits in these skills can subvert every aspect of the legal process.

A study examining the feasibility of screening and diagnosing for FASD in Western Australia's only juvenile facility, Banksia Hill Detention Centre, found nearly one in two of the representative sample of children and adolescents sentenced to detention had significant communication and language difficulties (Kippin, 2018). Communication and language difficulties were present among the sentenced youth with or without a diagnosis of FASD. Identifying specific communication and language needs, providing targeted and individualised support as early as the first engagement with justice services, can ensure best possible understanding and safety. Communication and language support is essential for both interactions within secure and detention settings and for any legal instructions during proceedings and prior to release.

The importance of early accommodation to prevent contributory outcomes

Individual's with FASD are encumbered with interrelated developmental impairments. During a child's engagement with the world from infancy to adolescence, their developmental learning is supported by their quotient of typical developmental skills. Developmental impairments without social and environmental adaptation and accommodation reduces the occasions of success. In addition to cumulative negative experiences from unrecognised or poorly accommodated developmental difficulties, individuals with FASD are exposed to higher than normal levels of family dysfunction and environmental stressors (Franklin et al., 2008; Molteno et al., 2014; Olson et al., 2009; Paley et al., 2005, 2006). For some, their adverse early life experiences may also include early engagement in statutory systems of out-of-home care and juvenile justice (Beardslee et al., 2019; Hayden & Graves, 2018; Robst, Armstrong & Dollard, 2017). Attributing adaptive and academic failure to early-life adversity alone without parallel consideration of the possibility of co-morbid developmental difficulties exacerbates the negative effects of iterative failure. PAE at each trimester is predictive of behaviour across the life-course. Day et al., (2013) found that PAE predicted increased behaviour problems on the Total Score, Internalising, Externalising, Attention, and Critical Items scales up to and including at 22 years of age. Also, alcohol exposure across pregnancy predicted a higher rate of behaviour problems compared to no PAE ever or PAE only during the first trimester (Day et al., 2013). There is proven benefit from early recognition and accommodation of all developmental impairments associated with PAE. Early recognition and accommodation of developmental impairment can delay onset and reduce the type and magnitude of lifelong contributory outcomes.

Secondary difficulties for an individual with FASD are many. Difficulties may include early disruption of circadian rhythms and sleep disorders (Inkelis & Thomas, 2018; Insana et al., 2014; Wengel, Hanlon-Dearman & Fjeldsted, 2011), victimisation and bullying (Thornton, 2013), disrupted and disengagement from schooling (Coles et al., 1991; Hafekost et al., 2017b; Larroque et al., 1995, 2000; Poitra et al., 2003), homelessness, unemployment, mental health disorders (Sayal, 2007), and early-age of substance misuse (Bower et al., 2018; Burns et al., 2009; Day et al., 2013; Drug and Alcohol Office, 2005; Elliott & Bower, 2004; Elliott et al., 2006, 2008; Grasso et al., 2013; Hafekost et al., 2017a; Hazel et al., 2008; Jones & Bower, 2016; Kinner et al., 2009; Nguyen-Louie et al., 2018; O'Connor & Paley, 2006; Olson et al., 2009; Ware et al., 2012). The life-long primary and secondary developmental impairments imposed on the lives of individuals with FASD increases their susceptibility to adaptive and social failure, victimisation, and early involvement in the criminal justice system (Fast & Conroy, 2009).

Children and adolescents with FASD have a higher incidence of the contributory outcomes of mental health issues and substance misuse, each contributing to adaptive failure and compound deficits of communication, executive function, attention, and memory. Individuals with FASD will try to ameliorate their deficits through acquiescence and confabulation. Difficulties with understanding time and remembering place can present to the neurodevelopmental novice as false testimony. Failure of a child and adolescent with FASD to learn from punitive consequences adds to the perception their behaviour is wilful and conduct disordered. They are not always understood to possess cognitive and adaptive abilities more typical of a younger child. The adult with FASD is even less likely to be understood as functioning with a cognitive ability of a child and may never have been afforded an assessment of their neurodevelopmental vulnerabilities. In other words, physical age does not match with developmental age or societal expectations that people act their age. This is another way in which individuals with FASD are disadvantaged in systems that are unaware of neurodevelopmental disability and dysmaturity. By early adult life, they are also likely to have acquired contributory outcomes. Only when an adult is perceived as living with a co-morbid intellectual disability is dispensation and service accommodation readily provided, rather than as routine for all individuals before justice services.

Age of criminality and age of detention

The United Nations (UN) Committee of the Rights of the Child (CRC) updated its general comment on children's rights in the child justice system in the second half of 2019, to reflect the increasing scientific knowledge about child and adolescent brain development, the negative consequences of prison on child and adolescent well-being, and the imperative to protect child rights. In light of the science confirming the typically developing adolescent does not possess the brain function and connectivity to understand punishment, the expert UN CRC recommended laws be changed to ensure that children under the age of 16 years 'may not legally be deprived of their liberty' (UN Committee on the Rights of the Child, 2019). The UN CRC experts also raised the minimum age at which children should be held legally responsible – from 12 years to 14 years.

In addition the UN CRC newly emphasised (point 28) that when the child or adolescent is not developing typically then they warrant exclusion from justice services:

> Children with developmental delays or neurodevelopmental disorders or disabilities (for example, autism spectrum disorders, fetal alcohol spectrum disorders or acquired brain injuries) should not be in the child justice system at all, even if they have reached the minimum age of criminal responsibility. If not automatically excluded, such children should be individually assessed.

Conclusion

The impairments associated with FASD are relevant to each stage of the criminal justice process, and yet FASD remains hidden in our justice systems and other sites of custodial care. The cases of Ella and LCM demonstrate the many challenges that young people with FASD face when in contact with justice and care services, and the pressing need for greater identification, diagnosis, and culturally safe and trauma-informed therapeutic services. They also demonstrate the urgent need for training of health, justice, and out-of-home care professionals to identify and support people with FASD.

In the next chapter, we outline research on the prevalence of FASD, and provide an in-depth account of the two leading Australian studies: the Lililwan project, and the Banksia Hill study. It will examine best practice in diagnosis and management, including current diagnostic assessments used by a multidisciplinary diagnostic team, and explore the problems of undiagnosed FASD, access to diagnosis, and trauma in Aboriginal communities.

References

Adelson, N. (2005). The embodiment of inequity: Health disparities in aboriginal Canada. *Canadian Journal of Public Health, 96*(2), S45–S61.

AH v The State of Western Australia [2014] WASCA 228.

American Psychiatric, A. (2013). Diagnostic and statistical manual of mental disorders.

Arstein-Kerslake, A., Gooding, P., Andrews, L., & McSherry, B. (2017). Human rights and unfitness to plead: The demands of the convention on the rights of persons with disabilities. *Human Rights Law Review, 17*(3), 399–419.

Astley, S. J. (2004). *Diagnostic guide for fetal alcohol spectrum disorders: The 4-digit diagnostic code.* Retrieved from http://depts.washington.edu/fasdpn/pdfs/guide2004.pdf

Astley, S. J. (2006). Comparison of the 4-digit diagnostic code and the Hoyme diagnostic guidelines for fetal alcohol spectrum disorders. *Pediatrics, 118*(4), 1532–1545.

Astley, S. J. (2011). Diagnosing fetal alcohol spectrum disorders (FASD). In S. A. Adubato & D. E. Cohen (Eds.), *Prenatal alcohol use and fetal alcohol spectrum disorders: Diagnosis, assessment and new directions in research and multimodal treatment.* Oak Park, IL: Bentham Books.

Astley, S. J., & Clarren, M. D. (1999). *Diagnostic guide for fetal alcohol syndrome and related conditions: The 4-digit diagnostic code* (2nd ed.). Seattle: University of Washington.

Astley, S. J., Bailey, D., Talbot, C., & Clarren, S. K. (2000). Fetal alcohol syndrome (FAS) primary prevention through FAS diagnosis: Identification of high-risk birth mothers through the diagnosis of their children. *Alcohol and Alcoholism, 35*(5), 499–508.

Baldry, E. (2014). Disability at the margins: Limits of the law. *Griffith Law Review, 23*, 1–19.

Baldry, E., Briggs, D. B., Goldson, B., & Russell, S. (2018). "Cruel and unusual punishment": An inter-jurisdictional study of the criminalisation of young people with complex support needs. *Journal of Youth Studies, 21*(5), 636–652.

Baldry, E., Clarence, M., Dowse, L., & Trollor, J. (2013). Reducing vulnerability to harm in adults with cognitive disabilities in the Australian criminal justice system. *Journal of Policy and Practice in Intellectual Disabilities, 10*(3), 222–229.

Beardslee, J., Miltimore, S., Fine, A., Frick, P. J., Steinberg, L., & Cauffman E. (2019). Under the radar or under arrest: How is adolescent boys' first contact with the juvenile justice system related to future offending and arrests? *Law & Human Behavior, 43*(4), 342–357.

Blagg, H., & Tulich, T. (2018). *Developing diversionary pathways for indigenous youth with foetal alcohol spectrum disorders (FASD): A three community study in Western Australia.* Report to the Australian Institute of Criminology.

Blagg, H., Tulich, T., & Bush, Z. (2015/2016). Placing country at the centre: Decolonising justice for indigenous young people with foetal alcohol spectrum disorders (FASD). *Australian Indigenous Law Review, 19*(2), 4–16.

Blagg, H., Tulich, T., & Bush, Z. (2017). Indefinite detention meets colonial dispossession: Indigenous youths with foetal alcohol spectrum disorders in a white settler justice system. *Social and Legal Studies, 26*(3), 333–358.

Boland, F. J., Chudley, A., & Grant, B. A. (2002). The challenge of fetal alcohol syndrome in adult offender populations. *Forum on Corrections Research, 14*, 61–64.

Bower, C., & Elliot, E. (2016). *Report to the Australian government of health: Australian guide to the diagnosis of fetal alcohol spectrum disorder (FASD).* Retrieved from https://www.fasdhub.org.au/siteassets/pdfs/australian-guide-to-diagnosis-of-fasd_all-appendices.pdf

Bower, C., Watkins, R. E., Mutch, R. C., Marriott, R., Freeman, J., Kippin, N. R., Safe, B., Pestell, C., Cheung, C. S., Shield, H., & Tarratt, L. (2018). Fetal alcohol spectrum disorder and youth justice: A prevalence study among young people sentenced to detention in Western Australia. *BMJ open, 8*(2), 1–11. doi:10.1136/bmjopen-2017–019605corr1

Brown, J., Carter, M. N., Haun, J., Judge Wartnik, A., & Zapf, P. A. (2019). Fetal alcohol spectrum disorder (FASD) and competency to stand trial (CST): A call on forensic evaluators to become informed. *Journal of Forensic Psychology Research and Practice, 19*(4), 315–340.

Burns, L., Black, E., & Elliott, E. (2009). Monograph of the intergovernmental committee on drugs working party on fetal alcohol spectrum disorders. Fetal Alcohol Spectrum Disorders in Australia: An update. Adelaide, Australia.

Chartrand, L. N., & Forbes-Chilibeck, E. M. (2003). The sentencing of offenders with fetal alcohol syndrome. *Health Law Journal, 11*, 35–70.

Chasnoff, I., Wells, A., & King, L. (2015). Misdiagnosis and missed diagnoses in foster and adopted children with prenatal alcohol exposure. *Paediatrics, 134*, 264–270.

Chudley, A. E. (2008). Fetal alcohol spectrum disorder: Counting the invisible - mission impossible? *Archives of Disease in Childhood, 93*(9), 721–722.

Chudley, A. E., Kilgour, A. R., Cranston, M., & Edwards, M. (2007). Challenges of diagnosis in fetal alcohol syndrome and fetal alcohol spectrum disorder in the adult. *American Journal of Medical Genetics, 145C*(3), 261.

Chudley, A. E., Conry, J., Cook, J. L., Loock, C., Rosales, T., & LeBlanc, N. (2005). Public health agency of Canada's National Advisory Committee on Fetal Alcohol Spectrum Disorder. Fetal alcohol spectrum disorder: Canadian guidelines for diagnosis. *Canadian Medical Association Journal, 172*(5), S1–S21.

Churnside v the State of Western Australia [2016] WASCA 146.

Coles, C. D., Brown, R. T., Smith, I. E., Platzman, K. A., Erickson, S., & Falek, A. (1991). Effects of prenatal alcohol exposure at school age. I. Physical and cognitive development. *Neurotoxicology and Teratology, 13*(4), 357–67.

Cook, J., Green, C. R., Lilley, C. M., Anderson, S. M., Baldwin, M. E., Chudley, A. E., ... Rosales, T. (2016). Fetal alcohol spectrum disorder: A guideline for diagnosis across the lifespan. *Canadian Medical Association Journal, 188*(3), 191–197.

Crawford, C. (2010). Families impacted by the criminal justice system on the frontier: A new model required. *Psychiatry, Psychology and Law, 17*(3), 464–475.

Crawford, C. (2014). "FASD clinicians forum" (Speech delivered at the Telethon Kids Institute), 18 November, Perth, Western Australia.

Crawford, C. (2015). *To examine how youth affected by fetal alcohol spectrum disorder, involved in the criminal justice system, are dealt with in other jurisdictions.* Report, Winston Churchill Memorial Trust of Australia.

Day, N. L., Helsel, A., Sonon, K., & Goldschmidt, L. (2013). The association between prenatal alcohol exposure and behavior at 22 years of age. *Alcoholism: Clinical & Experimental Research, 37*(7), 1171–1178.

Douglas, H., Hammill, J., Russell, E., & Hall, W. (2012). Judicial views of foetal alcohol spectrum disorder in Queensland's criminal justice system. *Journal of Judicial Administration, 21*(3), 178–188.

Drug and Alcohol Office, Government of Western Australia, and Department of Health. (2005). *Strong spirit strong mind. Western Australian Aboriginal alcohol and other drugs plan 2005–2009.* Retrieved from https://www.planitaerth.com/PDFs/drug-strategies/2005-2008/AboriginalAlcoholDrugPlan2005-2009.pdf

Elliott, E., Payne, J., Morris, A., Haan., E., & Bower, C.(2008). Fetal alcohol syndrome: A prospective national surveillance study. *Archives of Disease in Childhood, 93*, 732–737.

Elliott, E., Payne, J., Haan, E., & Bower, C. (2006). Diagnosis of foetal alcohol syndrome and alcohol use in pregnancy: A survey of paediatricians' knowledge, attitudes and practice. *Journal of Paediatrics and Child Health, 42*, 698–703.

Elliott, E. J., & Bower, C. (2004). FAS in Australia: Fact or fiction? *Journal of Paediatrics and Child Health, 40*, 8–10.

Famy, C., Streissguth, A. P., & Unis, A. S. (1998). Mental illness in adults with fetal alcohol syndrome or fetal alcohol effects. *American Journal of Psychiatry, 155*(4), 552–554.

Fast, D. K., & Conry, J. (2009). Fetal alcohol spectrum disorders and the criminal justice system. *Developmental Disabilities Research Reviews, 15*(3), 250–257.

Feldman, H. S., Jones, K. L., Lindsay, S., Slymen, D., Klonoff-Cohen, H., Kao, K., Rao, S., & Chambers, C. (2012). Prenatal alcohol exposure patterns and alcohol-related birth defects and growth deficiencies: A prospective study. *Alcoholism, Clinical and Experimental Research, 36*(4), 670–676.

Felske, A., Badry, D., Salmon, A., Harche, A., & Van Bibbe, M. (2012). Social determinants of health in Canada's North: FASD prevention. *Journal of Intellectual Disability Research, 56*(7–8), 770.

Franklin, L., Deitz, J., Jirikowic, T., & Astley, S. (2008). Children With fetal alcohol spectrum disorders: Problem behaviors and sensory processing. *American Journal of Occupational Therapy, 62*(3), 265–273.

Freckelton, I. (2016). Sentencing offenders with foetal alcohol spectrum disorder (FASD): The challenge of effective management. *Psychiatry, Psychology and Law, 23*(6), 815–825.

Freckelton, I. (2017). Assessment and evaluation of fetal alcohol spectrum disorder (FASD) and its potential relevance for sentencing: A clarion call from Western Australia. *Psychiatry, Psychology, and Law, 24*(4), 485–495.

Fuchs, D., Burnside L., Reinink, A., & Marchenski, S. (2010). *Bound by the clock: The voices of Manitoba youth with FASD leaving care.* Public Health Agency Canada. Retrieved from https://cwrp.ca/publications/bound-clock-voices-manitoba-youth-fasd-leaving-care

Gooding, P., McSherry, B., Arstein-Kerslake, A., & Andrews, L. (2017). Unfitness to stand trial and the indefinite detention of persons with cognitive disabilities in Australia: Human rights challenges and proposals for change. *Melbourne University Law Review, 40*(3), 816–866.

Grasso, D. J. P., Ford, J. D. P., &. Briggs-Gowan, M. J. P. (2013). Early life trauma exposure and stress sensitivity in young children. *Journal of Pediatric Psychology, 38*(1), 94–103.

Hafekost, K., Lawrence, D., O'Leary, C., Bower, C., Semmens, J., & Zubrick, S. R. (2017a). Maternal alcohol use disorder and risk of child contact with the justice system in Western Australia: A population cohort record linkage study. *Alcoholism: Clinical & Experimental Research, 41*(8), 1452–1460.

Hafekost, K., Lawrence, D., O'Leary, C., Bower, C., Semmens, J., & Zubrick, S. R. (2017b). Maternal alcohol use disorder and child school attendance outcomes for non-Indigenous and Indigenous children in Western Australia: A population cohort record linkage study. *BMJ Open, 7*(7), e015650.

Hamilton, S., Reibel, T., Maslen, S., Watkins, R., Freeman, J., Passmore, H., … Bower, C. (2020). Disability "In-Justice": The benefits and challenges of

"Yarning" with young people undergoing diagnostic assessment for fetal alcohol spectrum disorder in a youth detention center. *Qualitative Health Research, 30*(2), 314–327.

Hand, L., Pickering, M., Kedge, S., & McCann, C. (2016). Oral language and communication factors to consider when supporting people with FASD involved with the legal system. In M. Nelson, & M. Trussler (Eds.), *Fetal alcohol spectrum disorders in adults: Ethical and legal perspectives* (pp. 139–147). Cham, Switzerland: Springer.

Hayden, C., & Graves, S. (2018). Patterns of offending behaviour over time for different groups of children in relation to time spent in and out of care. *Child & Family Social Work, 23*(1), 25–32.

Hazel, N. A., Hammen, C., Brennan, P. A., & Najman, J. (2008). Early childhood adversity and adolescent depression: The mediating role of continued stress. *Psychological Medicine, 38*(4) 581–589.

Hoyme, H. E., May, P. A., Kalberg, W. O., Kodituwakku, P., Gossage, J. P., Trujilo, P. M., ... Robinson, L. K. (2005). A practical clinical approach to diagnosis of fetal alcohol spectrum disorders: Clarification of the 1996 institute of medicine criteria. *Pediatrics, 115*(1), 39–47.

Hughes, N., Clasby, B., Chitsabesan, P., & Williams, H. (2016). A systematic review of the prevalence of foetal alcohol syndrome disorders among young people in the criminal justice system. *Cogent Psychology, 3*, 1–8.

Hughes, N. (2015). Neurodisability in the youth justice system: Recognising and responding to the criminalisation of neurodevelopmental impairment. *Howard League What is Justice? Working Papers 17/2015.*

Inkelis, S. M., & Thomas, J. D. (2018). Sleep in infants and children with prenatal alcohol exposure. *Alcoholism: Clinical & Experimental Research, 42*(8), 1390–1405.

Insana, S. P., Foley, K. O., Montgomery-Downs, H. E., Kolko, D. J., & McNeil, C. B. (2014). Children exposed to intimate partner violence demonstrate disturbed sleep and impaired functional outcomes. *Psychological Trauma: Theory, Research, Practice, & Policy, 6*(3), 290–298.

Institute of Health Economics and Government of Alberta. (2013, September). *Consensus statements on legal issues of fetal alcohol spectrum disorder.* Presented at Institute of Health Economics Consensus Development Conference, Edmonton, Alberta.

Jones, H., & Bower, C. (2016). Addressing foetal alcohol spectrum disorders in Australia. *Journal of Intellectual Disability Research, 60*(7–8), 688.

Jones, K., & Smith, D. (1973). Recognition of fetal alcohol syndrome in early infancy. *Lancet, 302*, 999–1001.

Jones, K. L., Smith, D. W., Ulleland, C. N., & Streissguth, P. (1973). Pattern of malformation in offspring of chronic alcoholic mothers. *Lancet, 1*(7815), 1267–1271.

Kerig, P. K. (2019). Linking childhood trauma exposure to adolescent justice involvement: The concept of posttraumatic risk-seeking. *Clinical Psychology: Science & Practice, 26*(3), e12280.

Kinner, S. A., Degenhardt, L., Coffey, C., Sawyer, S., Hearps, S., & Patton, G. (2014). Complex health needs in the youth justice system: A survey of community-based and custodial offenders. *Journal of Adolescent Health, 54*(5), 521–526.

Kinner, S. A., Degenhardt, L., Coffey, C., Hearps, S., Spittal, M., Sawyer, S. M., & Patton, G. C. (2015). Substance use and risk of death in young offenders: A prospective data linkage study. *Drug & Alcohol Review, 34*(1), 46–50.

Kinner, S. A., Lennox, N. G., & Taylor, M. (2009). Randomized controlled trial of a post-release intervention for prisoners with and without intellectual disability. *Journal on Developmental Disabilities, 15*(2), 72–76.

Kinner, S. A. P., & Milloy, M. J. M. (2011). Collateral consequences of an ever-expanding prison system. *CMAJ Canadian Medical Association Journal, 183*(5), 632.

Kippin, N. R., Leitão, S., Watkins, R., Finlay-Jones, A., Condon, C., Marriott, R., Mutch, R. C., & Bower, C. (2018). Language diversity, language disorder, and fetal alcohol spectrum disorder among youth sentenced to detention in Western Australia. *International Journal of Law and Psychiatry, 61*, 40–49.

Kodituwakku, P. W. (2007). Defining the behavioral phenotype in children with fetal alcohol spectrum disorders: A review. *Neuroscience and Biobehavioral Reviews, 31*(2), 192–201.

Koren, G., & Navioz, Y. (2003). Historical perspective: The original description of fetal alcohol spectrum disorder in France, 1967. *Therapeutic Drug Monitoring, 25*(2), 131.

Landgraf, M. N., Nothacker, M., & Heinen, F. (2013). Diagnosis of fetal alcohol syndrome (FAS): German guideline version 2013. *European Journal of Paediatric Neurology, 17*(5), 437–446.

Larroque, B., Kaminski, M., Dehaene, P., Subtil, D., Delfosse, M. J., & Querleu, D. (1995). Moderate prenatal alcohol exposure and psychomotor development at preschool age. *American Journal of Public Health, 85*, 1654–1661.

Larroque, B., Kaminski, M., Dehaene, P., Subtil, D., & Querleu, D. (2000). Prenatal alcohol exposure and signs of minor neurological dysfunction at preschool age. *Developmental Medicine and Child Neurology, 42*, 508–514.

LCM v The State of Western Australia [2016] WASC 164.

Lemoine, P., Harousseau, H., Borteyru, J. P., Lemoine, P., Borteyru, J. P., & Menuet, J. C. (1968). Les enfants de parents alcooliques. Anomalies observees. A propos de 127 cas. *Ouest Medical, 8*, 476.

Lemoine, P., Harousseau, H., Borteyru, J. P., & Menuet, J. C. (2003). Children of alcoholic parents—Observed anomalies: Discussion of 127 cases. *Therapeutic Drug Monitoring, 25*(2), 132–136.

Leveque, E., & Badry, D. (forthcoming). Confabulation and FASD: Making sense of memory. *CanFASD*.

Lowenfels, A. B., & Tuyns, A. J. (1994). A historical note about the foetal-alcohol syndrome. A letter from Professor Lemoine. *Addiction, 89*, 1021–1023.

Martin, C. J. (2015, February). *Indigenous Incarceration Rates: Strategies for much needed reform.* Speech delivered at the Law Summer School, Perth. Retrievedfromhttp://www.supremecourt.wa.gov.au/_files/Speeches_Indigenous_Incarceration_Rates.pdf

Mattson, S. N., Bernes, G. A., & Doyle, L. R. (2019). Fetal alcohol spectrum disorders: A review of the neurobehavioral deficits associated with prenatal alcohol exposure. *Alcoholism: Clinical & Experimental Research, 43*(6), 1046–1062.

Mattson, S. N., Roesch, S. C., Fagerlund, A., Autti-Rämö, I., Jones, K. L., May, P. A., ... the CIFASD. (2010). Toward a neurobehavioral profile of fetal alcohol spectrum disorders. *Alcoholism: Clinical and Experimental Research, 34*(9), 1640–1650.

Mattson, S. N., & Riley, E. P. (1998). A review of the neurobehavioral deficits in children with fetal alcohol syndrome or prenatal exposure to alcohol. *Alcohol Clinical and Experimental Research, 22*(2), 279–294.

Mattson, S. N., & Riley, E. P. (1999). Implicit and explicit memory functioning in children with heavy prenatal alcohol exposure. *Journal of the International Neuropsychological Society, 5*(5), 462–471.

Mattson, S. N., & Riley, E. P. (2000). Parent ratings of behavior in children with heavy prenatal alcohol exposure and IQ-matched controls. *Alcoholism: Clinical and Experimental Research, 24*, 226–231.

Mattson, S. N., Schoenfeld, A. M., & and Riley, E. P. (2001). Teratogenic effects of alcohol on brain and behaviour. *Alcohol Research and Health, 25*, 185–191.

McLachlan, K. (2017). Fetal alcohol spectrum disorder in yukon corrections. Final report to yukon justice: Estimating the prevalece of FASD, mental health, and substance use problems in the justice system. Retrieved from http://www.justice.gov.yk.ca/pdf/Corrected_McLachlan_Final_Report_to_Yukon_August_2017.pdf

McLean, S., & McDougall, S. (2014). *Fetal alcohol spectrum disorders: Current issues in awareness, prevention and intervention* (CFCA Paper No. 29). Retrieved from https://aifs.gov.au/cfca/publications/fetal-alcohol-spectrum-disorders-current-issues-awareness-prevention-and

Milward, D. (2014). The sentencing of aboriginal accused with fetal alcohol spectrum disorder: A search for different pathways. *University of British Colombia Law Review, 47*(3), 1025.

Molteno, C. D., Jacobsen, J. L., Carter, R. C., Dodge, N. C., & Jacobson, S. W. (2014). Infant emotional withdrawal: A precursor of affective and cognitive disturbance in fetal alcohol spectrum disorders. *Alcoholism: Clinical & Experimental Research, 38*(2), 479–488.

Mutch, R. (2016a). Developmental risk factors associated with incarceration in the juvenile justice system. *Journal of Intellectual Disability Research July/August, 60*(7–8), 713.

Mutch, R. (2016b). Prevalence of foetal alcohol spectrum disorder and neurocognitive impairment among incarcerated youth. *Journal of Intellectual Disability Research July/August, 60*(7–8), 713.

Mutch, R., Peadon, E. M., Elliott, E. J., & Bower, C. (2009). Need to establish a national diagnostic capacity for foetal alcohol spectrum disorders. *Journal of Paediatrics and Child Health, 45*(3), 79–81.

Mutch, R., Watkins, R., Jones, H., & Bower, C. (2013). *Fetal alcohol spectrum disorder: Knowledge, attitudes and practices within the Western Australian justice system: Final Report.* Foundation for Alcohol Research and Education, Telethon Institute for Child Health Research, Perth.

Nguyen-Louie, T. T., Brumback, T., Worley, M. J., Colrain, I. M., Matt, G. E., Squeglia, L. M., & Tapert, S. F. (2018). Effects of sleep on substance use in adolescents: A longitudinal perspective. *Addiction Biology, 23*(2), 750–760.

Novick Brown, N., Connor, P. D., & Adler, R. S. (2012). Conduct-disordered adolescents with fetal alcohol spectrum disorder: Intervention in secure treatment settings. *Criminal Justice & Behavior, 39*(6), 770–793.

O'Connor, M. J. P., & Paley, B. P. (2006). The relationship of prenatal alcohol exposure and the postnatal environment to child depressive symptoms. *Journal of Pediatric Psychology Special Issue on Prenatal Substance Exposure: Impact on Children's Health, Development, School Performance, and Risk behavior, 31*(1), 50–64.

O'Leary, C. M. (2004). Fetal alcohol syndrome: Diagnosis, epidemiology, and developmental outcomes. *Journal of Paediatrics and Child Health, 40*, 2–7.

O'Leary, C. M., & Bower, C. (2009). Measurement and classification of prenatal alcohol exposure and child outcomes: Time for improvement. *Addiction, 104*(8), 1275–1276.

O'Leary, C. M., & Bower, C. (2012). Guidelines for pregnancy: What's an acceptable risk, and how is the evidence (finally) shaping up? *Drug and Alcohol Review, 31*(2), 170–183.

O'Leary, C., Nassar, N., Kurinczuk, J., & Bower, C. (2009). The effect of maternal alcohol consumption on fetal growth and preterm birth. *Obstetrical & Gynecological Survey, 64*(5), 299–300.

O'Leary, C. M., Nassar, N., Kurinczuk, J. J., De Klerk, N., Geelhoed, E., Elliott, E. J., & Bower, C. (2010). Prenatal alcohol exposure and risk of birth defects. *Pediatrics, 126*(4), e843–e850.

O'Leary, C. M., Nassar, N., Zubrick, S. R., Kurinczuk, J. J., Stanley, F., & Bower, C. (2010). Evidence of a complex association between dose, pattern and timing of prenatal alcohol exposure and child behaviour problems. *Addiction, 105*(1), 74–86.

Olson, H. C., Oti, R., Gelo, J., & Beck, S. (2009). "Family matters:" Fetal alcohol spectrum disorders and the family. *Developmental Disabilities Research Reviews, 15*(3), 235–249.

Paley, B., O'Connor, M. J., Frankel, F., & Marquardt, R. (2006). Predictors of stress in parents of children with fetal alcohol spectrum disorders. *Journal of Developmental & Behavioral Pediatrics, 27*(5), 396–404.

Paley, B., O'Connor, M. J., Kogan, N., & Findlay, R. (2005). Prenatal alcohol exposure, child externalizing behavior, and maternal stress. *Parenting, 5*(1), 29–56.

Parliament of Australia Senate Standing Committees on Community Affairs. (2017). *Inquiry into the indefinite detention of people with cognitive and psychiatric impairment in Australia.* Report, Parliament of Australia, Australia, November.

Parliament of Western Australia, Legislative Assembly, Education and Health Standing Committee. (2012). *Foetal alcohol spectrum disorder: The invisible disability, Report No. 15.* Parliament of Western Australia, Perth.

Peled, M., Smith., A., & McCreary Centre Society. (2014). *Breaking through the barriers: Supporting youth with FASD who have substance use challenges.* Vancouver, BC: McCreary Centre. Society.

Poitra, B. A., Marion, S., Dionne, M., Wilkie, E., Dawphinais, P., Wilke-Pepion, M., ... Burd, L. (2003). A school-based screening program for fetal alcohol syndrome. *Neurotoxicology and Teratology, 25*(6), 725–729.

Poole, N., Schmidt, R. A., Green, C., & Hemsing, N. (2016). Prevention of fetal alcohol spectrum disorder: Current Canadian efforts and analysis of gaps. *Substance Abuse: Research and Treatment, 10,* SART-S34545.

Rasmussen, C., Andrew, G., Zwaigenbaum, L., & Tough, S. (2008). Neurobehavioural outcomes of children with fetal alcohol spectrum disorders: A Canadian perspective. *Paediatrics & Child Health, 13*(3), 185–191.

Reid, N., Moritz, K. M., & Akison, L. K. (2019). Adverse health outcomes associated with fetal alcohol exposure: A systematic review focused on immune-related outcomes. *Pediatric Allergy and Immunology, 30*(7), 698–707.

Reid, N., Kippin, N., Passmore, H., & Finlay-Jones, A. (2020). Fetal alcohol spectrum disorder: The importance of assessment, diagnosis and support in the Australian justice context, *Psychiatry, Psychology and Law, 27*(2), 265–274.

Resendiz, M., Chen, Y., Oztürk, N. C., & Zhou, F. C. (2013). Epigenetic medicine and fetal alcohol spectrum disorders. *Epigenomics, 5*(1), 73–86.

Roach, K., & Bailey, A. (2009). The relevance of fetal alcohol spectrum disorder in Canadian criminal law from investigation to sentencing. *University of British Colombia Law Review, 42,* 1–68.

Robst, J., Armstrong, M., & Dollard, N. (2017). The association between type of out-of-home mental health treatment and juvenile justice recidivism for youth with trauma exposure. *Criminal Behaviour & Mental Health, 27*(5), 501–513.

Sayal, K. (2007). Alcohol consumption in pregnancy as a risk factor for later mental health problems. *Evidence-Based Mental Health, 10*(4), 98–100.

Sokol, R., Delaney-Black, V., & Nordstrom, B. (2003). Fetal alcohol spectrum disorder. *Journal of the American Medical Association, 290*(22), 2996–2999.

State of Western Australia v BB (A Child) [2015] WACC 2.

State of Western Australia v Tax [2010] WASC 208.

Stratton, K., Howe, C., & Battaglia, F. (Eds.) (1996). *Fetal alcohol syndrome: Diagnosis, epidemiology, prevention, and treatment.* Washington, DC: National Academy Press.

Streissguth, A. P., Aase, J. M., Clarren, S. K., Randels, S. P., LaDue, R. A., & Smith, D. F. (1991). Fetal alcohol syndrome in adolescents and adults. *Journal of the American Medical Association, 265,* 1961–1967.

Streissguth, A. P., Barr, H. M., Sampson, P. D., & Bookstein, F. L. (1994). Prenatal alcohol and offspring development: The first fourteen years. *Drug and Alcohol Dependence, 36*(2), 89–99.

Streissguth, A., & Kanter, J. (1997). *Primary and secondary disabilities in fetal alcohol syndrome, in The challenge of fetal alcohol syndrome: Overcoming secondary disabilities.* Seattle: University of Washington Press.

Thornton, L. C., Frick, P. J., Crapanzano, A. M., & Terranova, A. M. (2013). The incremental utility of callous-unemotional traits and conduct problems in predicting aggression and bullying in a community sample of boys and girls. *Psychological Assessment, 25*(2), 366–378.

United Nations Committee on the Rights of the Child. (2019). *General comment No. 24 (2019) on children's rights in the child justice system* (CRC/C/GC/24, 18 September). Retrieved from https://www.ohchr.org/Documents/HRBodies/CRC/GC24/GeneralComment24.pdf

van Dooren, K., Kinner, S. A., & Butler, T. (2010). Young prisoners: An important group for health research? *Journal of Correctional Health Care, 16*(4), 322–327.

Ware, A. L., Crocker, N., O'Brien, J. W., Dewesse, B. N., Roesch, S. C., Coles, C. D., ... Mattson, S. N. (2012). Executive function predicts adaptive behavior in children with histories of heavy prenatal alcohol exposure and attention-deficit/hyperactivity disorder. *Alcoholism: Clinical & Experimental Research, 36*(8), 1431–1441.

Wengel, T., Hanlon-Dearman, A. C., & Fjeldsted, B. (2011). Sleep and sensory characteristics in young children with fetal alcohol spectrum disorder. *Journal of Developmental & Behavioral Pediatrics, 32*(5), 384–392.

Williams, R. (2018). *Understanding fetal alcohol spectrum disorder through the stories of Nyoongar families and how may this inform policy and service delivery.* Unpublished Doctoral dissertation. Curtin University, Perth, Western Australia.

Wyper, K., & Pei, J. (2016). Neurocognitive difficulties underlying high risk and criminal behaviour in FASD: Clinical implications. In M. Nelson & M. Trussler (Eds.), *Fetal alcohol spectrum disorders in adults: Ethical and legal perspectives* (pp. 101–120). Cham, Switzerland: Springer.

3 FASD prevalence and assessment

Raewyn Mutch, Tamara Tulich, Harry Blagg, and Suzie Edward May

Introduction

This chapter outlines existing research on the prevalence of FASD including an in-depth account of the two leading Australian studies: the Lililwan project and the Banksia Hill Study. It examines the best practice model for diagnosis and management, including current diagnostic assessments used by a multidisciplinary diagnostic team, and explores the problems of undiagnosed FASD, access to diagnosis and trauma in Aboriginal communities. It argues that there is an urgent need for greater resources to ensure routine and universal assessment and diagnosis of health, well-being, and neurodevelopmental needs for all young people in contact with juvenile justice systems, and the provision of culturally safe, co-designed and trauma-informed rehabilitation, education and therapeutic programmes in justice and other settings.

The prevalence of FASD

The difficulty of obtaining accurate rates of FASD is well documented (Allen et al., 2007, p. 65; Douglas, 2010, p. 226; Fitzpatrick et al., 2015, p. 451; Harris & Bucens, 2003). The low reported rates in Australia are frequently attributed to under-diagnosis, under-reporting, lack of information regarding prenatal alcohol exposure, inconsistent diagnostic criteria, and under-representation of high-risk populations (Douglas, 2010, p. 226; Fast & Conroy, 2004, p. 162; Fitzpatrick et al., 2015, p. 451).

Most existing prevalence studies report only FAS. Existing Australian estimates of FAS in non-Indigenous populations have ranged from 0.14 to 1.7 per 100 children (Allen et al., 2007, p. 64; Bower et al., 2000; Harris & Bucens, 2003, pp. 530–531). Consistently with prevalence studies internationally (Chartrand & Forbes-Chilibeck, 2003, p. 40), FASD is disproportionately diagnosed amongst First Nations communities in Australia (Parliament of Australia, 2011, p. 96ff, 2012, p. 33ff). Australian estimates in Indigenous populations have ranged from 0.14 to 4.7 per 100 children (Parliament of Australia, 2011, p. 96ff, 2012, p. 33 ff). In 2015, Australia's first population-based study on the prevalence of FAS/pFAS, *the Lililwan Project,* reported rates of 12 per 100 children in the remote Aboriginal town of Fitzroy Crossing in Western Australia (Fitzpatrick et al., 2015). This is the highest reported prevalence of FAS/pFAS in Australia and similar to rates reported in 'high-risk' populations internationally (Fitzpatrick et al., 2015, p. 450).

In 2004 Streissguth et al., published a seminal paper on the longitudinal outcomes for a cohort of 415 young people diagnosed with Fetal Alcohol Syndrome and Fetal Alcohol Effects (median age 14 years at follow-up). Sixty percent had found themselves in trouble with the law and 35% had been incarcerated for a crime (Streissguth et al., 2004). Systematic reviews in 2011 and 2016 (Hughes, Clasby, Chitsabesan, & Williams, 2016; Popova et al., 2011a) identified four studies, all from Canada, of different methodologies seeking the prevalence of FASD among justice involved youth; two studies determined the prevalence of FASD through self-report survey (11.7% and 21%) (Fast, Conry & Loock, 1999), one retrospectively examined records of young people in a sexual offender programme (10.9%) (Murphy & Chittenden, 2005) and the other was an active case ascertainment of youth remanded to a forensic psychiatry unit (23.3%) (Rojas & Gretton, 2007). The most recent Canadian work actively seeking to determine the prevalence of FASD among justice-involved adults in the Yukon published their results in 2017. Professor Kaitlyn McLachlan's study found 14 of the 80 participants (17.5%) had FASD (McLachlan, 2017).

In Australia there have been recent studies to understand the nature of neurocognitive impairments (NCI) and mental health needs of justice-involved young people (Borschmann et al., 2014; Haysom, Indig, Moore, & Gaskin, 2014; Heffernan, Anderson, Davidson & Kinner, 2015; Howard, Lennings & Copeland, 2003; Royal Australasian College of Physicians, 2011). A New South Wales study reviewed cognitive abilities of young people from eight juvenile detention centres; 65% of all justice-involved youth completed the study (Indig et al., 2011). Nearly half (45.8%) had borderline or lower IQ including 14% with an IQ < 70; FASD had not been included in their clinical determination yet was likely present (Hughes et al., 2016). A Victorian study found 22% of justice-involved youth had engaged in self-harm and 17%

had psychosis (Borschmann et al., 2014). Mental health difficulties are common secondary difficulties manifest in young people with FASD (Olson et al., 2007; Streissguth et al., 2004). Mental health difficulties are more often manifest when persons with an FASD have lived sustained secondary trauma as a consequence of their FASD diagnosis not being considered and so accommodations to their needs have not being provided (House of Representatives, 2012; Streissguth et al., 1997; Parliament of Western Australia, 2012).

With Australia's unreconciled history of colonisation, sustained inequality between Aboriginal and other Australians including unmitigated gaps in health and educational outcomes, Aboriginal young people are 20 times more likely to be in detention compared with their non-Aboriginal young peers (Australian Institute of Health and Welfare, 2017). The Australian Institute of Health and Welfare (2017) reports that on an average day in 2016–2017 in Western Australia, the rate of Aboriginal young people in detention was a staggering 41 times the non-Aboriginal rate. According to the most recent available data, on 31 March 2020, 75% of youth detainees in Western Australia were of Aboriginal decent (that is, 87 out of 116), while they constitute roughly 7% of the relevant youth population (Department of Justice, Corrective Services, 2020).

The Lililwan project

The issue of FASD achieved prominence in Australia following campaigns initiated in 2007 by Aboriginal women in the West Kimberley town of Fitzroy Crossing to reduce the over-supply and over-consumption of alcohol due to the high number of alcohol and drug-related suicides in the Fitzroy Valley, extensive family violence and the increase in child protection issues associated with FASD (Aboriginal and Torres Strait Islander Social Justice Commissioner, 2011, p. 72). The Fitzroy Valley sits within the Kimberley regions of Western Australia. A high proportion of residents in the Fitzroy Valley are of Aboriginal heritage. Within the Fitzroy Valley there are four Aboriginal language groups – Bunuba, Gooniyandi, Walmajarri, and Wangkatjunga (Marninwartikura, 2009), spanning across approximately 40 communities and outstations. The town of Fitzroy Crossing is the regional hub of the Valley. One of the main reasons for this community-led action was the impact that alcohol was having on unborn children. Communities of the Fitzroy Valley were in crisis (Aboriginal and Torres Strait Islander Social Justice Commissioner, 2011, p. 69), with health professionals commenting on the devastating impacts of alcohol abuse within the community.

A coronial inquiry into the high rate of suicide in the area found that there had been a 100% increase in the number of self-harm deaths between 2005 and 2006, and that the rate of self-harm deaths in the Fitzroy Valley was exceptionally high (Hope, 2008). There was also great concern about the impact of alcohol consumption 'on the transfer of culture–stories, art and ceremony–from one generation to the next' (Elliott, Latimer, Fitzpatrick, Oscar, & Carter, 2012, p. 190). As concerns grew for the social and emotional well-being of Fitzroy Valley residents, Aboriginal women, including June Oscar (Bunuba), Emily Carter (Gooniyandi & Kija), and Maureen Carter (Gooniyandi & Kija), took charge. As a result of the communities, lobbying, the Director of Liquor imposed an initial six-month restriction on the sale of packaged liquor in the area (Elliott et al., 2012). This restriction was then extended indefinitely (Kinnane et al., 2010).

In 2015, three senior women, June Oscar (Bunuba), Emily Carter (Gooniyandi & Kija), and Maureen Carter (Gooniyandi & Kija), initiated and brokered a partnership between Nindilingarri Cultural Health Service and Marninwarntikura Women's Resource Centre, The George Institute for Global Health, and The University of Sydney Medical School to conduct the first population-based Australian study of FASD prevalence (Elliott et al., 2012). Known as *The Lililwan Project*, it also sought to develop individual treatment plans for children; educate the community on the risks of alcohol consumption during pregnancy; and provide support for parents, carers, and teachers. The name of the project derived from the Kimberley Kriol word 'Lililwanis', meaning 'all the little ones' (Elliott et al., 2012, p. 191). The research confirmed significant rates of FAS/pFASD of 12 per 100 children (Fitzpatrick et al., 2015). This is the highest reported prevalence of FAS/pFAS in Australia and similar to rates reported in 'high-risk' populations internationally (Fitzpatrick et al., 2015, p. 450).

The Banksia Hill Study

The complexity and risk for recidivism by a child and adolescent with unrecognised neurodevelopmental impairment such as FASD, is a global phenomenon (Greenmyer, 2018; Popova, 2011a, b). In light of this, the Western Australian child health research team completed a study examining the feasibility of screening and diagnosing FASD among sentenced children and adolescents. The study was completed at The Banksia Hill Detention Centre, the only juvenile detention facility of Western Australia. The study examined a representative sample of sentenced children and adolescents and found 89% had at least one domain of severe neurodevelopmental impairment. The sample included 99 young people (92 male, 6 female, 1 gender diverse) aged from 13 to 17 years, with a mean age of 15 years, with nearly three-quarter of the young people (n=73, 74%) self-identified as being Aboriginal-Australian. The Study found 89% had at least one domain of severe neurodevelopmental impairment.

Severity of impairment was assigned when standardised testing found individual measures fell two or more standard deviations less than the mean. The study employed a multidisciplinary team (MDT) of tertiary qualified health professionals to assess neurodevelopmental abilities. The team included a paediatrician, a speech and language pathologist, an occupational therapist and a clinical neuropsychologist, and a research officer. This MDT represents the minimum set of professional capabilities necessary to complete a comprehensive health and well-being assessment and to determine neurodevelopmental strengths and difficulties. In order to diagnose FASD, the MDT applied the Australian diagnostic guidelines for considering FASD. Normally ten domains are to be measured; however for the purposes of completing this study in a secure detention setting only nine of the required ten domains were measured. Adaptive functioning is imposed on all children and adolescents in a secure detention setting through daily scheduled routines for self-care expectations to complete group tasks.

A total of 36 young people were diagnosed with FASD, a prevalence of 36% (95% confidence interval 27%–46%). All diagnoses were made using the most recent iteration of the Australian FASD Diagnostic Guidelines and all were in the category of FASD with < 3 sentinel facial features; two were non-Aboriginal (FASD prevalence=8%), 34 were Aboriginal (FASD prevalence=49%). Two young people had a FASD diagnosis prior to entering the study. One was diagnosed 5–6 years previously, and one was a more recent diagnosis but had not had all domains assessed at that time. Both young people had the diagnosis of FASD confirmed using the new Australian criteria.

On completion of the clinical component of the Banksia Hill Study, the participating children and adolescents were found to be a representative sample of all children and adolescents sentenced to detention in Western Australia. As previously stated, nearly all participating children and adolescents had at least one domain of severe neurodevelopmental impairment (89%) not previously determined prior to participating in the study. Nearly two-thirds (65%) had three or more domains of impairment and the remaining third had five or more domains of impairment. These findings of profound neurodevelopmental impairment and unmet need demonstrate a failure of health, education, child protection, and justice systems to consider or seek to determine these neurodevelopmental vulnerabilities during their prior involvement with this children. There were common histories of the break down of out-of-home care and early school failure, yet none of these behavioural difficulties prompted requests for a comprehensive neurodevelopmental assessment.

Three or more domains of neurodevelopmental impairment meets eligibility criteria for accessing rehabilitative and therapeutic services of the Australian National Disability Insurance Scheme (NDIS). Access to NDIS services and the national free health services (Medicare) are prohibited for all children and adolescents on remand or sentenced under the justice system. Of all children and adolescents participating in the Banksia Hill Study, severe impairment was found in academic functioning (86%), attention (72%), executive functioning (78%), cognition (21%), memory (56%), fine and gross motor skills (50%), and language and communication (69%) (Bower et al., 2018; Kippin et al., 2018). Severe impairments were also noted with or without FASD (Bower et al., 2018).

Nearly one in two of the children and adolescents participating in the Banksia Hill Study also had a sibling previously engaged with juvenile justice services. This single fact highlights the need to routinely assess all children and adolescents when they first engage with statutory services and to consider their family of origin. The neurodevelopmental assessment must be applied in parallel with a comprehensive health and well-being assessment. The first child in a family coming under statutory services could be a means by which intensive services are directed to the family of origin. Comprehensive assessments for all siblings may prove a cost-saving and life-saving initiative, elevating opportunity for prevention, diversion and rehabilitation for all siblings and a mechanism for families to remain safe and together. Such initiatives also open the opportunity for recovery capital (Hamilton et al., 2020) and may interrupt the iterative intergenerational trauma of children being apprehended and families being fractured (Herman & Schatzow, 1987).

Principles to guide assessments and diagnosis: lessons learned from Banksia Hill Study

The children and adolescents with neurodevelopmental impairment and FASD have commonly endured adversity and trauma. The statutory systems engaging these same children and adolescents have an inconsistent record of mitigating risk and trauma as evidenced by their repeated inclusion in summaries and proceedings from royal commissions and coronial enquires. The conflict and adversities common among children and adolescents involved in justice services are the similar conflicts and trauma prevalent across their communities of origin. The trauma of the workplace for justice and custodial staff and the inter-sectorial tensions across out-of-home care, education, and justice services are characteristics commonly encountered in a humanitarian disaster.

The children and adolescents within the juvenile justice settings represent the human cost of unmet health and development needs and unmitigated lived-trauma. The over-representation of First Nations children and adolescents followed by the representation of children from migrant and refugee backgrounds, reflects indentured and intergenerational effects of colonisation. Considered together, these children represent a burden of need with equal characteristics and complexities as found in the theatre of humanitarian disasters. It is contended, therefore, that effective engagement with justice services by actors for child and adolescent health and well-being is best undertaken through referencing the internationally recognised and agreed practices known as humanitarian principles and humanitarian action.

The International Committee of the Red Cross and The United Nations remind us of the importance of humanitarian principles in maintaining access to individuals affected by natural disasters, armed conflict and other complex emergency situations to address human suffering wherever found (Swiss Federal Department of Foreign Affairs, 2019). The purpose of humanitarian action is to protect life and health and ensure respect for human beings in the framework of those principles. In recognition of the common adverse pathways leading children and adolescents into the juvenile justice systems, iterative trauma and unmet health and social well-being needs, the juvenile justice setting is equal to a complex emergency for any child and adolescent. During the Banksia Hill Study, it became evident that referencing the framework of humanitarian principles made certain the research team was able to engage effectively between the custodial staff and the sentenced children and adolescents. The team were able to complete unbiased assessments, and the staff and participants were able to trust health recommendations. The four pillars of humanitarian principles – humanity, impartiality, neutrality, and independence – are now considered and suggested for future application when working for system change in juvenile justice settings.

The first principle of humanity requires that human suffering must be addressed where it is found. The purpose of humanitarian action is to protect life and health and ensure respect for human beings. Children and adolescents in juvenile justice systems, by the very nature that they are there, indicates they have suffered. Even if their engagement is from their role as protagonist or perpetrator, their humanity is not diminished nor should be considered less. In accepting the humanitarian principle when working with the children and adolescents in justice settings, there is a requirement to determine the full nature of the lived experiences of the child and adolescent and have this pillar be one of the guiding principles when developing an individualised response to their assessment and restorative needs of all.

Humanitarian action must be carried out based on need alone. Impartiality, another of the four humanitarian principles, requires priority to be given to the most urgent cases of distress and make no distinctions based on gender, race, class, religious beliefs, nationality, or political opinions. Children and adolescents involved in juvenile justice systems have arrived there because their iterative needs were not recognised or not addressed in a manner capable of diverting them away from entering the system. Impartiality complements the principle of humanity, expecting no attribution of blame and providing compassionate space to seek reasons for the young person's distress. Identifying an individuals' reasons for their distress leading to juvenile justice is the beginning of resolution and informs essential mechanisms to restore each child and adolescent to health and well-being and return to community.

Neutrality needs to be understood as separate to impartiality. Neutrality requires the recognition of the complexities of negotiation and responsibilities shared between juvenile justice and other statutory systems and their separate and overlapping relationship with all children and adolescents under their jurisdictions. Adhering to humanitarian principles asks the humanitarian actor to not take sides in hostilities or engage in controversies. Although the original definition asks the humanitarian actor to not engage in hostilities and controversies of a political, racial, religious, or ideological nature, the domains of race and ideology are woven through juvenile justice services. Race and ideology cannot be ignored if the humanitarian actor is applying a decolonising and trauma-informed practice. System reformation rests on persuasive change. Existing ideologies of crime and punishment cannot be shifted to one of harm mitigation and restoration, if the humanitarian actor bringing health and well-being initiatives while also informing system change, is perceived to take sides.

The fourth of the humanitarian principles is independence and is not readily available to the child and adolescent under detention nor to the staff in charge of their care. In the case of research into juvenile justice systems, the research team can and should be independent from the very systems they are researching. The provision of health and well-being may originate from statutory systems of health and education and so be required to meet key performance indicators which in turn may constrain humanity and impartiality. Yet the provision of heath care must be independent and not altered by the moral judgement of the action or attributes of the person receiving care. Independence is most likely when the action is autonomous of political, economic, military, and other preconceived objectives. The three other pillars of humanity, impartiality and neutrality can support the boundaries of independence.

FASD assessment – a child development framework

From before conception until birth, the developing child is crafted according to inherited and novel genetic code. In-utero development is a stepwise and complex metamorphosis, modulated by proximal and external stimuli exerting advantageous and sometimes harmful effects. The developing child undergoes extraordinary change in structure and function in-utero informed by the genetic recipes, genes, encoded on deoxyribonucleic acid (DNA) and inherited from the biological parents. The genetic recipes unfold and through complex cellular processes are transcribed and inform how to make and build individual and complex interacting components for life. The in-utero milieu and the form and function of the developing child are in constant flux. The genetic processes are further influenced in real-time by the health and well-being of their parents (Grasso, Ford, & Briggs-Gowan, 2013; Hazel et al., 2008), the how and where they live (Brisbois, Farmer, & McCargar, 2012; Kato et al., 2013; Kawachi, Adler, & Dow, 2010; Siddiqi et al., 2007; Subramanian, Kawachi, & Smith, 2007). The genetic processes are moderated by real-time cellular factors as well as by epigenetic information, that is the heterogeneous and dynamic methylation of the DNA. Although there is no satisfactory explanation as yet for how tens of thousands of genes are orchestrated in their exclusive expression during differentiation (Resendiz et al., 2013), DNA-methylation, and histone codification influences how a genetic recipe is read and utilised. The lived experiences of biological parents can alter the methylation and coding of their own DNA (Labonte et al., 2012). Epigenetics can be inherited completely, or partially modified, and these changes can remain and in turn be passed on to offspring (Labonte et al., 2012; Perrin et al., 2010). Epigenetic effects can influence how DNA and genes are read across the whole of life (Taylor et al., 2016) and internalises external impacts to potentially redirect an established genetic course (Resendiz et al., 2013). Underlying epigenetic causes of FASD serve as an excellent example of the environmental impact on epigenetics (Resendiz et al., 2013).

Colonisation, dispossession, genocide, and cultural and spiritual destruction have been particularly harmful to First Nations peoples. War, famines, environmental crises, and forced migration are similarly harmful events (Betancourt et al., 2012; Finkelhor et al., 2015; Hanes et al., 2017; Seiler et al., 2016). Lived adversities can change the methylation and characteristics of DNA and these changes can be passed on to influence offspring and subsequent generations. In Australia, the transgenerational negative effects of colonisation and colonial trauma were amplified when generations of Aboriginal and Torres Strait Islander children were stolen from their parents and assimilated into statutory systems (Atkinson, 2002). The colonial-trauma is iterative across statutory systems and the negative effects are intergenerational and intracellular. There is global consensus informed from iterative research to recommend routine and universal screening of adverse childhood experiences (ACEs) (Purewal et al., 2016). The High Court of Australia has also stated that trauma is not extinguished across our lifetimes but must be considered on every occasion (*Bugmy v The Queen* [2013], para. 42; Maschi, Viola, & Koskinen, 2015; Maschi et al., 2013). Adversities and trauma, inherited, repetitive, and unremitting, contribute to the unacceptable, high and increasing rates of Indigenous incarceration and suicide (Dodson & IndigenousX, 2019; Gray et al., 2004, 2016).

'To us health is so much more than simply not being sick.

It's about getting a balance between physical, mental, emotional, cultural and spiritual health.

Health and healing are interwoven, which means that one can't be separated from the other.'

Dr Tamara Mackean, Chair of the Royal Australasian College of Physicians (RACP) Aboriginal and Torres Strait Islander Health Committee (Royal Australasian College of Physicians, Aboriginal and Torres Strait Islander Health Committee, 2018).

The Aboriginal and Torres Strait Islander Health Committee of the Royal Australasian College of Physicians defines health as a balance between five determinants: physical, mental, emotional, cultural, and spiritual health. Biology, psychosocial, culture and belief, place and environmental, each and together, influence in-utero development and influence an individual's development, health, and well-being across their life-course (Royal Australasian College of Physicians, 2018). Recognition, protection and provision of a full complement of each of the five determinants is a matter of rights, justice, and equity, and a certain means of ensuring best health and development (Goldhagen, 2020; Marmot, 2006, 2012, 2016). Provision of equitable and comprehensive, freely available health care together with well-resourced protective social determinants is a right for everyone and should never be considered as fee-for-service nor as a privilege (Bauchner & Fontanarosa, 2020).

Ages and stages of neurodevelopment and cognition

Childhood is a dynamic period of physical, psychosocial, and cognitive growth. Childhood and child development are advantaged when the child experiences a safe cohesive attachment to community and place. Esteem and dignity are endowed when a child acquires adaptive proficiency in language and culture (Fitzpatrick 2016, 2017; Aboriginal and Torres Strait Islander Social Justice Commissioner, 2017). Proficiency is especially important when language and culture may differ from the dominant practices of statutory systems such as education and health. Childhood allows time for iterative learning to develop and practice social, emotional, and physical competencies, and is successful when basic skills in these broad domains are attained. Outcomes such as well-being, resilience, and quality of life are best when additional factors such as safety, attachment, reduced, and removed inequities across domains such as education and healthcare provision are present.

From birth to two years of age typically developing children engage and explore their environment. The sensorimotor domain of development is at the forefront of how they engage in the world and learn. Here the vital developmental interplay of attachment, trust, and mistrust are laid down with a profound influence on future life (Madigan et al., 2016). From two years to six years the typically developing child begins to understand autonomy and shame; they experiment with initiative and can experience guilt; and they may or may not experience punishment and fear. Between two years and six years, the typically developing child may develop symbolic thought although the representations are typically considered pre-operational; this means the child cannot use logic or transform, combine, or separate ideas. From four years onwards in Australia, education is free and accessible until 18 years of age. Schooling is critical for optimal development and is causally related to health outcomes (Kawachi et al., 2010). Safe and supportive families together with safe and supportive schools help a child attain their best health and develop their full potential (Viner et al., 2012). From eight years to ten years, the typically developing child is accepted as industrious in their interaction with the world and can be observed to initially apply concrete reasoning to make sense of how things work. Transitioning to abstract thinking and applying logic may begin for the typically developing child at the start of their adolescence, yet for some typically developing adolescents, their acquisition of abstract thought and logical principles is yet to be achieved near the end of their teen years.

Adolescence is a time of renewed and rapid change in the body's structures, their internal and outward form and functions. The outward and striking visible changes in body habitus and function are paralleled by cognitive and psychosocial changes where the emerging adult experiments to find their place in community. Adolescence is a time for experimentation and risk-taking, practicing autonomy and independence ideally while still possessing a safe place to retreat to, a place where their younger self can be nurtured, regroup, and try again. Structural factors such as national wealth, income inequality, and access to education are the strongest determinants of adolescent health. Structural factors together with positive and supportive peers are crucial to helping young people develop to their full potential and attain the best health in the transition to adulthood (Viner et al., 2012). For some children their opportunity for a normal adolescence is truncated from failure of their structural factors, such as core or overwhelming psychosocial vulnerabilities (Oei, 2018) and for some, specific requirements of their culture-of-origin (Antonucci et al., 2019; Kidman, 2017). Truncated adolescence may shorten educational opportunities, removing the possibility for testing their adult identity and adaptive skills, and may reduce their economic and social advantage for the long term. This in turn diminishes their successful experimentation with social and reasoning abilities, to support negotiation of safe interpersonal relationships and spaces. Improving adolescent health requires improving young people's daily life with families, with peers, and in schools; addressing risk and protective factors in the social environment at a population level; and focussing on factors that are protective across various health outcomes (Viner et al., 2012).

The typically developing adolescent brain undergoes regional changes to refine brain function and connectivity (Spear, 2013). The cortical grey matter increases in size across adolescence up and until the beginning of the third decade (Donald et al., 2015; Giedd & Giedd, 2004). The typically developing adolescent brain does not possess matured inhibitory control systems. An adolescent's normal inhibitory control can be overcome under emotional circumstances. The typically developing adolescent brain has delayed maturation of the brain's frontal regions resulting in developmental immaturities in cognitive control, attentional regulation, response inhibition, and other relatively advanced cognitive functions (Casey, Getz & Galvan, 2008). The adolescent can utilise these cognitive functions until increased task demands, or increased emotion and arousal, can elicit performance impairment. Stressful and emotional situations can attenuate activity in frontal regions (Liston et al., 2009). Typically, the adolescent seeks iterative and immediate reward and their brain is less sensitive to aversive stimuli, meaning punishment cannot be a mechanism expected to induce change in adolescent behaviour or teach consequences. The normal neural networks of the typically developing adolescent brain rewards the adolescent seeking immediate and enjoyable experiences, the effects of which are heightened through risk-taking.

Recommended diagnosis

Diagnosis of FASD requires a comprehensive evaluation of primary and secondary neurodevelopmental strengths and difficulties, specialist knowledge of typical and non-typical development and an ability to differentiate between abnormalities or traits. In Australia, FASD is underdiagnosed and the effects of PAE and unrecognised FASD are life limiting and adverse (Bower et al., 2018; Elliott et al., 2006; Mutch, Wray & Bower, 2012). There is recognition of a higher rate of FASD in Aboriginal children born in Western Australian (Gray, 2004; Mutch, Watkins & Bower, 2015). In 2016, Australian guidelines for the screening and diagnosis of FASD were released to establish consistency for categorising FASD across the nation (Bower & Elliot, 2016). In Australia the diagnosis of FASD is to be completed by a multidisciplinary team of specialist clinicians (Jones, 1999) including a paediatrician, speech and language pathologist, occupational therapist, clinical neuropsychologist, and cultural navigator. Diagnosis requires evaluation of likely or actual PAE and carries with it complexities associated with maternal self-reporting (which may be subject to bias) (Eichler et al., 2016) and the use of alcohol biomarkers in pregnancy, which remains largely experimental.

Diagnosis of FASD also requires evaluation of primary and secondary neurodevelopmental difficulties, which are associated with poor long-term outcomes (Rasmussen et al., 2008). Secondary difficulties include repeated occasions of disrupted school experience, out-of-home care and detention, trouble with the law, inappropriate sexual behaviours, and substance misuse (Coriale et al., 2013). Nutritional and social deprivations, substance dependencies (Richardson, Day & Goldschmidt, 1995; Noland et al., 2003) misuse of prescription and non-prescription drugs and domestic violence (Devaney, 2008), negatively impact on typical development. Early life trauma (Labonte et al., 2012) and adverse childhood experiences, have proven negative association with cognitive abilities, attention, and affect regulation (Felitti et al., 1998; Finkelhor et al., 2015; Royal Australasian College of Physicians, 2018). Co-morbid or alternative diagnoses must be considered, including genetic aetiologies, when evaluating test outcomes (Emdad & Sondergaard, 2006) and weighing their likely contribution to measured abilities of anyone being considered for FASD.

In Australia, ten neurodevelopmental domains are considered (Kaemingk & Paquette, 1999) during a comprehensive assessment to determine FASD (Watkins et al., 2012), these include (i) brain structure/neurology; (ii) motor skills; (iii) cognition; (iv) language; (v) academic achievement; (vi) memory; (vii) attention; (viii) executive function, including impulse control and hyperactivity (ix) affect regulation, and (x) adaptive behaviour, social skills or social communication. A FASD diagnosis requires objective evidence of severe impairment of brain function in at least three of these ten specified neurodevelopmental domains. Evidence of severe impairment in three or more domains should be attributed to prenatal alcohol exposure only when other aetiologies have been considered. Criteria for severe impairment is when the global score or a major subdomain score on a standardised validated neurodevelopmental scale, is two or more standard deviations below the mean or less than the third percentile.

The current Australian Guide to the Diagnosis of FASD (2020) outlines the detail required to assess each domain and the 'clinical cut-off' criteria for assigning impairment and severity for each domain (Bower & Elliot, 2016). The Guide uses the clinical aids developed at the University of Washington by Susan Astley to assess facial dysmorphology associated with PAE (Astley, 2013; Astley & Clarren, 1999). A recent update to the Guide in February 2020 resulted in no amendments to the instrument or how to use it; however the Australian Guide is under a new tender from the Federal Government for the purpose of further revision at the time of writing this chapter.

There is an additional lens needed when considering the methods and outcomes of a comprehensive neurodevelopmental assessment and assigning strengths and vulnerabilities. This lens is for the necessary inclusion an individual's culture of origin and the cultural perspective regarding health and development; some cultures do not have terms for impairment or disability (see discussion in Chapter 6). The Aboriginal and Torres Strait Islander Health Committee of the Royal Australasian College of Physicians (2018) explains a measure of health among Aboriginal and Torres Strait Islander peoples must include consideration of an individuals' physical, mental, emotional, cultural, and spiritual domains. Cultural understandings are necessary when interpreting the health and well-being assessment measures. Co-design for cultural safety is recommended when planning individual recovery programmes and pathways for healing (Azzopardi, 2020; Freeman et al., 2019; Johnston et al., 2019; Hamilton, 2019; Hamilton et al., 2020; Smith, 2016; Smith et al., 2019).

Ten specific developmental domains considered for diagnosis of FASD in Australia

(i) Brain structure/neurology

Impairment in the brain structure and neurology domain is assigned when the following are present: (i) the occipitofrontal head circumference is abnormal; (ii) known structural brain abnormalities; (iii) a seizure disorder not due to known postnatal causes; and (iv) a significant neurological diagnosis not otherwise explained (e.g., visual impairment, cerebral palsy, and sensory-neuronal hearing loss). Assessment of the brain structure domain requires a physician or a paediatrician to consider the history, clinical signs, and available measures. Brain magnetic resonance imaging (MRI) studies of individuals with FASD show reduced total and regional brain volume (Astley et al., 2009). There is potential that multivariate analysis of brain volumes using MRI may in the future discriminate individuals with FASD; however, specificity of brain MRI to distinguish individuals with FASD is not yet available. Brain imaging such as MRI is not recommended to determine a diagnosis of FASD (Garrison et al., 2019; Harvey et al., 2019; Li et al., 2019; Little & Beaulieu, 2020; Treit et al., 2019).

(ii) Motor skills

Assessment of motor skills considers an assessment of an individual's fine motor, gross motor, and graphomotor skills as well as their integration of each skill. Motor assessment for the purposes of considering a diagnosis of FASD is best completed by an occupational therapist (Doney et al., 2017; Jirikowic, Gelo & Astley, 2008; Jirikowic, Gelo & Astley, 2010). Fine motor skill assessment considers an individual's manual dexterity, while gross motor skills assess an individual's balance, strength, co-ordination, and agility. Grapho-motor skills includes daily tasks of handwriting. Assessment of visuo-motor integration examines how an individual integrates these skills in accuracy and speed such as when catching a ball or deciding and committing to completing a manual task such as tracing or transcribing (Adnams et al., 2001; Bay & Kesmodel, 2010; Beery & Beery, 2010; Doney et al., 2017; Larroque et al, 1995; Richardson et al., 1995).

(iii) Cognition

Assessment of cognition requires an assessment of an individual's intelligent quotient (IQ) by a clinical and or neuropsychologist (Mattson et al., 1997; Mattson & Riley, 2000; Streissguth & Dehaene, 1993). Cognition assessment includes measures of verbal and non-verbal reasoning (Coles, Lynch, Kable, Johnson, & Goldstein, 2010; Mattson et al., 1996; Wechsler & Naglieri, 2006), processing speed (Burden et al., 2005), and working memory (Rasmussen, 2005; Burden et al., 2005). If working memory *alone* is severely impaired (below the clinically significant value agreed as a sensitive and specific cut-off), then working memory should be considered in the 'executive functioning' domain rather than in the 'cognition' domain (Kaemingk, Mulvaney, & Halverson, 2003).

Individuals who fulfil the criteria for an intellectual disability, by definition, will have impairment in three or more domains of neurodevelopment. A test that is independent of language and culture to consider an individual's cognition may be appropriate for certain populations; however there is an inherent risk of these tools overestimating or underestimating actual ability.

(iv) Language

Assessment of language requires a speech and language pathologist to analyse an individual's expressive and receptive language and communication skills. The language domain should be assessed as a single entity – it is inappropriate to use scores obtained during verbal IQ sub-tests as a measure of language proficiency (Kaemingk et al., 2003). Testing should always be completed in an individual's first language

(Rodriguez et al., 2015; Weatherburn, Snowball, & Hunter, 2008) and when necessary with the in-person assistance of an accredited interpreter (Kippin et al., 2018). Specific tests may be available for some Indigenous languages, but not always. When assessment is not possible using standardised tests or is not able to be applied utilising an individual's first language, then the clinical judgment of a specialised speech and language pathologist regarding severity of impairment is required (Kippin et al., 2018). This may be informed by the collaborative advice of the accredited interpreter. A longitudinal randomly selected, population-based sample of Australian children exposed to a binge pattern of maternal alcohol consumption in the second trimester of their in-utero life, had a three-fold increased odds of language delay. A similar three-fold increase was seen for those exposed to binge consumption during their third trimester and after controlling for covariates. Although the numbers did not reach significance, the trend is important (O'Leary et al., 2009a). O'Leary went on to show a link between maternal alcohol use disorders and child contact with justice systems (Hafekost et al., 2017a, b; O'Leary, 2009b).

Kippin et.al (2018) considered the language skills of a representative sample of young people sentenced to detention in Australia and found nearly one in two had a language disorder. Every aspect of the judicial process is completed with the expectation of competency in communication. Multiple studies across different jurisdictions consistently find communication and language difficulties among young people engaged in justice settings (Anderson, Hawes, & Snow, 2016; Draper et al., 2008; Hughes et al., 2017; Snow, Martine, & Sanger, 2012; Snow & Powell, 2005). Language and communication difficulties can exist independent of other developmental vulnerabilities including intellectual disability and FASD. Similarly, communication and language disorders can be a manifestation of other developmental impairments such as intellectual disability and FASD (Anderson et al., 2016). All justice services and environments need tools and systems to ensure safe communication processes. Accommodation to support communication vulnerabilities will prove most useful if routinely applied with an expectation that every second person has a communication and language disorder (Hamilton et al., 2020). We discuss courtroom accommodations in greater detail in Chapter 5.

(v) Academic achievement

Assessment of academic achievement requires an associated consideration of the measured abilities of cognition, attention, language, and phonological awareness. Cognitive and academic skills do not necessarily directly correlate, for example, some individuals with mild intellectual disability can perform in the low average range academically. Cognition and academic achievement domains should be tested and considered independently. Academic assessment considers an individual's skills in reading, mathematics, and/or literacy (including written expression and spelling). Access to and attendance at school or alternative instruction and/or remedial intervention, must be known and considered adequate before a deficit in academic achievement can be assigned. The type of schooling the young person needs must be understood, such as mainstream classes and educational support classes. This is in addition to challenges such as educational interruption, multiple placements, remote locations, new immigrants and whether the education is delivered in a language other than the first language of the young person. If they have a Specific Learning Disorder according to the Diagnostic and Statistical Manual of Mental Disorders, Fifth Edition (DSM-5), they fulfil criteria for severe impairment in academic achievement, providing testing shows evidence of impairment at clinical cut-off at or below two standard deviations (Glass et al., 2017).

(vi) Memory

Memory problems are to be considered separately to attentional problems for the purposes of diagnosing FASD in Australia (Pei et al., 2008). A deficit in working memory, impulse control and hyperactivity should be considered in the domain of executive function. Assessment of memory includes an individual's overall memory, verbal memory, and visual memory. Verbal learning impairment is seen in association with a high dose of PAE, while recall and recognition memory impairment is seen at moderate levels of PAE (Lewis et al., 2016). PAE is linked to impaired performance on tests of retrospective memory. Previous studies using the California Verbal Learning Test-Children's Version (CVLT-C) to examine effects of heavy PAE on verbal learning and memory, have reported impaired information acquisition (e.g., encoding), rather than retrieval, as the primary mechanism underlying learning and memory impairment (Lewis et al., 2015).

Prospective memory is the ability to remember and act on delayed intentions. Children and adolescents with FASD have prospective memory impairment only partially attributed to lower IQ, that is present after adjusting for socioeconomic confounders and executive function and there is no effect of Attention Deficit Hyperactivity Disorder (ADHD) (Lewis et al., 2016). PAE results in impaired verbal and visual-spatial episodic memory performance in affected individuals. Episodic memory deficit might be influenced, at least in part, by higher order cognitive processes (du Plooy et al., 2016).

(vii) Attention

Attention is not a singular or uniform phenomenon, qualifying terms are useful: selective attention, divided attention, alternating attention, and sustained attention. Selective attention is observed when an individual can focus on a single stimulus. Divided attention is when an individual attends to two or more stimuli simultaneously. Alternating attention is when switching focus from one stimulus to a different stimulus. Sustained attention is when an individual applies focussed attention for a long period of time and is simultaneously resistant to distraction. Deficits in attention can manifest in different ways. Attentional deficits include problems with giving and sustaining concentration, an inability to focus on any task and perseveration, that is, problems organising to initiate and complete work. Attention does overlap with executive function, discussed next. For diagnostic consideration of FASD in Australia, attention has been defined separately to executive function. Deficits in inhibition, impulse control or hyperactivity are not to be considered in the domain of attention rather these behaviours are to be considered under the domain of executive function. However, a diagnosis of inattentive or combined ADHD (based on DSM-5 criteria) (Psychiatrists, 2013) fulfils criteria for severe impairment in the domain of attention under Australian FASD Diagnostic guidelines.

(viii) Executive function, including impulse control
and hyperactivity

Executive function is an overarching term encompassing the various cognitive regulatory processes necessary for goal-directed behaviour. Executive functions are higher-order cognitive processes involving thoughts and actions which are under conscious control (Clark, Prior, & Kinsella, 2002). These processes include (but are not limited to) attentional and inhibitory control, self-regulation, working memory/updating, cognitive flexibility, set-shifting, planning and using effective strategies (Jacobson, Williford & Pianta, 2011; Pei et al., 2008; Rasmussen, 2005; Reader et al., 1994). Challenges with executive function are frequently observed in individuals with intellectual disability. Impaired executive function is common for individuals with FASD without an intellectual disability. The summative effects of impaired executive function are negative and contribute to risk for early school failure and early engagement with mental health and justice services (Fast et al., 1999; Moore & Green, 2004).

Impaired executive function is associated with poor impulse control and decreased ability to understand and anticipate consequences. Developmental difficulties of executive function are associated with unacceptable behaviours such as impulsivity to enter premises and remove objects, approach people unlawfully, seek and use recreational substances. Typically developing adolescents do not possess the neuronal connectivity to support impulse control. Deficits in executive function diminishes an individual's capability to choose and action socially appropriate behaviour (Ogilvie et al., 2011). Deficits in executive functioning are amplified for the child and adolescent with FASD and aggressive behaviours are common (De Brito et al., 2013; Giancola et al., 2001; Hughes, 2015).

(ix) Affect regulation

Affect regulation is the ability to modulate emotional arousal in response to all and changing situations. Proficient affect regulation assists with pro-social engagement and positive social inclusion, while impaired affect regulation and emotional dysregulation can result in social distancing and even exclusion (Shields & Cicchetti, 1997). Affect regulation can be impaired by prenatal and postnatal exposures including PAE, early life trauma, adversity, and impaired attachment, as well as inherited and acquired neurodevelopmental impairment including acquired brain injury from direct trauma and substance misuse (Konstantareas & Stewart, 2006; Niedtfeld et al., 2010). Children and adolescents acquire socially acceptable affect regulation through experiential and behavioural engagement with the world around them. The learning of how affect regulation modulates their experience of the world around them is acquired iteratively across the early years and entrains their habitual emotional and physical reactivity (Shields & Cicchetti, 1997). Difficulties with affect regulation are common for individuals with FASD. Indeed, having impaired affect regulation and FASD is associated with receiving a diagnosis of FASD at a later age than if the individual with FASD had effective affect regulation (Temple et al., 2019). Unresolved problems with affect regulation are associated with secondary difficulties such as substance abuse, mental health disorders and social exclusion which in turn can aggravate dysregulation (Rasmussen et al., 2008; Streissguth et al., 1997; Temple et al., 2019).

Data from the Canadian National FASD database considered affect regulation impairment in relation to suicidality and six associated mental health diagnoses: (i) ADHD; (ii) post-traumatic stress disorder (PTSD); (iii) conduct disorder; (iv) attachment disorder; (v) intellectual disability; and (vi) language disorder. Individuals with FASD and affect regulation impairment were significantly more likely to be diagnosed with conduct disorder (Odds Ratio[1] 4.8), attachment disorder (Odds Ratio 6.1), or PTSD (Odds Ratio 8.1), when compared to those without affect regulation impairment. Individuals with FASD and affect regulation impairment were also more likely to have a history of suicidality (Odds Ratio 8.6). Affect regulation impairment was most found in those with greater overall neurodevelopmental impairment and there was no relation to gender, intellectual disability, or language disorder (Temple et al., 2019). Together these co-morbidities and neurodevelopmental challenges elevate the risk of individuals with FASD and affect regulation to engage early in life with juvenile justice services.

(x) Adaptive behaviour, social skills, or social communication

Adaptive functioning is a developmental capability necessary for successful independent living and successful navigation of social systems, such as education, employment, and recreation. Adaptive functioning refers to daily personal and social skills, such as communication, living skills and socialization (Jirikowic et al., 2008). Individuals diagnosed with intellectual disability have impaired adaptive skills as well as impaired cognition (Clark et al., 2002; Jirikowic et al., 2008). Adaptive functioning is a common vulnerability for individuals with FASD with or without co-occurring intellectual disability (Mohr-Jensen, 2016; Spohr, Willms, & Steinhausen, 2007; Steinhausen et al., 2002, 2003). Impairment in the domain of adaptive functioning among individuals with FASD becomes more evident as they age and the impairments are less easily accommodated by typical community protocols and resources (Whaley, O'Connor & Gunderson, 2001). A young child being impulsive, excitable, and intrusive is accommodated, their affect regulation considered typical for their chronological age and their developmental age. An adult with developmental impairment and intrusive behaviour and impaired affect regulation can be accommodated when the behaviour is understood according to developmental age, not chronological age. Acceptance of impaired affect regulation is more immediate when the outward appearance of an individual is atypical, such as facial dysmorphisms or unusual habitus. Accommodation of impaired affect regulation is less forthcoming when the individual is of typical appearance and the possibility of immature developmental age and developmental impairment is not readily considered. Communication difficulties aggravate further an individual's social success if they also have impaired affect regulation. Typical communication supports all social skills and interpersonal cooperation and adaptive success. Individuals with FASD and communication and language impairment, display more frequent and dysregulated behaviours (Jirikowic, Kartin, & Olson, 2008; Mutch, 2016a,b).

Conclusion

There is an urgent need for greater resources to ensure routine and universal assessment and diagnosis of health, well-being and neuro-developmental needs for all children and adolescents entering juvenile justice systems globally. There is an equal and urgent need to provide culturally safe and trauma-informed rehabilitation, education, and therapeutic programmes to mitigate the effects of FASD and neuro-developmental impairments across out-of-home and justice settings (Bower et al., 2018). Inclusion of the child and adolescent and community voice can provide a way forward to improve programme engagement and retention. Cultural understandings are necessary when undertaking health and well-being assessments to decolonise and positively transform diagnostic methodology and renovate statutory systems (Freeman et al., 2019; Hamilton et al., 2019, 2020). Cultural safety and co-design are also necessary when planning individualised recovery programmes and pathways for healing (Azzopardi et al., 2020; Freeman et al., 2019; Hamilton, 2019; Hamilton et al., 2020; Smith, 2016; Smith et al., 2019; Johnston et al., 2019). Engagement and efficacy of health and well-being initiatives across juvenile justice settings are most likely to succeed, be trusted and permitted to remain as a routine capability, when the actors providing the health and well-being initiatives undertake their work guided by humanitarian principles and actions (Mutch, 2016a,b; Passmore et al., 2018).

Note

1 The Odds Ratio is the strength of association between the variable and the outcome, demonstrating how likely it is for the person to have certain impairments or issues.

References

Aboriginal and Torres Strait Islander Social Justice Commissioner. (2017). [Advocate for Indigenous Australian languages]. Retrieved from https://www.humanrights.gov.au/our-work/commission-general/june-oscar-ao-aboriginal-and-torres-strait-islander-social-justice.

Aboriginal and Torres Strait Islander Social Justice Commissioner. (2011). *Social justice report 2010.* Canberra, Australia: Report, Australian Human Rights Commission.

Adnams, C. M., Kodituwakku, P. W., Hay, A., Molteno, C. D., Viljoen, D., & May, P. A. (2001). Patterns of cognitive-motor development in children with fetal alcohol syndrome from a community in South Africa. *Alcoholism: Clinical and Experimental Research, 25*(4), 557–562.

Akison, L. K., Reid, N., Wyllie, M., & Moritz, K. M. (2019). Adverse health outcomes in offspring associated with fetal alcohol exposure: A systematic review of clinical and preclinical studies with a focus on metabolic and body composition outcomes. *Alcoholism: Clinical & Experimental Research, 43*(7), 1324–1343.

Allen, K., Riley, M., Goldfeld, S., & Halliday, J. (2007). Estimating the prevalence of FAS in Victoria using routinely collected administrative data. *Australian and New Zealand Journal of Public Health, 31*(1), 62–66.

American Psychiatric Association. (2013). *Diagnostic and statistical manual of mental disorders (DSM-5®).* American Psychiatric Pub.

Anderson, S. A. S., Hawes, D. J., & Snow, P. C. (2016). Language impairments among youth offenders: A systematic review. *Children and Youth Services Review, 65*, 195–203.

Antonucci, T. C., et al. (2019). The role of psychology in addressing worldwide challenges of poverty and gender inequality. *Zeitschrift fur Psychologie/ Journal of Psychology, 227*(2), 95–104.

Astley, S. J. (2013). Validation of the fetal alcohol spectrum disorder (FASD) 4-digit diagnostic code. *Journal of Population Therapeutics & Clinical Pharmacology, 20*(3), e416–e467.

Astley, S. J., et al. (2009). Neuropyschological and behavioral outcomes from a comprehensive magnetic resonance study of children with fetal alcohol spectrum disorders. *Canadian Journal of Clinical Pharmacology, 16*(1), e178–e201.

Astley, S. J., & Clarren, M. D. (1999). *Diagnostic guide for fetal alcohol syndrome and related conditions: The 4-digit diagnostic code* (2nd ed.). Seattle: University of Washington.

Atkinson, J. (2002). *Trauma trails, recreating song lines: The transgenerational effects of trauma in Indigenous Australia*, Spinifex Press, North Melbourne, Australia.

Australian Guide to the Diagnosis of FASD. (2020). Retrieved from https:// www.fasdhub.org.au/fasd-information/assessment-and-diagnosis/ guide-to-diagnosis/

Australian Institute of Health and Welfare. (2017) *Youth detention population in Australia 2017.* Bulletin 143. Australian Government, Australia, December.

Azzopardi, P., et al. (2020). Investing in the health of Aboriginal and Torres Strait Islander adolescents: A foundation for achieving health equity. *Medical Journal of Australia, 212*(5), 202–204e1.

Bauchner, H., & Fontanarosa, P. B. (2020). Health care is a right and not a privilege. *JAMA, 323*(11), 1049–1049.

Bay, B., & Kesmodel, U. S. (2010). Prenatal alcohol exposure – A systematic review of the effects on child motor function. *Acta Obstetrica et Gynecologica Scandinavica, 90*(3), 210–226.

Beery, K., & Beery, N. (2010). *The Beery-Buktenica development test of visual-motor integration, in administration, scoring and teaching manual.* Pearson, Minneapolis, MN.

Betancourt, T. S., et al. (2012). Trauma history and psychopathology in war-affected refugee children referred for trauma-related mental health services in the United States. *Journal of Trauma Stress, 25*(6), 682–690.

Borschmann, R. D., Coffey, C. P., Moran, P. M. D., Hearps, S., Degenhardt, L., Kinner, S. A., & Patton, G. (2014). Self-Harm in young offenders. *Suicide and Life Threatening Behavior, 44*(6), 641–652.

Bower, C., Watkins, R. E., Mutch, R. C., Marriott, R., Freeman, J., Kippin, N. R., ... Tarratt, L. (2018). Fetal alcohol spectrum disorder and youth justice: A prevalence study among young people sentenced to detention in Western Australia. *BMJ Open, 8*(2), 1–10.

Bower, C., & Elliot, E. (2016). *Report to the Australian government of health: Australian guide to the diagnosis of fetal alcohol spectrum disorder (FASD).* Retrived from https://www.fasdhub.org.au/siteassets/pdfs/australian-guide-to-diagnosis-of-fasd_all-appendices.pdf

Bower, C., Silvia, D., Henderson, T. R., et al. (2000). Ascertainment of birth defects: The effect on completeness of adding a new source of data. *Journal of Paediatrics and Child Health 36*, 574–576.

Brisbois, T. D., Farmer, A. P., & McCargar, L. J. (2012). Early markers of adult obesity: A review. *Obesity Reviews, 13*(4), 347–367.

Bugmy v The Queen [2013] HCA 37

Burden, M. J., Jacobson, S. W., & Jacobson, J. L. (2005). Relation of prenatal alcohol exposure to cognitive processing speed and efficiency in childhood. *Alcoholism: Clinical and Experimental Research, 29*(8), 1473–1483.

Burden, M. J., Jacobson, S. W., Sokol, R. J., & Jacobson, J. L (2005). Effects of prenatal alcohol exposure on attention and working memory at 7.5 years of age. *Alcoholism: Clinical and Experimental Research, 29*(3), 443–452.

Casey, B. J., Getz, S., & Galvan, A. (2008). The adolescent brain. *Developmental Review, 28*(1), 62–77.

Chartrand, L., & Forbes-Chilibeck, E. (2003). The sentencing of offenders with fetal alcohol syndrome. *Health Law Journal, 11*, 35–91.

Clark, C., Prior, M., & Kinsella, G. (2002). The relationship between executive function abilities, adaptive behaviour, and academic achievement in children with externalising behaviour problems. *Journal of Child Psychol Psychiatry, 43*(6), 785–796.

Coles, C. D., Lynch, M. E., Kable, J. A., Johnson, K. C., & Goldstein, F. C. (2010). Verbal and nonverbal memory in adults prenatally exposed to alcohol. *Alcoholism, Clinical and Experimental Research, 34*(5), 897–906.

Coriale, G., Fiorentino, D., Di Lauro, F., Marchitelli, R., Scalese, B., Fiore, M., ... Ceccanti, M. (2013). Fetal alcohol spectrum disorder (FASD):

Neurobehavioral profile, indications for diagnosis and treatment. *Rivista di Psichiatria, 48*(5), 359–69.

De Brito SA, Viding E, Kumari V, Blackwood N, Hodgins S (2013) Cool and Hot Executive Function Impairments in Violent Offenders with Antisocial Personality Disorder with and without Psychopathy. *PLoS ONE 8(6):* e65566. https://doi.org/10.1371/journal.pone.0065566

Department of Justice, Corrective Services, Government of Western Australia. (2020). *Quarterly statistics – Custodial (youth detainee) 2020 – Quarter 1.* Retrieved from https://www.wa.gov.au/sites/default/files/2020-06/2020-quarter1-youth-custodial.pdf

Devaney, J. (2008). Chronic child abuse and domestic violence: Children and families with long-term and complex needs. *Child & Family Social Work, 13*(4), 443–453.

Dodson, S., for IndigenousX. (2019, 26 March). Indigenous suicide shows our traumatic past is just too heavy a burden. *The Guardian.* Retrieved from https://www.theguardian.com/commentisfree/2019/mar/26/indigenous-suicide-shows-our-traumatic-past-is-just-too-heavy-a-burden

Donald, K. A., Eastman, E., Howells, F. M., Adnams, C., Riley, E. P., Woods, R. P., ... Stein, D. J. (2015). Neuroimaging effects of prenatal alcohol exposure on the developing human brain: A magnetic resonance imaging review. *Acta Neuropsychiatrica, 27*(5), 251–269.

Doney, R. B., Lucas, B. R., Jirikowic, T., Tsang, T. W., Watkins, R. E., Sauer, K., ... Elliott, E. J. (2017). Graphomotor skills in children with prenatal alcohol exposure and fetal alcohol spectrum disorder: A population-based study in remote Australia. *Australian Occupational Therapy Journal, 64*(1), 68–78.

Douglas, H. (2010). The sentencing response to defendants with foetal alcohol spectrum disorder. *Criminal Law Journal, 34*(4), 221–239.

Draper, B. M. D., et al. (2008). Long-term effects of childhood abuse on the quality of life and health of older people: Results from the depression and early prevention of suicide in general practice project. *Journal of the American Geriatrics Society, 56*(2), 262–271.

du Plooy, C. P., Malcolm-Smith, S., Adnams, C. M., Stein, D. J., & Donald, K. A. (2016). The effects of prenatal alcohol exposure on episodic memory functioning: A systematic review. *Archives of Clinical Neuropsychology, 31*(7), 710–726.

Eichler, A., Grunitz, J., Grimm, J., Walz, L., Raabe, E., Goecke, T. W., ... Kornhuber, J. (2016). Did you drink alcohol during pregnancy? Inaccuracy and discontinuity of women's self-reports: On the way to establish meconium ethyl glucuronide (EtG) as a biomarker for alcohol consumption during pregnancy. *Alcohol, 54*, 39–44.

Elliott, E., Payne, J., Haan, E., & Bower, C. (2006). Diagnosis of foetal alcohol syndrome and alcohol use in pregnancy: A survey of paediatricians' knowledge, attitudes and practice. *Journal of Paediatrics and Child Health, 42*(11), 698–703.

Elliott, E., Latimer, J., Fitzpatrick, J., Oscar, J., & Carter, M. (2012). There's hope in the valley. *Journal of Paediatrics and Child Health, 48*(3), 190–192.

Elliott, E. J., Payne, J., Morris, A., Haan, E., & Bower, C. (2008). Fetal alcohol syndrome: A prospective national surveillance study. *Archives of Disease in Childhood, 93*(9), 732.

Emdad, R., & Sondergaard, H. P. (2006). Short Communication: Visuoconstructional ability in PTSD patients compared to a control group with the same ethnic background. *Stress and Health, 22*(1), 35–43.

Fast, D. K., & Conry, J. (2004). The challenge of fetal alcohol syndrome in the criminal legal system. *Addiction Biology 9*, 161–166.

Fast, D., Conry, J., & Loock, C. (1999). Identifying fetal alcohol syndrome among youth in the criminal justice system. *Journal of Developmental and Behavioral Pediatrics, 20*(5), 370–372.

Felitti, V. J., Anda, R. F., Nordenberg, D., Williamson, D. F., Spitz, A. M., Edwards, V., … Marks, J. S. (1998). Relationship of childhood abuse and household dysfunction to many of the leading causes of death in adults. The Adverse Childhood Experiences (ACE) Study. *American Journal of Preventive Medicine, 14*(4), 245–258.

Finkelhor, D., Shattuck, A., Turner, H., & Hamby, S. (2015). A revised inventory of adverse childhood experiences. *Child Abuse and Neglect, 48*, 13–21.

Fitzpatrick, E., Macdonald, G., Martiniuk, A. L. C., Oscar, J., D'Antoine, H., Carter, M., … Elliott, E. J. (2017). The picture talk project: Starting a conversation with community leaders on research with remote aboriginal communities of Australia. *BMC Medical Ethics, 18*, 34–53.

Fitzpatrick, E. F., Martiniuk, A. L. C., D'Antoine, H., Oscar, J., Carter, M., & Elliott, E. J. (2016). Seeking consent for research with indigenous communities: A systematic review. *BMC Medical Ethics, 17*(1), 65–83.

Fitzpatrick, J. P., Latimer, J., Carter, M., Oscar, J., Ferreira, M. L., Carmichael Olson, H., … Elliott, E. J. (2015). Prevalence of fetal alcohol syndrome in a population-based sample of children living in remote Australia: The Lililwan Project. *Journal of Paediatrics and Child Health, 51*(4), 450–457.

Freeman, J., Condon, C., Hamilton, S., Mutch, R. C., Bower, C., & Watkins, R. E. (2019). Challenges in accurately assessing prenatal alcohol exposure in a study of fetal alcohol spectrum disorder in a youth detention center. *Alcoholism Clinical and Experimental Research, 43*(2), 309–316.

Garrison, L., Morley, S., Chambers, C. D., & Bakhireva, L. N. (2019). Forty Years of assessing neurodevelopmental and behavioral effects of prenatal alcohol exposure in infants: What have we learned? *Alcoholism: Clinical & Experimental Research, 43*(8), 1632–1642.

Giancola, P. R., Mezzich, A. C., & Tarter, R. E. (2001). Executive cognitive functioning, temperament, and antisocial behavior in conduct-disordered adolescent females. *Journal of Abnormal Psychology, 107*(4), 629–641.

Giedd, J., & Geidd, J.N. (2004). Structural magnetic resonance imaging of the adolescent brain. *Annals of the New York Academy of Sciences, 1021*(1), 77–85.

Glass, L., Moore, E. M., Akshoomoff, N., Jones, K. L., Riley, E. P., & Mattson, S. N. (2017). Academic difficulties in children with prenatal alcohol exposure: Presence, profile, and neural correlates. *Alcoholism: Clinical & Experimental Research, 41*(5), 1024–1034.

Goldhagen, J., Clarke, A., Dixon, P., Guerreiro, A. I., Lansdown, G., & Vaghri, Z. (2020). Thirtieth anniversary of the UN Convention on the rights of the child: Advancing a child rights-based approach to child health and well-being. *BMJ Paediatrics Open, 4*(1), e000589.

Grasso, D. J. P., Ford, J. D. P., & Briggs-Gowan, M. J. P. (2013). Early life trauma exposure and stress sensitivity in young children. *Journal of Pediatric Psychology, 38*(1), 94–103.

Gray, P., Baker, H. M., Scerif, G., & Lau, J. Y. F. (2016). Early maltreatment effects on adolescent attention control to non–emotional and emotional distractors. *Australian Journal of Psychology, 68*(3), 143–153.

Gray, D., Saggers, S., Atkinson, D., & Strempel, P. (2004). *Substance misuse and primary health care among Indigenous Australians.* Commonwealth Department of Health and Ageing: Canberra, Australia.

Greenmyer, J. R., Klug, M. G., Kambeitz, C., Popova, S., & Burd, L. (2018). A multicountry updated assessment of the economic impact of fetal alcohol spectrum disorder: Costs for children and adults. *Journal of Addiction Medicine November/December, 12*(6), 466–473.

Hafekost, K., Lawrence, D., O'Leary, C., Bower, C., Semmens, J., & Zubrick, S. R. (2017a). Maternal alcohol use disorder and risk of child contact with the justice system in Western Australia: A population cohort record linkage study. *Alcoholism: Clinical & Experimental Research, 41*(8), 1452–1460.

Hafekost, K., Lawrence, D., O'Leary, C., Bower, C., Semmens, J., & Zubrick, S. R. (2017b). Maternal alcohol use disorder and child school attendance outcomes for non-Indigenous and Indigenous children in Western Australia: A population cohort record linkage study. *BMJ Open, 7*(7), e015650.

Hamilton, S. (2019). *From locked up to linked up: Developing the recovery capital assets of justice-involved children and young people.* Retrieved from http://www.powertopersuade.org.au/blog/from-locked-up-to-linked-up-developing-the-recovery-capital-assets-of-justice-involved-children-and-young-people/26/6/2019

Hamilton, S., Reibel, T., Maslen, S., Watkins, R., Freeman, J., Passmore, H., … Bower, C. (2020). Disability "In-Justice": The benefits and challenges of "Yarning" with young people undergoing diagnostic assessment for fetal alcohol spectrum disorder in a youth detention center. *Qualitative Health Research, 30*(2), 314–327.

Hanes, G., Sung, L., Mutch, R., & Cherian, S. (2017). Adversity and resilience amongst resettling Western Australian paediatric refugees. *Journal of Paediatrics & Child Health, 53*(9), 882–888.

Harris, K. R., & Bucens, I. K. (2003). Prevalence of FAS in the top end of the NT. *Journal of Paediatrics and Child Health, 39*(7), 528–533.

Harvey, R. E., Berkowitz, L. E., Hamilton, D. A., & Benjamin, J. C. (2019). The effects of developmental alcohol exposure on the neurobiology of spatial processing. *Neuroscience & Biobehavioral Reviews December, 107*, 775–794.

Haysom, L., Indig, D., Moore, E., & Gaskin, C. (2014). Intellectual disability in young people in custody in New South Wales, Australia - Prevalence and markers. *Journal of Intellectual Disability Research, 58*(11), 1004–1014.

Hazel, N. A., Hammen, C., Brennan, P. A., & Najman, J. (2008). Early childhood adversity and adolescent depression: The mediating role of continued stress. *Psychological Medicine, 38*(4), 581–589.

Heffernan, E., Andersen, K., Davidson, F., & Kinner, S. A. (2015). PTSD among Aboriginal and Torres Strait Islander people in custody in Australia: Prevalence and correlates. *Journal of Trauma Stress, 28*(6), 523–30.

Herman, J. L. M. D., & Schatzow, E. M. E. (1987). Recovery and verification of memories of childhood sexual trauma. *Psychoanalytic Psychology Winter, 4*(1), 1–14.

Hope, A. (2008). *Inquest into the deaths of Edward John Riley, Rachael Henry, Chad Atkins, Teddy Beharral, Maitland Brown, Jonathon Dick, Lloyd Dawson, Benjie Dickens, Ivan Barry Gepp, Owen Gordon, Jonathan Hale, Ernest James Laurel, Joshua Middleton, William Robert Mille.* Perth: Office of the State Coroner of Western Australia.

Howard, J., Lennings, C. J., & Copeland, J. (2003). Suicidal behavior in a young offender population. *Crisis: Journal of Crisis Intervention & Suicide, 24*(3), 98–104.

Hughes, N. (2015). *Neurodisability in the youth justice system: Recognising and responding to the criminalisation of neurodevelopmental impairment in What is Justice?* Howard League. University of Birmingham, United Kingdom. Murdoch Childrens Research Institute, Australia. University of Melbourne, Australia.

Hughes, N., Chitsabesan, P., Bryan, K., Borschmann, R., Swain, N., Lennox, C., & Shaw, J. (2017). Language impairment and comorbid vulnerabilities among young people in custody. *Journal of Child Psychology & Psychiatry, 58*(10), 1106–1113.

Hughes, N., Clasby, B., Chitsabesan, P., & Williams, H. (2016). A systematic review of the prevalence of foetal alcohol syndrome disorders among young people in the criminal justice system. *Cogent Psychology, 3*, 1–8.

Indig, D., Vecchiato, C., Haysom, L., Beilby, R., Carter, J., Champion, U., ... Whitton, G. (2011). NSW young people in custody health survey: Full report. In *Justice Health and Juvenile Justice.* Sydney: Centre for Health Research in Criminal Justice (CHRCJ).

Jacobson, L. A., Williford, A. P., & Pianta, R. C. (2011). The role of executive function in children's competent adjustment to middle school. *Child Neuropsychology: A Journal on Normal and Abnormal Development in Childhood and Adolescence, 17*(3), 255–280.

Jirikowic, T., Kartin, D., & Olson, R. C. (2008). Children with fetal alcohol spectrum disorders: A descriptive profile of adaptive function. *Canadian Journal of Occupational Therapy, 75*(4), 238–48.

Jirikowic, T., Gelo, J., & Astley, S. (2010). Children and youth with fetal alcohol spectrum disorders: Summary of intervention recommendations after clinical diagnosis. *Intellectual and Developmental Disabilities, 48*(5), 330–344.

Johnston, I., Williams, M., Butler, T., & Kinner, S. A. (2019). Justice targets in closing the gap: Let's get them right. *Australian & New Zealand Journal of Public Health, 43*(3), 201–203.

Jones, K. L. (1999). Early recognition of prenatal alcohol effects: A pediatrician's responsibility. *Journal of Pediatrics, 135*, 405–406.

Kaemingk, K., & Paquette, A. (1999). Effects of prenatal alcohol exposure on neuropsychological functioning. *Developmental Neuropsychology, 15*(1), 111–140.

Kaemingk, K. L., Mulvaney, S., & Halverson, P. T. (2003). Learning following prenatal alcohol exposure: Performance on verbal and visual multitrial tasks. *Archives of Clinical Neuropsychology, 18*(1), 33–47.

Kato, T. P., Yorifuji, T., Inoue, S., Yamakawa, M., Doi, H., & Kawachi, I. (2013). Associations of preterm births with child health and development: Japanese population-based study. *Journal of Pediatrics, 163*(6), 1578–1584e4.

Kawachi, I., Adler, N. E., & Dow, W. H. (2010). Money, schooling, and health: Mechanisms and causal evidence. *Annals of the New York Academy of Sciences, 1186*(1), 56–68.

Kidman, R. (2017). Child marriage and intimate partner violence: A comparative study of 34 countries. *International Journal of Epidemiology, 46*(2), 662–675.

Kinnane, S., Farringdon, F., Henderson-Yates, L., & Parker, H. (2010). *Fitzroy valley alcohol restriction report: An evaluation of the effects of a restriction on take-away alcohol relating to measurable health and social outcomes, community perceptions and behaviours after a two year period.* Report for the Government of Western Australia. Perth: The University of Notre Dame.

Kippin, N. R., et al. (2018). Language diversity, language disorder, and fetal alcohol spectrum disorder among youth sentenced to detention in western australia. *International Journal of Law and Psychiatry,* No Pagination Specified.

Konstantareas, M. M., & Stewart, K. (2006). Affect regulation and temperament in children with autism spectrum disorder. *Journal of Autism and Development Disorders, 36*(2), 143–54.

Labonte, B. M., Suderman, M., Maussion, G., Navaro, L., Yerko, V., Mahar, I., ... Turecki, G. (2012). Genome-wide epigenetic regulation by early-life trauma. *Archives of General Psychiatry, 69*(7), 722–731.

Larroque, B., Kaminski, M., Dehaene, P., Subtil, D., Delfosse, M. J., & Querleu, D. (1995). Moderate prenatal alcohol exposure and psychomotor development at preschool age. *American Journal of Public Health, 85*, 1654–1661.

Lewis, C. E., Thomas, K. G. F., Dodge, N. C., Molteno, C. D., Meintjes, E. M., Jacobson, J. L., & Jacobson, S. W. (2015). Verbal learning and memory impairment in children with fetal alcohol spectrum disorders. *Alcoholism: Clinical & Experimental Research, 39*(4), 724–732.

Lewis, C. E., Thomas, K. G. F., Molteno, C. D., Kliegel, M., Meintjes, E., Jacobson, J. L., & Jacobson, S. W. (2016). Prospective memory impairment in children with prenatal alcohol exposure. *Alcoholism: Clinical & Experimental Research, 40*(5), 969–978.

Li, Y., Shen, M., Stockton, M. E., & Zhao, X. (2019). Hippocampal deficits in neurodevelopmental disorders. *Neurobiology of Learning & Memory November, 165*, 106945.

Liston, C., McEwen, B. S., & Casey, B. J. (2009). Psychosocial stress reversibly disrupts prefrontal processing and attentional control. *Proceedings of the National Academy of Sciences of the United States of America, 106*(3), 912–7.

Little, G., & Beaulieu, C. (2020). Multivariate models of brain volume for identification of children and adolescents with fetal alcohol spectrum disorder. *Human Brain Mapping, 41*(5), 1181–1194.

Madigan, S., Brumariu, L. E., Villani, V., Atkinson, L., & Lyons-Ruth, K. (2016). Representational and questionnaire measures of attachment: A meta-analysis of relations to child internalizing and externalizing problems. *Psychological Bulletin, 142*(4), 367–399.

Marmot, M. G. (2016). Empowering communities. *American Journal of Public Health, 106*(2), 230–231.

Marmot, M. G. (2012). Policy making with health equity at its heart. *JAMA, 307*(19), 2033–2034.

Marmot, M. G. (2006). Status syndrome: A challenge to medicine. *JAMA, 295*(11), 1304–1307.

Marninwarntikura Fitzroy Women's Resource & Legal Centre; Marra Worra Worra Aboriginal Corporation & Nindilingarri Cultural Health Services. (2009). *Creating a sustainable future together.* Joint submission to the Senate inquiry on remote and regional communities.

Maschi, T., Viola, D., & Koskinen, L. (2015). Trauma, stress, and coping among older adults in prison: Towards a human rights and intergenerational family justice action agenda. *Traumatology, 21*(3), 188–200.

Maschi, T., Baer, J., Morrissey, M. B., & Moreno, C. (2013). The aftermath of childhood trauma on late life mental and physical health: A review of the literature. *Traumatology, 19*(1), 49–64.

Mattson, S. N., Riley, E. P., Gramling, L., Delis, D. C., & Jones, K. L. (1997). Heavy prenatal alcohol exposure with or without physical features of fetal alcohol syndrome leads to IQ deficits. *Journal of Pediatrics, 131*(5), 718–721.

Mattson, S. N., Riley, E. P., Delis, D. C., Stern, C., & Jones, K. L. (1996). Verbal learning and memory in children with fetal alcohol syndrome. *Alcoholism: Clinical and Experimental Research, 20*(5), 810–816.

Mattson, S. N., & Riley, E. P. (2000). Parent ratings of behavior in children with heavy prenatal alcohol exposure and IQ-matched controls. *Alcoholism: Clinical and Experimental Research, 24*, 226–231.

McLachlan, K. (2017). *Fetal alcohol spectrum disorder in yukon corrections. Final report to yukon justice: Estimating the prevalece of FASD, mental health, and substance use problems in the justice system.* Y. Justice, Editor. Department of Justice, Government of Yukon: Policy and Communications Unit.

Mohr-Jensen, C., & Steinhausen, H. C. (2016). A meta-analysis and systematic review of the risks associated with childhood attention-deficit hyperactivity disorder on long-term outcome of arrests, convictions, and incarcerations. *Clinical Psychologocal Review, 48*, 32–42.

Moore, T. E., & Green, M. (2004). Fetal alcohol spectrum disorder (FASD): A need for closer examination by the criminal justice system. *Criminal Reports, 19*(1), 99–108.

Murphy, A., & Chittenden, M. (2005). *Time out II: A profile of BC youth in custody.* Vancouver.

Mutch, R. (2016a). Developmental risk factors associated with incarceration in the juvenile justice system. *Journal of Intellectual Disability Research, 60*(7–8), 713.

Mutch, R. (2016b). Prevalence of foetal alcohol spectrum disorder and neurocognitive impairment among incarcerated youth. *Journal of Intellectual Disability Research, 60*(7–8), 713.

Mutch, R., Wray, J., & Bower, C. (2012). Recording a history of alcohol use in pregnancy: An audit of knowledge, attitudes and practice at a child development service. *Journal of Population Therapeutics & Clinical Pharmacology, 19*(2), e227–33.

Mutch, R., Watkins, R., & Bower, C. (2015). Fetal alcohol spectrum disorders: Notifications to the Western Australian register of developmental anomalies. *Journal of Paediatrics and Child Health, 51*(4), 433–436.

Niedtfeld, I., Schulze, L., Kirsch, P., Herpertz, S. C., Bohus, M., & Schmahl, C. (2010). Affect regulation and pain in borderline personality disorder: A possible link to the understanding of self-injury. *Biological Psychiatry, 68*(4), 383–391.

Noland, J. S., Singer, L. T., Arendt, R. E., Minnes, S., Short, E. J., & Bearer, C. F. (2003). Executive functioning in preschool-age children prenatally exposed to alcohol, cocaine, and marijuana. *Alcoholism: Clinical and Experimental Research, 27*(4), 647–656.

Oei, J. L. (2018). Adult consequences of prenatal drug exposure. *Internal Medicine Journal, 48*(1), 25–31.

Ogilvie, J. M., Stewart, A. L., Chan, R. C. K., & Shum, D. H. K. (2011). Neuropsychological measures of executive function and antisocial behavior: A meta-analysis. *Criminology, 49*(4), 1063–1107.

Ogloff, J. R., Pfeifer, J. E., Shepherd, S. M., & Ciorciari, J. (2017). Assessing the mental health, substance abuse, cognitive functioning, and social/emotional well-being needs of aboriginal prisoners in Australia. *Journal of Correctional Health Care, 23*(4), 398–411.

O'Leary, C. M., Nassar, N., Kurinczuk, J. J., & Bower, C. (2009a). The effect of maternal alcohol consumption on fetal growth and preterm birth. *Obstetrical & Gynecological Survey, 64*(5), 299–300.

O'Leary, C. M., Nassar, N., Zubrick, S. R., Kurinczuk, J. J., Stanley, F., & Bower, C. (2009b). Evidence of a complex association between dose, pattern and timing of prenatal alcohol exposure and child behaviour problems. *Addiction, 105*(1), 74–86.

Olson, H. C., Jirikowic, T., Kartin, D., & Astley, S. (2007). Responding to the challenge of early intervention for fetal alcohol spectrum disorders. *Infants & Young Children, 20*(2), 172–189.

Parliament of Australia House of Representatives Standing Committee on Aboriginal and Torres Strait Islander Affairs. (2011). *Doing time - Time for doing indigenous youth in the criminal justice system.* Report, Parliament of Australia, Australia, June.

Parliament of Australia House of Representatives Standing Committee on Social Policy and Legal Affairs. (2012). *FASD: The hidden harm inquiry into the prevention, diagnosis and management of fetal alcohol spectrum disorders.* Inquiry, Parliament of Australia, Australia, November.

Parliament of Western Australia, Education and Health Standing Committee. (2012). *Foetal alcohol spectrum disorder: The invisible disability.* Report 15, Parliament of Western Australia, Perth.

Passmore, H. M., Mutch, R. C., Burns, S., Watkins, R., Carapetis, J., Hall, G., & Bower, C. (2018). Fetal alcohol spectrum disorder (FASD): Knowledge, attitudes, experiences and practices of the Western Australian youth custodial workforce. *International Journal of Law & Psychiatry, 59*, 44–52.

Pei, J. R., Rinaldi, C. M., Rasmussen, C., Massey, V., & Massey, D. (2008). Memory patterns of acquisition and retention of verbal and nonverbal information in children with fetal alcohol spectrum disorder. *Canadian Journal of Clinical Pharmacology, 15*(1), e44–e56.

Perrin, M., Kleinhaus, K., Messinger, J., & Malaspina, D. (2010). Critical periods and the developmental origins of disease: An epigenetic perspective of schizophrenia. *Annals of the New York Academy of Sciences, 1204*(1), 8–13.

Popova, S., Lange, S., Bekmuradov, D., Mihic, A., & Rehm, J. (2011a). Fetal alcohol spectrum disorder prevalence estimates in correctional systems: A systematic literature review. *Canadian Journal of Public Health, 102*, 336–340.

Popova, S., Stade, B., Bekmuradov, D., Lange, S., & Rehm, J. (2011b). What do we know about the economic impact of fetal alcohol spectrum disorder? A systematic literature review. *Alcohol & Alcoholism, 46*(4), 490–497.

Psychiatrists, American Psychiatric Association. (2013). *Diagnostic and statistical manual of mental disorders.* Arlington, VA: A.P. Publishing, Editor.

Purewal, S. K., Bucci, M., Wang, L. G., Koita, K., Marques, S. S., Oh, D., & Harris, N. B. (2016). Screening for adverse childhood experiences (ACEs) in an integrated paediatric care model. *Zero to Three, 36*(3), 10–17.

Rasmussen, C. (2005). Executive functioning and working memory in fetal alcohol spectrum disorder. *Alcoholism: Clinical and Experimental Research, 29*(8), 1359–1367.

Rasmussen, C., Andrew, G., Zwaigenbaum, L., & Tough, S. (2008). Neurobehavioural outcomes of children with fetal alcohol spectrum disorders: A Canadian perspective. *Paediatric Child Health, 13*(3), 185–191.

Reader, M. J., Harris, E. L., Schuerholz, L. J., & Denckla, M. B. (1994). Attention deficit hyperactivity disorder and executive dysfunction. *Developmental Neuropsychology, 10*(4), 493–512.

Resendiz, M., Chen, Y., Oztürk, N. C., & Zhou, F. C. (2013). Epigenetic medicine and fetal alcohol spectrum disorders. *Epigenomics, 5*(1), 73–86.

Richardson, G. A., Day, N. L., & Goldschmidt, L. (1995). Prenatal alcohol, marij cxx uana, and tobacco use: Infant mental and motor development. *Neurotoxicology and Teratology, 17*, 479–487.

Rodriguez, M., Kratochvilova, Z., Kuniss, R., Vorackova, V., Dorazilova, A., & Fajnerova, I. (2015). Case report: Is verbal cognitive performance in bilingual neuropsychiatric patients test–language dependent? *Psychological Journal, 4*(4), 208–217.

Rojas, E., & Gretton, H. (2007). Background, offence characteristics, and criminal outcomes of Aboriginal youth who sexually offend: A closer look at Aboriginal youth intervention needs. *Sex Abuse, 19*, 257–83.

Royal Australasian College of Physicians. (2018). *Indigenous strategic framework 2018–2028.* Retrieved from https://www.racp.edu.au/about/board-and-governance/governance-documents/indigenous-strategic-framework-2018-2028/indigenous-strategic-framework

Royal Australasian College of Physicians, Aboriginal and Torres Strait Islander Health Committee. (2018). *Aboriginal and Torres Strait Islander health position statement.* Retrieved from https://www.racp.edu.au/docs/default-source/advocacy-library/racp-2018-aboriginal-and-torres-strait-islander-health-position-statement.pdf?sfvrsn=cd5c151a_4

Royal Australasian College of Physicians. (2011). The health and well-being of incarcerated adolescents. Sydney. Retrieved from https://www.racp.edu.au/docs/default-source/advocacy-library/the-health-and-wellbeing-on-incarcerated-adolescents.pdf

Seiler, A., Kohler, S., Ruf-Leuschner, M., & Landolt, M. A. (2016). Adverse childhood experiences, mental health, and quality of life of chilean girls placed in foster care: An exploratory study. *Psychological Trauma: Theory, Research, Practice, & Policy, 8*(2), 180–187.

Shields, A., & Cicchetti, D. (1997). Emotion regulation among school–Age children: The development and validation of a new criterion Q–sort scale. *Developmental Psychology, 33*(6), 906–916.

Siddiqi, A., Subramanian, S. V., Berkman, L., Hertzman, C., & Kawachi, I. (2007). The welfare state as a context for children's development: A study of the effects of unemployment and unemployment protection on reading literacy scores. *International Journal of Social Welfare, 16*(4), 314–325.

Smith, A., Cox, K., Poon, C., & Stewart, D. (2013). Time out III: A profile of BC youth in custody. Vancouver.

Smith, P. (2016). Australian doctors condemn "horrific" treatment of children in juvenile detention. *BMJ, 6*(354). doi:10.1136/bmj.i4329

Smith, W., Sitas, M., Rao, P., Nicholls, C., McCann, P., Jonikis, T., ... Waters, F. (2019). Intensive community treatment and support "Youth Wraparound" service in Western Australia: A case and feasibility study. *Early Intervention in Psychiatry, 13*(1), 151–158.

Snow, P. C., Martine, B. P., & Sanger, D. D. (2012). Oral language competence, young speakers, and the law. *Language, Speech, and Hearing Services in Schools, 43*(4), 496–506.

Snow, P. C., & Powell, M. B. (2005). What's the story? An exploration of narrative language abilities in male juvenile offenders. *Psychology, Crime & Law, 11*(3), 239–253.

Spear, L. P. (2013). Adolescent neurodevelopment. *Journal of Adolescent Health, 52*(2), S7–S13.

Spohr, H., Willms, J., & Steinhausen, H. (2007). Fetal alcohol spectrum disorders in young adulthood. *Journal of Pediatrics, 150*(2), 175–179.

Steinhausen, H. C., Von Gontard, A., Sophr, H-L., Hauffa, B. P., Eiholzer, U., Backes, M., ... Malin, Z. (2002). Behavioral phenotypes in four mental retardation syndromes: Fetal alcohol syndrome, Prader–Willi syndrome, Fragile X syndrome, and Tuberosis sclerosis. *American Journal of Medical Genetics, 111*, 381–387.

Steinhausen, H. C., Willms, J., Metzke, C. W., & Spohr, H. L. (2003). Behavioural phenotype in foetal alcohol syndrome and foetal alcohol effects. *Developmental Medicine and Child Neurology, 45*(3), 179–182.

Streissguth, A. P., Bookstein, F., Barr, H., Sampson, P. D., O'Malley, K., & Young, J. K. (2004). Risk factors for adverse life outcomes in fetal alcohol syndrome and fetal alcohol effects. *Journal of Developmental and Behavioural Pediatrics, 25*(4), 228–238.

Streissguth, A. P., & Dehaene, P. (1993). Fetal alcohol syndrome in twins of alcoholic mothers: Concordance of diagnosis and IQ. *American Journal of Medical Genetics, 47*, 857–861.

Streissguth, A., & Kanter, J. (1997). *Primary and secondary disabilities in fetal alcohol syndrome, in the challenge of fetal alcohol syndrome: Overcoming secondary disabilities*. Streissguth, A., & Kanter J., editors. University of Washington Press, Seattle.

Subramanian, S. V., Kawachi, I., & Smith, G. D. (2007). Income inequality and the double burden of under- and overnutrition in India. *Journal of Epidemiology & Community Health, 61*(9), 802–809.

Swiss Federal Department of Foreign Affairs. (2019). *Humanitarian principles here and now.* Retrieved from http://www.elysee.ch/fileadmin/user_upload/elysee/Expositions_itinerantes/Humanitarian_Principles/ELY_DDC_brochure_WEB.pdf

Taylor, J., Bradbury-Jones, C., Lazenbatt, A., & Soliman, F. (2016). Child maltreatment: Pathway to chronic and long–term conditions? *Journal of Public Health, 38*(3), 426–431.

Temple, V. K., Cook, J. L., Unsworth, K., Rajani, H., & Mela, M. (2019). Mental health and affect regulation impairment in fetal alcohol spectrum disorder (FASD): Results from the Canadian National FASD Database. *Alcohol & Alcoholism, 54*(5), 545–550.

Treit, S., Jeffrey, D., Beaulieu, C., & Emery, D. (2019). Radiological findings on structural magnetic resonance imaging in fetal alcohol spectrum disorders and healthy controls. *Alcoholism: Clinical & Experimental Research, 44*(2), 455–462.

Viner, R. M., Ozer, E. M., Denny, S., Marmot, M., Resnick, M., Fatusi, A., & Currie, C. (2012). Adolescence and the social determinants of health. *Lancet, 379*(9826), 1641–52.

Watkins, R. E., Elliott, E. J., Mutch, R. C., Latimer, J., Wilkins, A., Payne, J. M., ... Bower, C. (2012). Health professionals' perceptions about the adoption of existing guidelines for the diagnosis of fetal alcohol spectrum disorders in Australia. *BMC Pediatrics, 12*, 69.

Weatherburn, D., Snowball, L., & Hunter, B. (2008). Predictors of Indigenous arrest: An exploratory study. *Australian & New Zealand Journal of Criminology, 41*, 307–322.

Wechsler, D., & Naglieri, J. (2006). *Wechsler nonverbal scale of ability.* San Antonio, TX: Harcourt Assessment.

Whaley, S. E., O'Connor, M. J., & Gunderson, B. (2001). Comparison of the adaptive functioning of children prenatally exposed to alcohol to a nonexposed clinical sample. *Alcoholism: Clinical & Experimental Research, 25*(7), 1018–1024.

4 FASD in the courts

Fitness to stand trial

Tamara Tulich

Introduction

It is estimated that there are approximately 100 people detained in prisons and psychiatric facilities across Australia who have been found unfit to stand trial and therefore not tried, convicted, or sentenced for any offence, and at least half identify as Aboriginal and Torres Strait Islanders peoples (Parliament of Australia, 2016, p. 14). In Western Australia, at 30 June 2019, there were 42 people subject to custody orders following a finding of unfitness, with 10 of those detained in prison (Mentally Impaired Accused Review Board, 2019, p. 5). FASD, along with other cognitive impairments, is relevant to whether an accused person is fit to stand trial. An accused person's mental fitness to stand trial relates to his or her ability to comprehend the proceedings and communicate at the time of a criminal trial, and is crucial to the fairness of the trial process. While differences exist between the Commonwealth, states, and territories in Australia, a person found unfit to stand trial in Australia may be detained – often indefinitely and in a custodial setting – for a longer period than if they had plead guilty to the offence. Members of the High Court have repeatedly emphasised that, 'it should not be overlooked …that the usual consequence of a finding that a person is unfit to plead is indefinite incarceration without trial. It is ordinarily in the interests of an accused person to be brought to trial, rather than suffer such incarceration' (*Eastman v The Queen* (2000), para. 24 (Gleeson CJ); *Kesavarajah* (1994), p. 249, (Deane & Dawson JJ)).

The application of fitness regimes to persons with cognitive impairment have been heavily criticised by international bodies, state, and federal parliamentary committees, the judiciary, disability advocates, and researchers. Criticisms have concentrated on the place and duration of detention (Australian Human Rights Commission ('AHRC'),

2014, p. 30; Blagg & Tulich, 2018; Blagg, Tulich & Bush, 2016, 2017; Crawford 2010, 2014; Martin, 2015; Parliament of Western Australia, 2012; *State of Western Australia v BB (a Child)*, [2015]; *State of Western Australia v Tax*, [2010]); the lack of appropriate accommodations for persons with cognitive impairment to exercise their right to a fair trial and participate in proceedings (Arstein-Kerslake Gooding, Andrews & McSherry, 2017; McCausland, Reeve & Gooding, 2019; McSherry et al., 2017; Gooding, McSherry, Arstein-Kerslake & Andrews 2017; Parliament of Australia, 2016); and the absence of an opportunity, in some Australian jurisdictions, to test the evidence through a trial or special hearing process (ALRC, 2014; Blagg et al., 2016, 2017). At the same time, critical disability scholars have highlighted the need to 'disable' forensic detention: illustrating, as Steele (2017, p. 329) does, that reform of laws governing fitness will not 'interrupt the ongoing processes of control of criminalized people designated as disabled if it does not also acknowledge and challenge the temporal and carnal logics underpinning the carcerality of the disabled body itself.'

This chapter begins by outlining the challenges legislative regimes governing fitness to stand trial pose for persons with FASD and other cognitive impairments using the case studies of Rosie Anne Fulton (Northern Territory), Gene Gibson (Kiwirrkura), and Marlon Noble, a Yamatji man whose indefinite detention was subject to an adverse finding by the United Nations Committee on the Rights of Persons with Disabilities. It explores decolonising reform options to improve outcomes for unfit accused with FASD through a multidisciplinary and community-focussed approach, drawing on international best practice examples – including the FASD Justice Program and new FASD Court in Manitoba, Canada, and the New Zealand needs and cultural assessment model. It argues that reform to fitness regimes must prioritise Aboriginal leadership, knowledges, and pathways to healing.

Fitness and fairness

An accused person's fitness to stand trial is central to the fairness of the trial process (*R v Presser* (1958); *Eastman* (2000)). In *Proceedings in the Case of John Frith for High Treason* (1790, pp. 317–318), the Lord Chief Justice, Lord Kenyon, explained the rationale and basis for the doctrine of fitness to stand trial:

the humanity of the law of England falling into that which common humanity, without any written law would suggest, has prescribed, that no man shall be called upon to make his defence at a time when his mind is in that situation, as not to appear capable of so doing; for, however guilty he may be, the enquiring into his guilt, must be postponed to that season, when, by collecting together his intellects, and having them entire; he shall be able so to model his defence, as to ward off the punishment of the law...

The common law principles relating to fitness to stand trial have been traced to Medieval England when a person could be tried for a felony or treason *only if* he or she entered a plea of guilty or not guilty to the charged offence(s) (Walker, 1968; Grubin, 1996; Loughnan, 2012). An accused person who refused to enter a plea to a felony or treason, or was unable to do so due to illness or incapacity, could not be convicted and executed and, crucially, their property could not be forfeited to the Crown. When this occurred, the Court was required to determine if the person refused to enter a plea due to 'malice' or 'by visitation of God' (Loughnan, 2012, p. 77). When found to have refused due to 'malice', the accused person was, from the turn of the fifteenth Century, subjected to *peine forte et dure:* withholding of food coupled with the imposition of increasing weights on the chest until the person agreed to enter a plea, or died (Grubin, 1996, p. 10; Walker, 1968, pp. 220–221). A person found mute by 'visitation of God' would be assumed to have entered a plea of not guilty, and the trial postponed. It was only after 1827, that a person found mute by 'malice' was similarly regarded as entering a plea of not guilty. While the *peine* was abolished in 1772 (but last used, according to Grubin [1996, p. 11], in 1736), in the intervening years those found to be mute by 'malice' were immediately convicted and sentenced (Grubin, 1996, p. 11).

In Australia, the common law test of fitness to stand trial was articulated by Smith J in the Victorian case of *R v Presser* (1958) and based on the formulation of Baron Alderson in *R v Pritchard* (1836). The *Presser* test identifies the minimum standards that an accused person must meet before being considered fit to stand trial for an offence, and constitutes the legal test in Australian jurisdictions (incorporated into legislation in all Australian jurisdictions except for NSW and Qld where it is incorporated through the common law: Gooding et al., 2017, p. 824). The test requires the accused person (*Kesavarajah*, [1994], p. 245 (Mason CJ, Toohey & Gaudron JJ)):

1 to understand the nature of the charge;
2 to plead to the charge and to exercise the right of challenge;

3   to understand the nature of the proceedings, namely that it is an inquiry as to whether the accused committed the offence charged;
4   to follow the course of the proceedings;
5   to understand the substantial effect of any evidence that may be given in support of the prosecution; and
6   to make a defence or answer the charge.

A person with FASD who fails to meet these minimum standards will be found unfit to stand trial and dealt with under statutory regimes governing unfit accused persons, as opposed to the ordinary criminal justice process. Statutory regimes governing unfit accused persons, while designed to achieve fairness, so often lead to injustice. Injustice, as Ms Fulton's and Mr Noble's cases demonstrate, in the operation of the regime, and injustice, as Mr Gibson's case highlights, when it is bypassed.

Rosie Anne Fulton (Northern Territory)

Ms Fulton, an Aboriginal woman from the Northern Territory, was born with FASD. It is reported that she was diagnosed with FASD at age 11 (Guilliatt, 2016). In 2012, she was arrested on charges of reckless driving and motor vehicle theft in Kalgoorlie, Western Australia. On the basis of medical evidence before the Court, the Magistrate found Ms Fulton unfit to stand trial pursuant to the *Criminal Law (Mentally Impaired Accused) Act* 1996 (WA) ('CLMIA Act'). In Western Australia, where a court finds a person is unfit to stand trial, and 'will not become mentally fit to stand trial within 6 months', the court has two options: unconditionally release the accused; or make a custody order (where imprisonment is a sentencing option) (CLMIA Act ss 16(5), 19(4)). A custody order commits an accused person to indefinite detention, at the Governor's pleasure. In deciding whether or not to make a custody order, the court must be satisfied such an order 'is appropriate having regard to' (CLMIA Act ss 16(6), 19(5)):

a   the strength of the evidence against the accused;
b   the nature of the alleged offence and the alleged circumstances of its commission;
c   the accused's character, antecedents, age, health and mental condition; and
d   the public interest.

In contrast to most Australian jurisdictions, the Western Australian regime does not involve a special hearing as to guilt or innocence.

Special hearings were introduced in many Australian jurisdictions because an accused person found to be unfit did not otherwise have an opportunity to test the evidence against them, raise defences and, crucially, be acquitted (NSW Law Reform Commission, 2013, p. 141; see also Gooding et al., 2017). Where special hearings exist, an accused person found to be unfit to stand trial is only subject to the coercive provisions of the regime if found to have engaged in the conduct constituting the offence (often referred to as a qualified finding of guilt).

Following the making of the custody order, and without the benefit of a special hearing process, Ms Fulton spent 21 months in Eastern Goldfields Regional Prison, Western Australia, without support or treatment, and away from her family and nation. Through the advocacy of her guardian, former Northern Territory police officer Ian McKinlay, media attention, and a petition to the government signed by 120,000 people, Ms Fulton was released in 2014 (see, e.g., O'Brien, 2014, p. 366; Parliament of Australia, 2016; Stewart, 2014). Since her release, Rosie has cycled in and out of prison (Steele, 2017) – denied, her guardian Mr McKinlay reported to a Senate Standing Committee in 2016, a transitional support plan and 'placed under a clearly designed-to-fail support plan, which has seen her under conviction for 70% of the time since her return to the Northern Territory' (Parliament of Australia, 2016, p. 51).

Marlon James Noble (Yamatji)

> I'm from Geraldton. I went to prison for the rest of my life. Been there for ten years of my life. No … I am not free. I am out of prison, but I am not free yet.
>
> Marlon Noble (Yamatji) (Unfinished Business, 2020)

Mr Noble, a Yamatiji man, was hospitalised with meningitis, an inflammation of the membranes covering the brain and spinal cord, when he was four months of age. It is reported that, due to this, Mr Noble 'experiences difficulties with literacy and numeracy and following complex instructions' (McSherry, 2018, p. 159; see also Freckelton & Keyzer, 2017). It is not suggested that Mr Noble has FASD; however, his cognitive impairment manifests similarly to FASD, making his experience relevant to understanding the challenges people with FASD and other cognitive impairments face when navigating the legal process. The United Nations Committee on the Rights of Persons with Disabilities (2016, para 4.11) described medical reports regarding Mr Noble as follows:

> several clinical psychologists' reports expressed ongoing concern about the author's "eagerness to please" leaving him "potentially

vulnerable to coercion in the presence of negative peer influences" and "to manipulation and exploitation". That conclusion prompted concern among medical experts that "the author's intellectual disability is such that he will need continual 24-hour care and support while in the community." The reports also expressed concern about the author's "impulsive and opportunistic" behaviour and his "aggressive, unpredictable outbursts."

Mr Noble was 19 years of age when, in October 2001, he was arrested and charged with sexual offences against two girls pursuant to ss 320 and 321 of the *Criminal Code 1913* (WA). He was detained in Hakea Prison and refused bail. Mr Noble's fitness to stand trial was raised in early 2002, and he was remanded in custody for psychiatric assessment. Mr Noble remained in Hakea Prison until 7 March 2003, when the District Court of Western Australia made a finding that he was unfit to stand trial under the *Criminal Law (Mentally Impaired Defendants) Act 1996* (WA) (since renamed the CLMIA Act) and ordered Mr Noble be subject to a custody order (Committee on the Rights of Persons with Disabilities, 2016, p. 2). Mr Noble was detained in Greenough Prison from March 2003 to January 2012, from which time he was released on a conditional release order, subject to 10 conditions.

The injustice possible by the absence of the safeguard of a special hearing became acutely apparent in Mr Noble's case. In 2010, a forensic psychiatrist concluded Mr Noble was capable of standing trial with appropriate supports. Mr Noble's legal team sought orders from the District Court that he was fit to plead, and that an indictment or discontinuance be presented for the offences charged in 2001. The Committee on the Rights of Persons with Disabilities (2016, para. 2.6) reported:

> The Western Australian Director of Public Prosecutions advised the Court that he did not intend to proceed with any further prosecution of the author because: (a) the substantial time he had already spent in custody far exceeded any reasonable term of imprisonment should he be convicted of all charges; and (b) there were very limited prospects of securing a conviction on the charges because of the low quality of the evidence available.

In relation to the low quality of evidence, it was widely reported in the media that the alleged victims denied the allegations against Mr Noble (Brul, 2011; McSherry, 2018). Mr Noble spent 10 years and 32 months in prison without trial. There remains no opportunity for him to clear his name.

In 2012, Mr Noble took his matter to the United Nations Committee on the Rights of Persons with Disabilities, claiming that his rights under the *United Nations Convention on the Rights of Persons with Disabilities* had been breached. In September 2016, the Committee found in favour of Mr Noble, finding that Australia had failed to fulfil its obligations under articles 5 (1) & (2) (equal protection and benefit of the law), 12 (2) & 3 (equal enjoyment of legal capacity and supports), 13 (1) (access to justice), 14 (1) (b) (liberty and security of person), and 15 (freedom from inhuman or degrading treatment) of the Convention. In particular, the Committee found that the CLMIA Act operated to suspend the right to a fair trial, and the lack of appropriate support to exercise the right to a fair trial and access to justice violated the Convention (McGaughey, Tulich & Blagg, 2017, p. 68; Gooding et al., 2017). The Committee recommended that the Australian Government compensate Mr Noble, pay his legal costs, and immediately revoke the conditions of his release. The Committee called on the Government to take measures to prevent similar violations by amending the CLMIA Act and any equivalent or related laws, and ensuring that persons with mental and cognitive impairments before the courts have adequate support and accommodation measures to enable them to exercise their legal capacity. In response, the Australian Government stated it 'respectfully disagrees with a number of the Committee's views' (Australian Government, n.d.). The Western Australian Government is currently in the process of reforming the CLMIA Act; however the reform Bill is yet to be introduced into Parliament.

These cases demonstrate the many challenges experienced by people with cognitive impairment in the justice system – and particularly at the critical juncture of fitness to stand trial. Neither Ms Fulton nor Mr Noble were provided with appropriate accommodations to exercise their right to a fair trial. Neither were – and neither has since been – given an opportunity to test the case against them through a trial or special hearing process. Culturally embedded alternatives to custody, such as on country, therapeutic alternatives led by Aboriginal people were not available to either Ms Fulton or Mr Noble. Mr Noble spent over ten years in prison. Ms Fulton spent nearly two years in prison. Without an opportunity for acquittal – or, indeed, compensation as was provided to Mr Gibson.

These cases also illustrate the pervasive impact of FASD on families and communities, as unhealed intergenerational and transgenerational trauma linked to colonial violence and dispossession corrodes social, emotional, and cultural well-being (Blagg et al., 2016, 2017; Blagg & Tulich, 2018; Dudgeon, Milroy & Walker, 2014; Williams, 2018). Ms Fulton was placed in care at a young age (Steele, 2017, p. 335). She was, from a young age, at the mercy of a system that continuously failed her. Even with a diagnosis of FASD at age 11, the necessary accommodations and throughcare support did not exist to support Ms Fulton – an issue explored further in Chapter 6. These two cases show one part of the picture: the invidious operation of the CLMIA Act on those found unfit to stand trial due to cognitive impairment. Mr Gibson's case illustrates the unfairness caused by undiagnosed FASD and the confluence of factors that can lead to the making of improper admissions and a plea of guilty.

Gene Gibson (Pintupi)

In 2012, Mr Gibson, a young Kiwirrkura man from a remote Aboriginal community was charged with murder. He entered a plea of not guilty and the matter was set down for trial in August 2014. In July 2014, the Supreme Court of Western Australia ruled that police interviews, in which Mr Gibson made admissions, were inadmissible as they were not voluntary and in breach of the *Criminal Investigation Act* 2006 (WA) (*The State of Western Australia v Gibson,* [2014], para. 183 (Hall J)). Following this ruling, in July 2014, Mr Gibson entered a plea of guilty, on advice of his lawyer, to the lesser charge of manslaughter. He was sentenced to seven years and six months imprisonment (see *State of Western Australia v Gibson* [2014] (Jenkins J); Tulich, Blagg & Hill–de Monchaux, 2017). In November 2016, Mr Gibson was granted leave to appeal against his conviction. In April 2017, the Court of Appeal unanimously quashed Mr Gibson's conviction. The Court of Appeal found that a miscarriage of justice occurred as Mr Gibson entered a plea of guilty when he likely did not adequately understand the legal process, the case against him or legal advice about the nature and implications of his plea of guilty, and because of the real risk 'that the plea was not attributable to a genuine consciousness of guilt' (*Gibson v The State of Western Australia* [2017] para. 157 (Buss P, Mazza & Beech JJA)).

It was only on appeal that FASD was raised (Parliament of Western Australia, 2018, p. 8). This followed on from media reports that experts were of the view that Mr Gibson should be assessed for FASD (Christodoulou, 2015). The Court of Appeal found that Gibson had 'significant and pervasive' cognitive impairments, English language difficulties, and a 'tendency for gratuitous concurrence' at all material times (*Gibson v The State of Western Australia* [2017] paras. 161, 200 (Buss P, Mazza & Beech JJA)). Further issues raised on the appeal included the lack of resources for expert assessment of cognitive impairment, the lack of resources for interpreters, and the pressures placed on lawyers working in remote areas. Following the decision of the Court of Appeal, Mr Gibson was released from custody after spending nearly five years in prison. In 2018, Gibson received a $1.3 million ex-gratia payment from the Western Australian Government (Kagi, 2018).

Mr Gibson's case reinforces the need for, and challenges to, identification and assessment of persons suspected of having FASD when they come into contact with the criminal justice system. The need for identification and recording of FASD is further explored in Chapter 6 in relation to Ms Clarke. Mr Gibson's case also demonstrates the continuing need for the training of all justice and out-of-home care personnel in identifying FASD and supporting people with FASD, as is discussed in more detail in Chapters 5, 6, and 7.

Improving outcomes for accused persons with FASD found unfit to stand trial: a supported, therapeutic, and community-based approach

It should be axiomatic that, as recommended by the Senate Standing Committees on Community Affairs (2016) and the Australian Human Rights Commission (2014, p. 30), where a person who has been found unfit to stand trial is to be held in detention, it must be demonstrated that all reasonable steps have been taken to avoid this outcome, and the person must be held in a place of therapeutic service delivery – not a prison. It should be similarly axiomatic that where an accused person found unfit to stand trial is detained, the detention should be of limited duration and subject to periodic review (ALRC, 2014, p. 210). The recent General Comment by the United Nations Committee on the Rights of the Child (2019, para. 28), outlined in Chapter 2, bears repeating:

> Children with developmental delays or neurodevelopmental disorders or disabilities (for example, autism spectrum disorders, fetal alcohol spectrum disorders or acquired brain injuries) should not be in the child justice system at all, even if they have reached the minimum age of criminal responsibility. If not automatically excluded, such children should be individually assessed.

To facilitate this, training is essential for all stakeholders in the justice system. Internationally, the Canadian Consensus Statement on Legal Issues of FASD (Institute of Health Economics, 2013, p. 7) recommends ongoing mandated training for all stakeholders in the legal system both in courts and corrections; and in the community. In Australia, similar calls have been made and are outlined in more detail in Chapters 5 and 6.

In addition, to achieve a multidisciplinary and community-focussed approach, that maximises therapeutic outcomes and responds to the needs and strengths of accused persons with FASD, number of changes need to occur:

- Standardised screening, diagnosis and individualised support is needed for young people and adults coming in contact with police, legal practitioners, courts and the justice system with suspected or diagnosed FASD.
- Provision for courtroom accommodations to support a person with FASD to exercise their legal capacity.
- Resourcing for community-based orders and community-based service provision that address the needs and strengths of an accused person. For Aboriginal offenders with FASD, the resourcing of Aboriginal owned services and on-country programs.

Reform to fitness regimes must prioritise Aboriginal leadership, knowledges, and pathways to healing. This would ideally be effectuated at the court stage, as discussed in Chapters 5 and 7, through innovations such as Neighbourhood Justice Centres and Aboriginal Courts with a focus on triage, co-located services, a no wrong door approach, trauma informed practice, and strong engagement with Aboriginal communities as leaders in justice partnerships and service provision.

Identification and assessment: court-based clinicians

As noted in Chapter 2, a full assessment of FASD can require input from a team of clinicians, including a developmental paediatrician, a speech pathologist, a neuropsychologist, an occupational therapist, and a psychologist. The process can be slow and expensive. The programmes discussed in relation to sentencing in Chapter 5 – the FASD Youth Justice Program in Manitoba and the New Zealand Youth Court list days – would also assist the court in relation to fitness to stand trial dispositions. Programmes like this, if resourced appropriately, could aid Australian courts by expediting multidisciplinary assessments to ensure judicial officers have the requisite information to be able to make orders not only on sentence, but also on a finding of unfitness, which are responsive to needs and strengths of persons with

FASD. While much of the scholarship is focussed on sentencing dispositions, there is no reason why dispositions at the fitness to stand trial stage are not similarly resourced.

The *FASD Youth Justice Program in Manitoba,* for example, would be equally important at the fitness stage. The Program was established in 2006, following a successful pilot and evaluation (Longstaffe et al., 2017). The Program is designed to ensure that at-risk youth who enter the criminal justice system are screened for FASD, and receive a timely assessment and diagnosis; that a sentencing court receives recommendations as to sentencing dispositions; capacity is built within families and communities while enhancing supports and services; and meaningful multidisciplinary intervention and reintegration plans for youth following custody are implemented (Longstaffe et al., 2017). The Program manager explained the value of the programme as 'building the relationship with the person who has a FASD diagnosis, their family and other supports' (Geary, 2020).

Where an accused person is Aboriginal, the assessment should address cultural needs. Aotearoa New Zealand provides a best practice example of how this might occur. In the early 2000s, New Zealand significantly reformed its unfitness legislative regime to both modernise the law and accommodate the needs of persons with an intellectual disability who were not covered by the prior regime. Fitness to stand trial is now governed by the *Intellectual Disability (Compulsory Care and Rehabilitation) Act 2003* (NZ) (IDCCR) and the *Criminal Procedure (Mentally Impaired Persons) Act 2003* (NZ) (CPMIP), and a person found unfit to stand trial cannot be detained in prison (s 9(4), IDCCR).

Once a person is found unfit to stand trial, the court must order the person to either attend specified places or be detained in a hospital or secure facility for the purpose of conducting an inquiry into what order would be most appropriate (CPMIP, s 23). The inquiry must take no longer than 30 days and, if the person has an intellectual disability, the needs assessment under the IDCCR must take place as part of the inquiry (CPMIP, s 23(4)-(5)). The purposes of the *needs assessment* are to assess the kind of care that the care recipient needs, identify suitable services capable of providing care for the person, and prepare a care and rehabilitation plan (IDCCR, s16). If the person is Māori, the care co-ordinator must also make a cultural assessment. That is, he or she must 'try to obtain the views of any suitable Māori person or Māori organisation concerned with, or interested in, the care of persons who have an intellectual disability' (IDCCR, s23(2)). The Māori person should be a member of the person's whānau, hapu, or iwi, if possible. The care and rehabilitation plan must, under ss 25 and 26, address a person's 'social, cultural, and spiritual needs', which must take into account the cultural assessment completed by the coordinator if the person is Māori.

The New Zealand Ministry of Health (2004) has developed *Guidelines for Cultural Assessment – Māori* to promote best practice in assessments undertaken under the IDCCR. The Guidelines (2004, p. 3) outline the principles and goals of cultural assessment:

> To provide an holistic picture of a person's needs.
>
> It is an inherent right of an individual to receive a culturally appropriate assessment, care and service.
>
> That the individual is heard and considered throughout their assessment, care and rehabilitation.
>
> To enhance the cultural perspective on the needs of the person and their whänau through appropriate assessment, care and rehabilitation.
>
> To establish and maintain a culturally effective and safe assessment and care under the IDCCR Act 2003.
>
> To ensure the quality and effectiveness of assessment and service delivery for people with an intellectual disability.
>
> To ensure that people assessed are cared for in the least restrictive environment and their rights upheld.
>
> To ensure that assessors undertaking the cultural assessment are competent in the area of intellectual disability.
>
> To ensure the involvement of Māori in the development and delivery of intellectual disability services.
>
> To respect the wishes of a person who may not wish to have contact with their whänau.

The Guidelines (2004, p. 12) provide a recommended process for the Māori *cultural assessment,* to be applied in accordance with local tribal tikanga or customary practice.

Research demonstrates that the New Zealand regime is not a panacea – and has been controversial in many respects (Brookbanks, 2013; Diesfeld, 2013; Prebble et al., 2013). Care managers have articulated the tensions inherent in their prescribed role under the Act, including balancing risk and rehabilitation, and creating environments that promote individual autonomy and self-control while managing risk (Prebble et al., 2013).

Research undertaken by Blagg and Tulich (2018) in the West Kimberley revealed strong support amongst community members and justice professionals for the introduction of a similar needs and cultural assessment in Western Australia. However, community members and justice professionals expressed concern about who would undertake a cultural assessment and how. A local process of cultural assessment must be developed in consultation with each community. While legislative prescription of a cultural assessment would be preferable, a form of cultural or needs assessment may be possible under existing legislative arrangements.

Courtroom accommodations

The Noble case highlights the need for appropriate accommodations to be provided to support individuals subject to unfitness proceedings to exercise their legal capacity. In 2016, a team of researchers piloted a Disability Justice Support Program in NSW, Victoria, and the Northern Territory to test whether a Non-Legal Disability Justice Support Person 'could assist accused persons with cognitive disabilities, by working alongside legal counsel and helping clients participate in criminal proceedings' (McSherry et al., 2017, p. 29). It was hypothesised that this support would, amongst other things, reduce the need for fitness to stand trial determinations and thereby prevent indefinite forensic detention.

The Support Persons were co-located in community legal centres and provided assistance related to decision-making, advocacy, and communication (McSherry et al., 2017, p. 38). The research team evaluated the programme, including undertaking a costs-benefits analysis. The team undertook a cost-benefit analysis and found 'significant cost savings to government', explaining (McSherry et al., 2017, p. 57):

> The findings indicate significant short-term savings associated with the intervention by the Disability Justice Support Worker which cost $5,033.88 per client on average, compared to the maximum cost associated with full unfitness to plead proceedings totaling upwards of $390,000. The longer-term savings are likely to be even more pronounced. While criminal proceedings and pathways and associated costs may vary between jurisdictions, this cost-benefit ratio is likely to still apply or provide even greater savings in circumstances where clients may face indefinite detention.

The support people were also found to have an educative effect on the lawyers in the community legal centres that were part of the study.

A FASD court, with Aboriginal leadership

These accommodations could be facilitated through a specialist FASD court. In Canada, the success of the *Manitoba FASD Youth Justice Program* has led to the creation of the *FASD Court in Winnipeg, Manitoba Canada*. The Court was established in 2019 for youth and adults who have been diagnosed with FASD, with judicial officers who understand FASD and support workers who can advise and connect people with FASD with community programmes (Provincial Court of Manitoba, 2019). It has been described as a 'game changer' (Malone, 2019). The Chief Judge of the Provincial Court of Manitoba, Margaret Wiebe, issued a Notice on 14 March 2019 which outlined the new docket:

> One of the goals of these dockets is to provide the accused with a court environment that takes into account the specific deficits identified in the FASD assessment report and how they might be related to the offender's moral blameworthiness or degree of responsibility for an offence. If there is a link between the deficits resulting from FASD and the offending behaviour, the Court would explore how the sentence imposed would best reflect and respond to that link.

The Court's features have been described as (Pro Bono Students Canada, 2019):

1   A smaller, quieter courtroom;
2   Judges with a specialized understanding of FASD;
3   Support workers available to provide connections to community programs; and
4   Access to help for obtaining a medical diagnosis.

May (2019) reported on the Court's first sitting on 28 March 2019:

> The familiar fluorescent glare of institutional overhead lights is gone. So is the click-clack of the court clerk's keyboard — it's been replaced with a sleek and silent model. A sign outside the Winnipeg courtroom, illustrated with a cartoon gavel, cautions spectators not to walk in and out — the swinging of the heavy wooden door would be yet another distraction.

Since its first sitting, demand for the Court has 'skyrocketed' (Geary, 2020) and sittings have more than doubled.

The FASD Court is, like most specialist courts, a sentencing court (discussed in more detail in Chapter 5). That is, it requires an accused person to enter a plea of guilty before they can be admitted into the programme. However, there is no reason in principle why a similar court could not also determine fitness matters. Indeed, consideration should be given to a similar court innovation in Australia. At the fitness stage, a 'reg flags' referral to timely assessment and diagnosis could lead to a referral to specialist court that would facilitate court-based management, judicial monitoring and a non-adversarial problem solving approach – for both fitness and, where relevant, sentencing. It would also facilitate, through the co-location of services, the efficient development of supported treatment and diversion plans.

As discussed in Chapter 5, this could be built around innovations already in existence in Australia such as Neighbourhood Justice Centres (NJC) that do not require a plea of guilty to access the services of the centre. Blagg and Tulich (2018) found strong support for a hybrid justice centre, drawing on the NJC and Aboriginal Court models, that emphasises the co-location of services, a trauma informed practice, a no wrong door approach to treatment, and respect for Aboriginal knowledges, leadership and pathways to healing. Such an innovation would, of course, be well placed to promote the use of courtroom accommodations to support an accused person to exercise their legal capacity.

Conclusion

While designed to avoid unfairness to an accused person, fitness to stand trial regimes often produce unfairness for persons with FASD and other cognitive impairments. The cases discussed in this chapter illustrate, on the one hand, the unfairness caused by the pernicious operation of the CLMIA Act on those found unfit to stand trial due to cognitive impairment, and, on the other, the unfairness occasioned by undiagnosed FASD and to the improper entering of a plea of guilty. The case studies also demonstrate the pervasive impact of FASD on individuals, families, and communities, as unhealed trauma linked to colonisation and dispossession undermines social, emotional, and cultural well-being, and is coupled with the systemic failure of mainstream justice and out-of-home care systems. This chapter has explored reform options to improve outcomes for unfit accused with FASD through a multidisciplinary and community-focussed approach, drawing on international best practice examples – including the new FASD Court in Manitoba, Canada, and the New Zealand needs and cultural assessment model – and the centring of Aboriginal knowledges, leadership, and pathways to healing.

References

Arstein-Kerslake, A., Gooding, P., Andrews, L., & McSherry, B. (2017). Human rights and unfitness to plead: The demands of the convention on the rights of persons with disabilities. *Human Rights Law Review, 17*(3), 399–419.

Australian Government. (n.d.). *Response of Australia to the views of the committee on the rights of persons with disabilities in communication No. 7/2012 (Noble v Australia)*. Retrieved from https://www.ag.gov.au/rights-and-protections/publications/noble-v-australia-72012-australian-government-response

Australian Human Rights Commission. (2014). *Equal before the law: Towards disability justice strategies*. Report, Australian Human Rights Commission, Australia, February.

Australian Law Reform Commission. (2014). *Equality, capacity and disability in commonwealth laws*, Report No. 124, Sydney, Australia: Law Reform Commission, August.

Blagg, H., & Tulich, T. (2018). *Developing diversionary pathways for indigenous youth with foetal alcohol spectrum disorders (FASD): A three community study in Western Australia: Report to the criminology research advisory council (Grant: CRG 34/14–15) August 2018*. Australia: University of Western Australia.

Blagg, H., Tulich, T., & Bush, Z. (2016). Placing country at the centre: Decolonising justice for indigenous young people with foetal alcohol spectrum disorders (FASD). *Australian Indigenous Law Review, 19*(2), 4–16.

Blagg, H., Tulich, T., & Bush, Z. (2017). Indefinite detention meets colonial dispossession: Indigenous youths with foetal alcohol spectrum disorders in a white settler justice system. *Social and Legal Studies, 26*(3), 333–358.

Brookbanks, W. (2013). Managing the challenges and protecting the rights of intellectually disabled offenders. In B. McSherry, & I. Freckelton (Eds.), *Coercive care: Rights, law and policy* (pp. 218–240). Abingdon, UK: Routledge.

Brull, M. (2011, 9 December) "The sad story of Marlon noble." *ABC Ramp Up*. Retrieved from https://www.abc.net.au/rampup/articles/2011/12/09/3387845.htm

Christodoulou, M. (2015, 2 November). Expert casts doubt on Gene Gibson murder confession, wants FASD assessment. *ABC Online*. Retrieved from https://www.abc.net.au/news/2015-11-02/expert-casts-doubt-on-gene-gibson-murder-confession/6905426

Committee on the Rights of the Child. (2019). *General comment No. 24 (2019) on children's rights in the child justice system*. CRC/C/GC/24. 18 September 2019.

Committee on the Rights of Persons with Disabilities. (2016). *Views adopted by the Committee under article 5 of the Optional Protocol, concerning communication No. 7/2012*. CRPD/C/16/D/7/2012. Adopted by the Committee at its sixteenth session (15 August–2 September 2016).

Crawford, C. (2010). Families impacted by the criminal justice system on the frontier: A new model required. *Psychiatry, Psychology and Law, 17*(3), 464–475.

Crawford, C. (2014). "FASD clinicians forum" (Speech delivered at the Telethon Kids Institute, 18 November 2014). Retrieved from http://alcoholpregnancy.telethonkids.org.au/media/1020099/fasd_clinicians_forum_magistrate_crawford_presentation.pdf

Criminal Code 1913 (WA)

Criminal Investigation Act 2006 (WA)

Criminal Law (Mentally Impaired Accused) Act 1996 (WA)

Criminal Law (Mentally Impaired Defendants) Act 1996 (WA)

Criminal Procedure (Mentally Impaired Persons) Act 2003 (NZ)

Diesfeld, K. (2013). The expected and unexpected issues raised by New Zealand's Intellectual Disability (Compulsory Care and Rehabilitation) Act 2003. In B. McSherry & I. Freckelton (Eds.), *Coercive care: Rights, law and policy* (pp. 241–257). Abingdon, UK: Routledge.

Dudgeon, P., Milroy, H., & Walker, R. (Eds.) (2014). *Working together: Aboriginal and Torres Strait Islander mental health and wellbeing principles and practice* (2nd ed.). Canberra, Australia: Commonwealth of Australia.

Eastman v The Queen (2000) 203 CLR 1

Freckelton, I. & Keyzer, P. (2017). Fitness to stand trial and disability discrimination: An international critique of Australia. *Psychiatry, Psychology and Law, 24*(5), 770–783.

Geary, A. (2020, January 13). As demand explodes, Manitoba's new FASD court expands to meet need. *CBC News.*

Gibson v The State of Western Australia [2017] WASCA

Gooding, P., McSherry, B., Arstein-Kerslake, A., & Andrews, L. (2017). Unfitness to stand trial and the indefinite detention of persons with cognitive disabilities in Australia: Human rights challenges and proposals for change. *Melbourne University Law Review, 40*(3), 816–866.

Grubin, D. (1996). *Fitness to plead in England and Wales.* East Sussex, UK: Psychology Press.

Guilliatt, R. (2016, August 19). What happened to Rosie Ann?. *The Weekend Australian Magazine.*

Institute of Health Economics. (2013). *Consensus statements on legal issues of fetal alcohol spectrum disorder.* Prepared at Institute of Health Economics Consensus Development Conference, Edmonton, Alberta, 18–20 September 2013.

Intellectual Disability (Compulsory Care and Rehabilitation) Act 2003 (NZ).

Kagi, J. (2018, April 18). Gene Gibson gets $1.3m payment after wrongful conviction over Josh Warneke's Broome Death. *ABC (online).* Retrieved from http://www.abc.net.au/news/2018-04-18/gene-gibson-gets-payment-after-josh-warneke-wrongful-conviction/9671792

Kesavarajah (1994) 181 CLR 230

Longstaffe, S., Chudley, A. E., Harvie, M. K., Markesteyn, T., Neault, D., & Brown, T. (2018). The Manitoba youth justice program: Empowering and supporting youth with FASD in conflict with the law. *Biochemisty and Cell Biology, 96*(2), 260–266.

Loughnan, A. (2012). *Manifest madness: Mental incapacity in the criminal law.* Oxford, UK: Oxford University Press.

Malone, K. G. (2019, 3 February). New Manitoba court for people with FASD could be game changer: Experts. *The Canadian Press.*

Martin, W. (2015). "Indigenous Incarceration Rates: Strategies for much needed reform" (Speech delivered at the Law Summer School, Perth, 20 February 2015). Retrieved from http://www.supremecourt.wa.gov.au/_files/Speeches_Indigenous_Incarceration_Rates.pdf

May, K. (2019, 28 March). First case for Canada's first FASD Court. *Winnipeg Free Press.*

McCausland, R., Reeve, R., & Gooding, P. (2019). The economic case for improving legal outcomes for accused persons with cognitive disability: An Australian study. *International Journal of Law in Context, 15*(4), 367–389.

McGaughey, F., Tulich, T., & Blagg, H. (2017). UN Decision on Marlon Noble case– Imprisonment of an Aboriginal man with intellectual disability found unfit to stand trial in Western Australia. *Alternative Law Journal, 42*(1), 67–70.

McSherry, B. (2018). "Unfit" to Plead. *Meanjin Quarterly, 77*(1), 158–165.

McSherry, B., Baldry, E., Arstein-Kerslake, A., Gooding, P., McCausland, R., & Arabena, K. (2017). *Unfitness to plead and indefnite detention of persons with cognitive disabilities.* Melbourne: Melbourne Social Equity Institute, University of Melbourne.

Mentally Impaired Accused Review Board. (2019). *Annual report 2018/2019.* Perth, Australia: Government of Western Australia.

New Zealand Ministry of Health. (2004). *Guidelines for cultural assessment – Māori: Under the intellectual disability (Compulsory Care and Rehabilitation) Act 2003.* Auckland, New Zealand, August.

NSW Law Reform Commission. (2013). *People with cognitive and mental health impairments in the criminal justice system: Criminal responsibility and consequences.* Report No. 138, Sydney, Australia: Law Reform Commission, May.

O'Brein, K. (2014). Boots, blankets, and bomb tests: First Australian petitioning and resistance to colonisation. *Griffith Journal of Law & Human Dignity, 2*(2), 357–376.

Parliament of Australia, Senate Standing Committee on Community Affairs. (2016). *Inquiry into the indefinite detention of people with cognitive and psychiatric impairment in Australia.* Report, Parliament of Australia, Australia, November.

Parliament of Western Australia, Legislative Assembly, Education and Health Standing Committee. (2012). *Foetal alcohol spectrum disorder: The invisible disability, Report No. 15.* Parliament of Western Australia, Perth.

Parliament of Western Australia, Legislative Assembly, Joint Standing Committee on the Corruption and Crime Commission. (2018). *The more things change... Matters arising from the corruption and crime commission's report on operation aviemore: Major crime squad investigation into the unlawful killing of Mr Joshua Warneke, Report No. 8*. Parliament of Western Australia, Perth.

Prebble, K., Diesfeld, K., Frey, R., Sutton, D., Honey, M., Vickery, R., & McKenna, B. (2013). The care manager's dilemma: Balancing human rights with risk management under the intellectual disability (Compulsory care and rehabilitation) Act 2003. *Disability & Society, 28*(1), 110–124.

Pro Bono Students Canada. (2019). Fetal alcohol syndrome disorder (FASD): New studies suggest that the prevalence of fetal alcohol syndrome disorder (FASD) in the Canadian population is higher than previously thought. *Marl* (Manitoba Association for Rights and Liberties) 9 October 2019.

Proceedings in the Case of John Frith for High Treason. (1790). 22 Howell's State Trials 307.

Provincial Court of Manitoba. (2019). *Notice re: FASD Dockets – Adults and Youth*. 14 March 2019.

R v Presser [1958] VR 45

R v Pritchard (1836) 173 ER 135

State of Western Australia v BB (A Child) [2015] WACC 2

State of Western Australia v Gibson [2014] WASCSR 203

State of Western Australia v Tax [2010] WASC 208

Steele, L. (2017). Disabling forensic mental health detention: The carcerality of the disabled body. *Punishment & Society, 19*(3), 327–347.

Stewart, J. (2014, June 25). Intellectually impaired Aboriginal woman Rose Fulton to be freed after 21 months in jail with no convictions. *ABC Online*. Retrieved from https://www.abc.net.au/news/2014-06-25/aboriginal-woman-in-jail-without-conviction-to-be-freed/5550790

The State of Western Australia v Gibson [2014] WASC 240

Tulich, T., Blagg, H., & Hill-de Monchaux, A. (2017). Miscarriage of justice in Western Australia: The case of Gene Gibson. *Griffith Journal of Law and Human Dignity, 5*(2), 118–142.

Unfinished Business. (2020). *Stories from Australian Aboriginal and Torres Strait Islander people with disabilities: Marlon Noble*. Retrieved from http://www.unfinishedbusiness.net.au/portfolio/marlon-noble-2/

United Nations Convention on the Rights of Persons with Disabilities, opened for signature 30 March 2007, 2515 UNTS 3 (entered into force 3 May 2008).

Walker, N. (1968). *Crime and insanity in England, volume one: The historical perspective*. Edinburgh, UK: Edinburgh University Press.

Williams, R. (2018). Understanding fetal alcohol spectrum disorder (FASD) through the stories of Nyoongar families and how may this inform policy and service delivery. Unpublished doctoral thesis. Health Sciences. Curtin University.

5 Sentencing and courts

Suzie Edward May

Introduction

FASD, along with other mental impairments, may be taken into account as a mitigating factor when sentencing an offender, be relevant to the type of sentence imposed, and how certain sentencing principles, such as individual and general deterrence, are weighed in the exercise of sentencing discretion. This chapter outlines the challenges of sentencing offenders with FASD and why sentencing responses to FASD have been criticised as inadequate, through an analysis of current case law and commentary. It explores reform options to improve sentencing outcomes for Aboriginal youth with FASD by maximising therapeutic outcomes with community-based alternatives, drawing on Australian, Canadian, and New Zealand best practice examples. Building on the issues raised in preceding chapters, this chapter will also explore courtroom accommodations, building effective sentencing options, mandatory sentencing regimes, and the role of innovative specialist courts, namely, Community Justice Centres and Aboriginal Courts.

Challenges of sentencing persons with FASD

Each jurisdiction in Australia has its own sentencing laws; however the procedural process, presumptions, and objectives of sentencing are the same. The criminal law assumes that offenders have free will, are capable of making choices, understanding the consequences of their actions, and taking individual responsibility for these actions. The sentencing process also presumes that sentences imposed by courts will have the effect of specific and general deterrence, denunciation, incapacitation, and rehabilitation, resulting in a person learning from their mistakes and not repeating their offending behaviour, creating a safer society.

These assumptions are incompatible with the impairments associated with FASD, as discussed in Chapter 3. Judge Lilles in the Canadian decision of *R v Harper* [2009], stated that if an offender has been diagnosed with FASD, then a failure to take this diagnosis into consideration when sentencing is an injustice to not only the offender, but the community. Judge Lilles also stated [(37)–[39]) that to ignore this diagnosis would hold the offender to a standard they were unable to reach due to their impairment, which was manifestly unfair and would not result in a safer and just society. His Honour went so far as to say that imposing a sentence without consideration of FASD could have 'a substantially more severe effect on someone with the impairments associated with FASD.'

Australian and New Zealand courts have followed this approach by recognising that a diagnosis of FASD is relevant to the sentencing process. This includes the person's cognitive, social, and behavioural problems associated with FASD; impulsive and unplanned offending; secondary participation with other offenders; lack of memory and inability to understand the concept of cause and effect; inappropriate sexual behaviour; and substance abuse (Douglas, 2010). The recognition of this by courts has had the effect of reducing the person's moral culpability (but not his or her legal responsibility) for the offence, impacting on the weight given to punishment and denunciation as a sentence purpose; influencing the type and conditions of a sentence; reducing the weight given to deterrence as a sentencing purpose, depending on the nature and severity of the mental impairment and how it might affect the mental capacity of the person at both the time of the offending and at sentencing; increasing the hardship experienced by a person in prison if they had a mental impairment at the time of sentencing; and justifying a less severe sentence where there was a serious risk that imprisonment could have a significant adverse effect on their mental health (Victorian Court of Appeal in *R v Verdins* (2007)).

The consideration of the impairments associated with FASD by some Australian courts has resulted in a number of cases where the moral culpability of the person has been reduced, along with the retributive, denunciatory, and deterrent aspects of sentencing. In the case of *Churnside v the State of Western Australia* [2016], the Western Australian Court of Appeal stated that although burglary offences committed by the offender were serious, 'deterrence, both general and specific, is of much reduced significance in the sentencing process because of the disabilities [FASD] which the appellant suffers through no fault of his own' (para 78). The Court also stated that there was an obvious connection between the offending behaviour and the person's FASD, and therefore the moral culpability of the behaviour was diminished. Similarly, in the case of *R v MBQ: ex parte A-G (Qld)* [2012] the Queensland Court of Appeal heard an appeal by the prosecution against the sentence imposed on a 12-year-old boy with FASD who had pleaded guilty to raping a three-year-old girl. The appeal was dismissed with McMurdo P (para 44) stating that due to the mental age of the respondent (nine years old) caused by FASD, he had a 'limited grasp of the consequences and moral blameworthiness of his actions at the time he committed the offences' which was considered 'highly relevant to the exercise of the sentencing discretion', resulting in a reduction of the moral culpability for the offending, so the retributive, denunciary, and deterrent aspects of sentencing were less relevant than they otherwise would have been.

In the case of *AH v The State of Western Australia* [2014], the Western Australian Court of Appeal stated that the trial judge's imposed sentence of imprisonment on a 21-year-old Aboriginal woman with suspected FASD should only have been made if the court was satisfied that prison was the *only* justifiable sentence. The Court determined that given the age, antecedents, vulnerability, and disabilities of the offender, prison was unlikely to have a deterrent effect and instead, 'it should have been concluded that the reduction of AH's risk of re-offending through a process of rehabilitation was a most significant sentencing factor, and in which punishment and deterrence were less significant factors' (para 125, (Martin CJ, Mazza JA and Hall J)). The Court of Appeal went so far as to say that imprisonment had 'repeatedly worsened her condition thereby increasing the risk to the community' (para 119, (Martin CJ, Mazza JA and Hall J)).

The 2013 Canadian Consensus Statement on Legal Issues of Fetal Alcohol Spectrum Disorder (Institute of Health Economics, 2013) recommends sentencing courts give primary consideration to the objective of rehabilitation and impose community-based sanctions by deeming FASD a mitigating factor in sentencing. Traditionally, the term 'rehabilitation' is understood as a process that relies on the ability of a person to understand, learn, remember, and make choices, which may be contrary to the abilities of people with FASD. However, the Statement recommends 'rehabilitation' be defined in relevant legislation to include 'a reasonable prospect of managing the offender in the community' (p. 20) which is a shift in goal from the neurodevelopmental ability of the individual, to an achievement facilitated by family, community, and organisational support. In determining sentencing options, the Statement recommends a focus on 'those measures most likely to provide opportunities for the offender to be rehabilitated and reintegrated peacefully into society' (p. 21).

Reform options to improve sentencing outcomes

In order for courts to impose sentences that are beneficial to Aboriginal youth with a diagnosed or suspected FASD, their families, and communities, there are a number of things that need to exist within the justice and court systems. These include therapeutic place-based, community-owned sentencing options; education of judicial officers, legal practitioners, police, and other professionals within the justice and court systems (and professionals intersecting with these systems) on FASD and its impact; appropriate community-based, culturally responsive multidisciplinary services to support individuals, families, and communities; and courtroom policy and practice reform allowing for more appropriate engagement with people diagnosed with or suspected of having FASD. The remainder of this chapter will discuss these essential elements and the ways in which their implementation would greatly improve the experience of young people with FASD in the justice system while resulting in more effective justice outcomes for individuals, families, and communities.

Therapeutic and community-based sentencing options

Both courts and commentators have made clear that custodial sentences should be used as a last resort for people with suspected or diagnosed FASD as people with FASD are unlikely to be able to comply with prison/detention rules due to difficulties with memory and linking actions with consequences; they may be victimised, exploited, and manipulated due to their suggestibility (Chudley et al., 2007, p. 269; Douglas, 2010.p. 228, Fast & Conroy, 2009, p. 252; Institute of Health Economics, 2013, p. 25); and their FASD could be exacerbated by the prison environment (*AH v The State of Western Australia* [2014]). However, some jurisdictions of Australia (such as Western Australia and the Northern Territory) still have mandatory sentencing legislation, that requires judicial officers to order a minimum or fixed penalty when a person is convicted of a particular offence. The court is stripped of its usual discretion to consider mitigating factors and to order alternative sentencing dispositions in response to that mitigation. This type of legislation disproportionately affects vulnerable groups, such as Indigenous Australians, young people, and people with intellectual disabilities (The Law Society of Western Australia, 2019, p. 2). While there have been calls for the repeal of mandatory sentencing legislation in Australia (Law Council of Australia, 2016, p. 6), it does still exist and therefore continues to negatively impact people with FASD. Blagg, Tulich, Mutch, Williams, & May (2018, p. 44) call for State and Territory mandatory sentencing legislation in Australia to be amended to give wide judicial discretion and allow departure from the legislation where there is evidence of FASD. Other jurisdictions such as Canada have recommended a statutory exemption to mandatory sentencing for offenders with FASD, recognising the disproportionate and harmful impact its imposition would have. The Canadian Consensus Statement states that 'Judges should have the fullest range of sentencing discretion in dealing with the diverse circumstances of offenders with FASD' and that courts should develop 'an appropriate and case-sensitive sentencing jurisprudence for offenders with FASD' (Institute of Health Economics, 2013, pp. 22–23).

However, even if mandatory sentencing laws are repealed and custodial sentences avoided, sentencing dispositions such as community-based orders will only have a chance of being effective if they are tailored to the needs and strengths of the individual with FASD. For example, a community-based order may require a young person to regularly report to another person, attend meetings, reside at a particular location, or refrain from an activity. A young person with FASD will be set up to fail and be put at risk of breaching their court order and being detained in custody if they are held to these expectations, as the challenges they experience when adhering to instructions, keeping appointments, reasoning, impulse control, and judgement, are likely to prevent them from being compliant with these conditions. It is therefore imperative that community-based orders include rigorous family, community, government, and non-government scaffolding which includes 'comprehensive and consistent supports to provide them with ongoing advice, direction, and structure, as well as to advocate on their behalf' (FASD Justice Committee, 2007–2008) to give the person the best chance of success. The Court of Appeal in *Churnside* emphasised that courts need to investigate the family, community, and organisational supports available before imposing a community-based order. Referred to as an 'external scaffolding', this network of support must be present to successfully maintain the person in the community.

For Aboriginal children and young people with FASD, this scaffolding would include extended family, community, and Aboriginal organisations, and, as we discuss in later chapters, embedded on-country. Keeping Aboriginal children in a culturally secure environment on-country, connected to culture and language has proven successful in supporting at-risk young people. The Yiriman Project, run by Cultural Bosses from around Fitzroy Crossing in Western Australia, has been used by Magistrates as an alternative to juvenile detention. Young people are taken out onto traditional country and taught bush skills from Elders who are able to nurture them, improve their diets and minimise their involvement in the justice system (Palmer, 2013, p. 122). This is in stark contrast to the outcomes that occur when young people from remote communities of Western Australia are disconnected from their families, communities and lands, and transported hundreds of kilometres away to the State's only juvenile detention facility, where they have limited if any support. However, to facilitate essential scaffolding and cultural programmes for at-risk young people, Aboriginal organisations require start up and secure ongoing funding for mentoring, family support services and on-country camps that work to stabilise and heal young people and their families, reducing the likelihood of the young person reoffending.

This therapeutic, community-based, culturally responsive, and multidisciplinary approach requires courts and judicial officers to not simply focus on whether a young person is guilty of an offence or not, but to consider and address some of the social and health issues behind their offending behaviour. To effectively examine these issues in Aboriginal youth with FASD, their unique circumstances need to be recognised by courts in the sentencing process. The Canadian Supreme Court in *R v Gladue* [1999] (para 68) expressed this well:

> [T]he circumstances of aboriginal offenders differ from those of the majority because many aboriginal people are victims of systemic and direct discrimination, many suffer the legacy of dislocation, and many are substantially affected by poor social and economic conditions... Aboriginal offenders are, as a result of these unique systemic and background factors, more adversely affected by incarceration and less likely to be "rehabilitated" thereby, because the internment milieu is often culturally inappropriate and regrettably discrimination towards them is so often rampant in penal institutions.

The result of this decision was the application of the '*Gladue* factors', which ask judicial officers to recognise the adverse backgrounds and cultural impact of Canadian Aboriginal peoples when sentencing, via a *Gladue* report or pre-sentence cultural report. In contrast to a traditional pre-sentence report, a *Gladue* report is completed with the assistance of a person who has a link or understanding of the Indigenous community the person comes from. The report aims to provide the court with a background of the person's community and 'place the offender's circumstances within an Indigenous framework in order to assist the judge in crafting a sentence that is culturally sensitive' and focussed on rehabilitation (Hundal, 2018).

Practically, *Gladue* factors mitigate the culpability of the offender and could result in the reduction of time in prison or the avoidance of custody, instead allowing for restorative justice processes that focus on healing all those affected by the crime including the person who committed the offence.

The High Court of Australia in *Bugmy v The Queen* [2013] discussed *Gladue* in relation to the relevance of an offender's background of profound social deprivation when sentencing and the majority of the Court held that this principle should be applied in a race-neutral way to maintain the delivery of justice in an individualised manner. This means that the background of an Aboriginal person may mitigate the sentence imposed for an offence, just as the background of a non-Aboriginal person may mitigate that person's offence. They also stated that 'the effects of a childhood deprivation do not diminish over time' and should be given full weight when determining an appropriate sentence. While these cases legitimise evidence of disadvantage and cultural impacts of Aboriginality for the purpose of sentencing, unless there is a wider understanding of FASD, courts will either fail to be presented with this relevant evidence or will risk giving the evidence insufficient weight when imposing non-custodial orders.

Judicial and legal practitioner education

The best practice model of a multidisciplinary, community-focussed approach that maximises therapeutic outcomes and responds to the needs, including cultural needs, of young people with FASD who come into contact with the justice system, can only occur if judicial officers, legal practitioners, police, and others involved in our justice systems (and in professions that intersect with the justice system) are educated on the prevalence, effects, and far-reaching impact of FASD on individuals, families, and communities.

Australian studies have found that justice professionals require more training on FASD than they currently receive. A survey conducted in 2011 of Queensland barristers and solicitors, highlighted that 82% wanted guidelines on how to deal with a person diagnosed with or suspected of having FASD (Douglas, Hammill, Russell, & Hall, 2012). Similarly, a 2011–2012 Western Australian study examining the awareness and knowledge of FASD amongst judges, magistrates, lawyers, corrections staff, and police, identified a need for training and education to improve awareness of the specific impairments associated with FASD that impact on the treatment of individuals with FASD across the justice system (Mutch et al., 2013, p. 39). In the Northern Territory, the North Australian Aboriginal Justice Agency and the Central Australian Aboriginal Legal Aid Service (2014, p. 2) have recommended urgent targeted training of the judiciary, lawyers, prosecutors, police and corrections officers to increase their awareness of FASD and facilitate earlier identification, referral, and assessment. Internationally, the Canadian Consensus Statement (Institute of Health Economics, 2013, p. 7) recommends ongoing mandated training on FASD for all stakeholders in the legal system in the courts, corrections, and the community.

A court can only act on the information presented to it, as Canadian Justice Melvyn Green (2006) explains:

> ...judges only know (or are permitted to know) what counsel, by way of evidence and submissions, are prepared to tell them. My seat may be the best in the courtroom, but I can only see what counsel allow me to see...In too many cases, I suspect, judges are hamstrung because they're denied the information they need. This doesn't serve the interests of justice or the public or, perhaps most importantly, the interests of defendants with FASD who, far too often, find themselves in conflict with the law...Crown as well as the defense – whose job it is to inform judges when a defendant is FASD compromised. A FASD-educated judge will then have the ken to ask the salient questions: How impaired? What history of therapeutic intervention and with what success? What alternatives to jail are available? How effective are they likely to be *in this one, single, individual case*? Judges are at the far end of the forensic food chain. Please give us the tools to do our job.

This not only includes the legal professionals presenting to the court, but also the other members of the multidisciplinary team involved in the assessment of a young person with FASD, such as the developmental paediatrician, speech pathologist, neuropsychologist, occupational therapist, and psychologist. It is only with evidence in the form of reports presented to the court, from these other professionals, that the judicial officer can both understand and fully consider the young persons' FASD when sentencing.

While FASD is increasingly recognised in youth detention (Blagg & Tulich, 2018), it is a difficult task to create culturally secure, trauma-informed detention centres; hence the importance of informing and upskilling staff in this area. All detention centre staff should receive education and training on FASD to prevent unrealistic expectations of what young people can achieve in terms of following instructions and conforming with regulations while in custody. A Western Australian study (on both adults and children in custody) also identified intensive case management, mentoring, and throughcare planning as both essential and best practice when working with young people with FASD in detention (Tubex, Rynne, & Blagg, 2020).

Innovative courtroom policy and practice

The education and training of judicial and legal professionals (and others involved in the justice and court systems) are not only essential to ensuring that appropriate sentencing dispositions are made by courts but also to ensuring that courtroom accommodations are made to assist people with FASD in their understanding of the processes, practices, and outcomes of a busy courtroom.

The Canadian FASD Justice Committee (2007–2020) have highlighted that people with FASD may not be able to behave according to courtroom conventions; may not understand the severity of the offences before the court; may act inappropriately or impulsively or without inhibition; may show no remorse or consideration for others involved in the case; may be only be able to hear every third or fourth word that is spoken; may misinterpret judicial and legal processional' non-verbal gestures; may be easily led and manipulated during questioning; may provide information which is off the topic, inappropriate or confusing; may be able to read court documents but not comprehend them; and may not correctly interpret visual information presented in court.

While this poses a challenge, a judicial officer who receives education and training on FASD can easily ensure the person with FASD is engaged in the proceedings of the court by making a number of simple accommodations, including speaking slowly, scheduling more time than usual for a trial, keeping statements and questions short and to the point, breaking information into small pieces, confirming that what the person heard is what was said, allowing the person more time to respond to questions, reading all materials out loud, checking the person's understanding of what he or she is being asked, not assuming that what they see is indifference, providing one direction or rule at a time, using repetition, establishing a mentor/buddy/role model system, developing and utilising diversion programmes, utilising support persons, using simple wording on release forms and probation orders, and being consistent in probation/parole follow-up (Dubovsky, 2006).

For the person with FASD, these adjustments to the usual courtroom process and practice can make a big difference to not only their experience and understanding of the court system, but on their compliance with court orders which they are now more likely to understand.

Specialist courts and FASD

While FASD education and training of judicial officers and other professionals in the justice system is essential to ensure sentencing dispositions are responsive to the needs and strengths of young people with FASD, some jurisdictions are leading the way with specialist courts that are focussed on addressing the social, economic, and health issues behind offending behaviour, while also delivering fair justice to individuals and communities.

The *FASD Youth Justice Program in Manitoba Canada* is the leading example of an innovative specialist justice programme for young people with FASD. It ensures that young people receive a timely diagnosis; makes recommendations to the court regarding sentencing dispositions; builds capacity within families and communities while enhancing supports and services; and implements meaningful multidisciplinary intervention and reintegration plans for youth following custody (Longstaffe, Chudley, Harvie, Markesteyn, Neault, & Brown, 2017). The *New Zealand Youth Court* list days involve specialist mental health, alcohol, and drug services, which assist the court by screening and assessing offenders for mental health, intellectual disability, and alcohol and drug issues. They also offer liaison services, treatment and clinical care, and specialist consultation for health and justice staff. Education Officers in Youth Justice Courts also provide the court with information about the education history of the young person which prompts screening for FASD and earlier intervention than in a regular court. This multitude of disciplines provide reports to the court, which can be taken into consideration by the judicial officer when sentencing is determined (Crawford, 2015).

In Australia, existing court innovations, such as the Neighbourhood Justice Centre in Victoria, and specialist Aboriginal courts, such as the Victorian Koori Court, which focus on triage, co-located services, a no wrong door approach, trauma-informed practice, and strong engagement with Aboriginal communities as justice partners and service providers, could be expanded to specifically deal with young people with FASD. These solution focussed court models have a number of essential elements to successfully meet the legal and social needs of the people appearing before the court, including consistency of judicial officers; judicial monitoring and motivational interviewing; multidisciplinary, multi-agency integrative teamwork; linkages to community-based service provision; co-location of court, legal, and social welfare support services; dedicated legislation; and clear judicial boundaries (Murray, Blagg, & May, 2018, p. 9). These elements, coupled with mandatory training in FASD for all professionals involved in the justice and court systems, along with access to therapeutic community-based sentencing options, would greatly enhance outcomes for young people with FASD.

Necessary community-based scaffolding

Despite the existence of educated judicial and legal professionals; court recognition of disadvantage via *Gladue* or cultural reports (discussed in Chapter 4); the abolition of discriminatory mandatory sentencing legislation; and innovative courtrooms to make therapeutic, community-based sentencing orders, if the community structures to facilitate this do not exist, or are not adequately explored by courts as viable sentencing options, custodial sanctions will continue to be imposed on vulnerable people with FASD.

As discussed earlier, in the Western Australian Court of Appeal case of *Churnside*, the offender was assessed as having FASD and medical, neurological, and paediatric experts recommended therapeutic interventions including on-country or basic workplace programmes; a male mentor; and engagement with occupation, sporting, and leisure activities. Despite this, the sentencing judge imposed a custodial sentence because it was argued that the level of intensive, structured support required to manage the person in the community was unavailable. Allowing the appeal, quashing the prison sentence, and imposing a community-based order, the appellate court found that there were in fact opportunities that could have been explored further by the sentencing court to support the person in the community. The Court of Appeal held that the sentencing judge (82):

> ...was 'obliged to use 'every means at its disposal' to arrive at a disposition which would offer some degree of protection to the community by reducing the risk of [Churnside] reoffending and at the same time provide some measure of justice to [Churnside], who would otherwise be destined to an indefinite and perhaps escalating cycle of offending and imprisonment as a result of his pre-birth and childhood experiences.

This case highlighted the effort that courts (as well as legal represent-atives) should make to break the cycle of reoffending that is often part and parcel of the life experience of young Aboriginal offenders with FASD. The Court of Appeal stated that it is not enough for courts to simply presume that community supports needed to maintain the per-son in the community are unavailable or inadequate, courts need to actually engage with government and non-government agencies with the aim of assisting the person to reform their life and their behaviours. In addition, family members and communities must be consulted to understand their willingness and capacity to support a person on a community-based order. By making these detailed enquires, courts are then able to make informed sentencing dispositions, utilising the realistic support of the young persons' family, wider community, and access to multidisciplinary support services – a practice already used by specialist courts.

Conclusion

The significant negative impact of mainstream court practices, custo-dial sentences, and community-based orders with unrealistic condi-tions; and a lack of community embedded support for young people with FASD, is becoming clearer. There is recognition of the need to: educate all professionals engaged with young people with suspected or diagnosed FASD; develop therapeutic, community-based sentencing options for courts; and reform our courtroom practices and processes to better engage young people with FASD. Specialist courts are re-sponding with a focus on the social and health needs (as well as legal needs) of individuals in many areas such as mental health and alcohol and drug misuse, working to keep our most vulnerable out of prison and detention, instead facilitating rehabilitation and engagement in supportive communities. Expansion to include the vulnerable cohort of young people with FASD is essential to ensure our justice and court systems are delivering fair and responsive justice to all.

References

AH v The State of Western Australia [2014] WASCA 228

Blagg, H., & Tulich, T. (2018). *Developing diversionary pathways for indigenous youth with foetal alcohol spectrum disorders (FASD): A three community study in western Australia: Report to the criminology research advisory coun-cil (Grant: CRG 34/14–15) August 2018.* Australia: University of Western Australia.

Blagg, H., Tulich, T., Mutch, R., Williams, R., & May, S. (2018). *FASD and the criminal justice system: Report to the Australian National Advisory Council on Alcohol and Drugs* (ANACAD) Secretariat (Reference ID: 6000078020).

Bugmy v The Queen [2013] HCA 37

Chudley, A. E., Kilgour, A. R., Cranston, M., & Edwards, M. (2007). Challenges of diagnosis in fetal alcohol syndrome and fetal alcohol spectrum disorder in the adult. *American Journal of Medical Genetics, 145C*(3), 261.

Churnside v the State of Western Australia [2016] WASCA 146

Crawford, C. (2015). *To examine how Youth affected by fetal alcohol spectrum disorder, involved in the Criminal Justice System, are dealt with in other Jurisdictions.* Report, Winston Churchill Memorial Trust of Australia.

Douglas, H. (2010). The sentencing response to defendants with foetal alcohol spectrum disorder. *Criminal Law Journal, 34*(4), 221–239.

Douglas, H., Hammill, J., Russell, E., & Hall, W. (2012). Judicial views of foetal alcohol spectrum disorder in Queensland's criminal justice system. *Journal of Judicial Administration 21*(3), 178–188.

Dubovsky, D. (2006). *Improving outcomes for children and adolescents in the juvenile justice system.* Retrieved from https://www.fasdjustice.ca/what-works/resources-what-works.html and https://fasdjustice.ca/trial/strategies-to-get-relevant-information.html

FASD Justice Committee. (2007–2018). *FASD and the justice system.* Canada. Retrieved from http://fasdjustice.ca/trial/evidentiary-challenges/information-processing-and-language.html and http://fasdjustice.ca/trial/courtroom-behaviour.html

Fast, D. K., & Conry, J. (2009). Fetal alcohol spectrum disorders and the criminal justice system. *Developmental Disabilities Research Reviews, 15*(3), 250–257.

Green, J. M. (2006). *A judicial perspective.* Paper presented at the Fetal Alcohol Syndrome Disorders Symposium for Justice Professionals, Toronto, Ontario, 1 March 2006. Retrieved from http://fasdjustice.ca/media/JudgeGreenSpeech.pdf

Hundal, B. (2018). The impact of the gladue case on indigenous peoples within the context of the criminal justice system. *CanLII Authors Program*, CanLIIDocs 10982.

Institute of Health Economics and Government of Alberta. (2013). Consensus statements on legal issues of fetal alcohol spectrum disorder. Prepared at *Institute of Health Economics Consensus Development Conference*, Edmonton, Alberta, 18–20 September.

Law Council of Australia. (2016). *Federal election policy platform.* Retrieved from https://www.lawcouncil.asn.au/docs/074a7e93-837d-e711-93fb-005056be13b5/LCA_2016_Federal_Election_Policy_Platform.pdf

Longstaffe, S., Chudley, A. E., Harvie, M. K., Markesteyn, T., Neault, D., & Brown, T. (2017). The Manitoba youth justice program: Empowering and supporting youth with FASD in conflict with the law. *Biochemisty and Cell Biology, 96*(2), 260–266.

Murray, S., Blagg, H., & May, S. (2018). *Doing justice differently: A community justice centre for Western Australia: A feasibility study*. Perth, Australia: The University of Western Australia.

Mutch, R., Watkins, R., Jones, H., & Bower, C. (2013). *Fetal alcohol spectrum disorder: Knowledge, attitudes and practices within the Western Australian justice system: Final Report*. Foundation for Alcohol Research and Education, Telethon Institute for Child Health Research, Perth.

Palmer, D. (2013). *We know they healthy cos they on country with old people: Demonstrating the value of the Yiriman Project 2010–2013*. Report, Yiriman Project, Australia.

R v Gladue [1999] 1 SCR 688

R v Harper [2009] YKTC 18

R v MBQ: ex parte A-G (Qld) [2012] QCA 202

R v Verdins (2007) 16 VR 269

The Law Society of Western Australia. (2019). *Briefing paper: Mandatory sentencing*. Retrieved from https://www.lawsocietywa.asn.au/wp-content/uploads/2015/10/Law-Society-Briefing-Papers-Mandatory-Sentencing.pdf

The North Australian Aboriginal Justice Agency and the Central Australian Aboriginal Legal Aid Service. (2014). *Joint submission to the NT parliamentary inquiry into foetal alcohol syndrome disorders (FASD)*, May 2014, 17. Retrieved from https://parliament.nt.gov.au/__data/assets/pdf_file/0004/363217/Submission_Number_21_NAAJA_CAALAS.pdf

Tubex, H., Rynne, J., & Blagg, H. (2020). *Building effective throughcare strategies for Indigenous offenders in Western Australia and the Northern Territory*. Australia: Australian Institute of Criminology.

6 A decolonising and human rights approach to FASD training, knowledge, and case practice for justice involved youth in correctional contexts

Robyn Williams and Dorothy Badry

Introduction

This chapter will examine the challenges people with FASD encounter in correctional settings from a decolonising lens. Drawing on current research and best practice, it will identify concerns regarding the need for training on FASD for correctional staff and provide guidance on delivering culturally secure training. A review of recent studies on the needs of carers and families, health, and justice professionals, and FASD in the youth justice system has informed this work. The Royal Commission Report into the Protection and Detention of Children in the Northern Territory (2017) highlights young people's vulnerability to abuse in youth detention, such as the Don Dale Youth Detention Centre and demonstrates that youth are at risk of multiple forms of vulnerability in detention. Youth with FASD are at risk of involvement with the justice system as so many aspects of their lives remain fragmented including a lack of a secure home environment, early exposure to substance use, entrenched cycles of poverty, leaving school early, limited employment opportunities, and a lack of support for their disability. We argue that cumulative disadvantages and inherited disparity deeply contribute to the current state of youth justice in Australia, and marginalised youth with FASD are particularly at high risk of victimisation when they enter into this system. The need for intensive, formalised education, and training on FASD in the youth justice system, from first contact with the law through to community-based prevention programmes and institutional care, is an ethical imperative in the justice system as individuals with FASD are often in conflict with the law.

Baldry, McCausland, Dowse, & McEntyre (2015) indicate that Indigenous people in Australia are more likely to have 'been in out of home care, to come into contact with police at a younger age and

at a higher rate as a victim and offender, to have higher numbers...
of convictions...and higher rates of homelessness' (p. 10). Baldry,
McCausland, Dowse, & McEntyre (2015) point out that multiple
systemic challenges exist relating to vulnerability that is connected to
a history of adverse childhood experiences, poverty, and systemic racism.
Youth with FASD who become criminally involved are entering a
system that presumes that they are cognizant and aware of the impact
of their criminal activity on others and have the capacity to learn from
their behaviour (Pei, Leung, Jampolsky, & Alsbusy, 2016). It is critical
to recognise that factors contributing to youth with FASD becoming
involved with the youth justice system are biological, psychological,
and social (Pei et al., 2016). It is essential to apply an intersectionality
lens to the experience of youth with FASD in the youth and criminal
justice system as this experience is deeply entrenched in the history of
colonisation in Australia.

Impact of colonisation

The unfolding legacy of colonisation continues to be mirrored in high
rates of incarceration, suicide, substance use disorders, and child
welfare involvement in the Indigenous population in Australia. The
Australian Government, Institute of Health, and Welfare [AIHW]
(2019) report highlighted that Indigenous children, in contrast to
non-Indigenous children, were eight times more likely to receive
child protection services, have more substantiated cases of abuse
and neglect and were more likely to have protection orders in place.
Gatwiri, McPherson, Parmenter, Cameron & Rotumah (2019) report
that Aboriginal children were 11 times more likely to be in out-of-
home care, based on 2019 AIHW data.

It is noted by Gatwiri et al., (2019) that the overrepresentation of
Indigenous children is connected to the unfolding legacy of colonisation
and children continuing to be displaced and disconnected from
culture. Cumulative disadvantage is a key factor in the representation
of Indigenous children in child protection and justice systems. Indigenous
youth are 17 times more likely to be involved in youth justice
supervision than youth who are not; and children involved with child
protection are nine times more likely to also be involved in the youth
justice system than the general population (AIHW, 2019). The prevalence
of FASD in Australia remains relatively unknown. A systematic
review undertaken on FASD, found a higher incidence within special
populations, including, children in care, Aboriginal populations,
criminal justice, and psychiatric care (Lange et al., 2017). This review

noted that, due to limited awareness of FASD, most children in care were not likely to be assessed for FASD and, as a consequence, receive no access to early interventions to improve their quality of life. There is no doubt that many young people in detention in Australia have prenatal alcohol exposure, but most have never been assessed or diagnosed, as evidenced in the Banksia Hill Study (discussed in Chapter 3). This recent study undertaken at the Banksia Hill Detention Centre in Western Australia found a FASD prevalence rate of 36% (Bower et al., 2018).

It is critical to decolonise FASD as a disability and to recognise the connection between FASD and inherited disparity as a consequence of colonisation. Disability compounds the disparities confronting Indigenous populations, and racism further contributes to the disproportionate social, health, and economic disadvantages (Green et al., 2018). Fitts & Soldatic (2020) identify the prevalence rate of disability is higher amongst Indigenous populations than mainstream in settler colonial nations including Australia, Canada, and the United States. Notably, Australia has the highest rate of disability amongst Indigenous populations and this has not changed in the past decade. Further, disability is often not recognised in the criminal justice system and those with 'borderline intellectual disability, foetal alcohol spectrum disorder or acquired brain injury, are often seen as just poorly behaved and as wilfully offending. Without timely therapeutic support in the community, both groups are set on a trajectory of criminal justice contact' (McCausland, Baldry, Segrave, Spivakovsky & Eriksson, 2017, p. 302). Blagg, Tulich, and May (2019) demonstrate the high incidence of lack of diversion from policing of Aboriginal youth. Aboriginal youth with FASD were found to have more involvement in the justice system than non-Aboriginal youth with FASD (Brownell et al., 2019). Therefore, it is important to understand protective factors against increased justice system involvement for Aboriginal youth with FASD, that work to decolonise their experiences. Findings from this report demonstrated that Aboriginal youth reported improved mental health after participating in cultural activities that increased their sense of connection and belonging, and subsequently, results found decreased police involvement in these youth (Peled, Smith, & McCreary Centre Society, 2014).

The Aboriginal languages of Australia do not have a defined term to represent disability due to cultural factors, and individuals who are Indigenous and disabled are considered to have a dual disadvantage (Green et al., 2018). A lack of recognition of FASD and a general lack of diagnostic capacity, poses serious disadvantages for children and youth from Aboriginal communities in Australia who already face a life of inherited disparity. The Aboriginal worldview of disability implies applying a cultural/strength-based approach in caring for family members and is part of looking after family. Research by Hill, Cass, Newton, and Valentine (2012) highlights a great deal of caring occurs on an informal basis within Aboriginal families and can also be seen as part of the legacy of colonisation. The report by Hill highlights the differences between Aboriginal and mainstream carers; and that the majority of Aboriginal carers undertake caring responsibilities whilst experiencing chronic health conditions and intergenerational trauma, contributing to a lack of trust by Aboriginal carers when engaging services (Eades, 2020).

Literature review: FASD awareness, diagnosis, and training

FASD is not well recognised in justice systems due to a lack of training in both the disability itself, and in supportive case management techniques. There has been strong resistance to responding to FASD in justice systems which need to be understood and challenged. Freckelton (2017) notes that it is critical to recognise FASD as a mitigating factor for criminally involved youth. Justice systems often inherit what departments of child protection do not deal with when it comes to FASD. Baldry (2013, p. 371) indicates that 'thousands of people with mental and cognitive disability are being "managed" by Australian criminal justice systems rather than being supported in the community.' A lack of FASD awareness continues to be influenced by stigma, and the fear of labelling children with a disability (Choate & Badry, 2019). Mela, Coons-Harding and Anderson (2019) identified that a significant proportion of individuals are diagnosed with FASD due to their involvement in the criminal justice system, noting that many of these individuals had previously been diagnosed with mental health conditions. Similarly, Bower et al. (2018) found that only two of the 36 adolescents diagnosed with FASD as part of the Banksia Hill Study had, prior to the study, had access to a diagnosis. Mela et al. (2019) not only indicated that youth with FASD are 19 times more likely to be incarcerated than their peers without FASD but also cautioned that the majority of individuals with FASD do not become involved in the criminal justice system. A common narrative emerging from FASD literature is the lack of FASD awareness, depth of knowledge, and confidence of health sector professionals in ways to work with this population (Mukherjee, Wray, Curfs, & Hollins, 2015).

This lack of awareness and confidence is also influenced by a lack of FASD content in university curriculums, and certificate qualifications (Paley et al., 2009).

Research undertaken in Australia and New Zealand found the level of FASD awareness was low and in some cases, knowledge of FASD was informed by misconceptions (Bagley & Badry, 2019; Payne et al., 2005). Whilst research on FASD awareness and prevalence studies has emerged in the past decade, Australia remains behind countries such as Canada and the United States in terms of FASD diagnostic services, FASD informed practice and interventions. Mutch, Jones, Bower, Watkins (2016) undertook a quantitative study exploring FASD awareness in Western Australia amongst the criminal justice sector, police, lawyers, and judicial officers. Findings from the 427 participants identified that the majority had heard of Fetal Alcohol Syndrome; however only 16% indicated an awareness of FASD as a permanent condition. The findings also supported further training for staff involved in the criminal justice system and suggested that FASD training should include information on behaviours, FASD support organisations, information for referrals and diagnosis, and access to qualified specialists.

In Manitoba, Canada, in 2004, a pilot programme on FASD and youth justice was developed to provide access to FASD diagnosis; build capacity of families and communities on FASD; and offer post-release support including the co-ordination of relevant services for the young person and their family (Longstaffe et al., 2017). This FASD Youth Justice Program is likely to be one of the longest running programmes and provides good insight into the priority areas of adapting service delivery in justice for youth with FASD. The results of FASD diagnosis from this pilot confirmed that 17.5% of youth had FASD and significant cognitive impairment, addiction, and mental health issues. Some of the identified areas and strategies for improved outcomes included mandatory FASD training for staff. The pilot was further strengthened by the establishment of a steering committee made up of the Winnipeg Police, Manitoba Corrections, Manitoba Treatment Centre, and two Winnipeg Court Judges.

In Alberta, Canada, a FASD community of practice training and research project took place from 2009 to 2011 within Alberta Children's Services and included training on FASD for caseworkers and foster parents. Workforce development in Alberta also included advanced case consultation and a model of collaborative training with foster parents, caseworkers, and supervisors (Badry, Pelech, & Milne, 2014). Recent Canadian research conducted by Stewart (2016), explored the awareness by police of FASD. Findings showed a lack of awareness of FASD, and a preference for face to face training, involving case scenarios and role plays.

In 2011, the Canadian Alexis Nakota Sioux Nation initiative was developed to improve service delivery for adults suspected of having FASD involved in justice. This initiative involved the combination of the Alexis Justice Model with the Northwest Central Alberta FASD Services Network Clinical Network. An evaluation of this project included service providers from clinical and justice sectors. The results were promising and indicated improved collaboration of services, as well as improvements in building capacity of both the sector and families, with the benefit of better access to services. The researchers cautioned on loss and grief felt by families and the community and recognised the link to colonisation. They also highlighted the need for cultural security and understanding of intergenerational trauma by trainers, and the need for Aboriginal trainers (Flannigan, Pei, Rasmussen, Potts & O'Riordan, 2018).

Carers, family awareness, and societal lack of knowledge

Universal narratives have emerged over the past decade of the ongoing challenges and adversity impacting on carers and families raising children with FASD, throughout the world (Reid, Moritz, & Akison, 2019). A recent study conducted in the US on carers, found multiple levels of system barriers for service delivery to families. The key barriers identified were: delayed diagnosis, qualifying for services, availability of services, implementation of services, maintaining services, and the overarching barrier was lack of knowledge of FASD (Petrenko, Alto, Hart, Freeze, & Cole, 2014). Another study by Watson, Coons, & Hayes (2013) found raising children with FASD to be more stressful than raising children with Autism.

Domeij et al. (2018) undertook a systemic review of 18 studies examining families raising children with FASD and found families faced a range of challenges and often reported feeling isolated. Concerns included the fear of their child not having the ability to have an independent life as an adult (Brown, Harr, Morgan, Varga, & Fenrich, 2017; Domeij et al., 2018). Isolation was compounded by carers and families reporting that relevant services, including health care and education, had limited understanding of FASD (Domeij et al., 2018). Lack of FASD awareness increased the need for carers and families to be advocates for their child across multiple settings (Reid et al., 2019).

Reid et al., (2019) recently conducted an international online survey of 109 carers of children with FASD. The majority of carers included adoptive parents and foster carers, and were recruited online from Australia (33%), the USA (31%), New Zealand (16%), Canada (13%), the UK (3%), and South Africa (2%). The findings of the study were consistent with previous studies of high caregiver stress and lack of societal knowledge on FASD. Furthermore, this was seen to have an impact on the mental health of carers, with the likelihood of having an impact on caring for their child.

Aboriginal kinship carers

One of the strengths of Aboriginal culture and families is the extended family system and the obligation and roles for families to care for family members. Hill (2012) conducted a landmark study on Indigenous Carers in Australia, with the key findings identifying a contrasting worldview of how Aboriginal people relate to disability, and the high rate of informal caring undertaken in comparison to mainstream Australia (Hill, Cass, Newton & Valentine, 2012). Whilst it is well established that raising a child with a disability has a profound impact on the health of carers, Aboriginal carers are often living with chronic health conditions themselves (Eades, 2020; Hill, 2012).

It is critical to examine the challenges and experiences of Aboriginal carers, given the global over-representation of Aboriginal children in both out-of-home care and the criminal justice system. Corrado, Freedman, and Blatier (2011) identify the long association between the child protection system, criminal justice system, and the tragic historical policies of removal, impacting on generations of First Nations children in Canada and Australia. The literature on carers largely represents the experiences of non-Aboriginal carers, with the experiences of biological parents and Aboriginal carers rarely being presented. Stewart, Lawley, Tambour, & Johnson (2018) discuss colonisation and child welfare, identifying that more First Nations children are in welfare today than during the period of residential schools. Similarly, the rates continue to escalate within Australia, with Aboriginal children being 9.2 times more likely to be in care, particularly under the age of four (Libesman, 2014).

Many Aboriginal children in Australia are likely to be placed with kinship carers (Libesman, 2014). Kinship carers are often older women with health issues, living in poverty and receiving less support from social services than non-kinship carers, further marginalising children, and kinship carers (Mann-Johnson & Kikulwe, 2018). Another significant disadvantage for Aboriginal families is the high mortality rates and the majority of the population being under the age of 25, impacting on the capacity of Aboriginal families. Professor Anne-Marie Eades, a Noongar woman from Western Australia, undertook research on 72 Aboriginal women across Australia and found that all had at least one chronic health condition, and several had to cease caring for multiple young children due to their chronic health conditions (Eades et al., 2020). Similarly, Noongar scholar, Dr Robyn Williams (2018) found, in a study of Aboriginal kinship carers raising children with FASD, chronic health conditions had an impact on placements, resulting in several placements ceasing. Often placements of Aboriginal children will be impacted by a health crisis of kinship carers or early death (Eades et al., 2020; Williams, 2018).

Fitts and Soldatic (2020) further identify limited research has been undertaken on Aboriginal carers with a disability and chronic health conditions, finding that Aboriginal women often have extended multiple care responsibilities and will prioritise the health of others before themselves. Green et al. (2018) examined the barriers confronting Aboriginal carers, which included racism, mistrust of mainstream services, and lack of culturally appropriate services. Reported barriers to culturally competent service delivery included mainstream workloads and lack of provider interest in cultural competency training (Green, et al., 2018). In a recent study of Aboriginal carers, housing and poverty emerged as having a devastating impact on the carer and impacted on accessing services for their child (Green et al., 2018). The same study found the majority of carers resided in public housing and several carers were living in crisis accommodation. Green et al. believe that an intersectionality framework has the potential to create new ways of describing disparities and developing sustainable and meaningful solutions.

Mental health

Brown et al., (2017) identify the importance of FASD training for mental health professionals and the need for training to incorporate the following key areas: understanding the need for early diagnosis and intervention; addressing myths and misconceptions relating to FASD; best practice on screening tools and measures; and the DSM-5 definition of Neurobehavioral Disorder associated with PAE criteria. Further, it is imperative for mental health professionals to understand the significant disadvantages in treatment when providers lack appropriate awareness and understanding of FASD. Brown et al.,

(2017) cautioned that without adequate FASD training for mental health professionals, the cost to the client is likely to be immeasurable. Riches, Parmenter, Wiese, and Stancliffe (2006) note that most disability support systems in Australia are structured to provide care to individuals with either intellectual developmental disability or mental health problems, but limited crossover exists for complex individuals with other co-morbid or co-existing conditions. Supports and services provided to individuals with FASD in Australia have limited infrastructure in contrast to developmental disabilities. As Baldry (2013) notes, thousands of people with complex disabilities are incarcerated in the absence of these community-based services.

Within FASD literature, the high rates of mental health disorders and higher rates of suicide, are well documented (O'Connor, Portnoff, Lebsack-Coleman, & Dipple, 2019). In a recent sample of 54 adolescents with FASD aged between 13 and 18, it was found that 13% reported to have made a serious suicide attempt in the past 12 months, in comparison to 2.4% of their peers without FASD (O'Connor et al., 2019). O'Connor et al., (2019) reported 94% of this sample lived with an adopted or foster carer.

Recognising trauma

A profile of BC youth in custody (Smith, Cox, Poon, Stewart, & McCreary Centre Society, 2013) reported on findings of a survey of 114 youth in custody in the province of British Columbia Canada, with 52% identified as Indigenous. Of these 114 youth, 21 were female and 93 were male, and 36% reported having an FASD diagnosis. Common problems the youth identified included housing instability, historical abuse, and victimisation, and a high level of experiencing the death of a person close to them. Experiences of loss and grief amongst incarcerated youth is not well documented in the literature. The manner of deaths included violence (34%), suicide (32%), and overdose (32%), implying a significant majority of youth experience trauma for both the victim and the bereaved. At the time of entry into youth custody, 32% were in government care and had histories of physical and sexual abuse. It is important to note that researchers identify FASD informed and trauma-informed approaches as protective factors in positive outcomes for youth with FASD. If we unpack this concept, the key message is that a requirement exists for all those working with youth, to have at least a basic knowledge of FASD and specific knowledge about case management in child welfare and corrections, including youth justice.

Service delivery

Lack of FASD awareness by health and social services contributes to a lack of services for children struggling with FASD and their families. Further, the lack of FASD specialisation of sector professionals contributes to a reluctance and apprehension in delivering services and being uncomfortable working with individuals with FASD (Brown et al., 2019; Petrenko et al., 2014). In a recent study by Brown et al. (2019), carers expressed their concerns regarding a lack of services and for the future of their child. This included their fears of transition from youth to adulthood, and the reality of a lifetime commitment. Carers also expressed their anxiety about the risks of their child becoming involved in criminal activity, unplanned pregnancy, and abusive relationships. Importantly, carers also believed that with access to adequate support services, their child would be able to have a productive life. Furthermore, the fear expressed by carers for their child having no access to FASD informed services as they transition to adulthood, is well founded.

In the study noted earlier by Peled et al., (2014) relating to challenges in accessing services, youth cited long waiting times for services and the lack of programme flexibility, as a major issue for them. In some cases, youth were informed by alcohol treatment centres that they would not have received access to services if they had disclosed their FASD diagnosis. In other cases, the lack of a FASD diagnosis was a barrier to being able to access services. Both youth and caregivers reported the challenge of navigating health and social services. Notably, caregivers cautioned that access to health, social systems, and disability funding is impossible for an individual with FASD, without the support of an advocate. In terms of treatment for alcohol and drug use, youth reported that traditional programmes had unrealistic expectations and youth struggled with attending appointments at the correct time. In accessing mental health services, youth reported transport as an issue, along with no mental health services available in their community. Youth with FASD expressed strong views against group work as they are easily overstimulated by too many people in their surroundings, making group sessions highly ineffective. Sports and activities such as horse therapy and others involving animals, was also found to increase mental health and reduce suicidal ideation.

Youth with FASD will more likely respond to treatment that is inclusive of the following principles: FASD informed (trained workforce); flexible; holistic in nature; and consistent (Brown et al., 2017). Youth identified the following as service delivery best practice:

self-determination and the opportunity to be consulted and have input in the direction of their lives; and attending programmes that are willing to be flexible in their approach.

Cultural security

For the past decade there has been emerging evidence and recognition that connection to culture and use of culture as treatment is a legitimate form of intervention (Gatwiri et al., 2019). It is inherently an ethical, cultural, and human right to have access to culturally grounded interventions for children and adults in Aboriginal families. Connection to cultural identity sustains and nurtures child health, well-being, and development. This access to culturally grounded programmes remains imperative for Aboriginal youth who are involved in the justice system. Traditional diversion programmes that provide an alternative pathway for youth who become criminally involved, need to address cultural needs – not added on to programmes but included as a mandated part of the programme, in all institutions. The need exists for a cultural diversionary pathway as an integral part of the care of Aboriginal youth who are in custody.

The strength and resilience of Aboriginal culture is often overlooked in the literature, while the deficits of statistics dominate and reduce the potential for Aboriginal agency and knowledges. Prior to colonisation, there was no word for 'disability' and 'suicide' amongst Indigenous languages (Barker, Goodman & DeBeck, 2017; Hill, et al., 2012). Tait (2003), Salmon (2011), and Badry and Felske (2013) identify that FASD interventions and delivery for Indigenous people must be decolonised. Samaroden (2018) recognises that FASD for Aboriginal people is the result of colonisation and intergenerational trauma. Further, Barker et al., (2017) identify the emerging framework of 'culture as treatment' as another important tool, alongside social strategies that alleviate poverty, homelessness, and access to services. In a study on Aboriginal youth with FASD, youth reported improved mental health after participating in cultural activities and an increase in their sense of connection and belonging (Peled et al., 2014). Williams (2018) recently undertook a quantitative study on FASD amongst 180 Aboriginal people in Western Australia and found the majority of participants were keen to have training on FASD and only 10% of participants were confident in their knowledge of FASD awareness. Further, Aboriginal participants identified the culturally secure approach to FASD training was face to face in community forums and small groups, in preference to online training (Williams, 2018).

FASD training – most effective approaches

Training on FASD is important to the human services sector and essential in terms of providing FASD informed care. FASD is a distinct disability requiring training that acknowledges factors such as the challenges individuals and families with FASD face in relation to child protection, legal/justice systems, where other factors intersect such as poverty, addictions, and homelessness. In order to highlight some of the complexities that training on FASD would need to encompass we include the case of Ms Clarke who died in Geraldton, Western Australia on September 18, 2019. For cultural reasons, we will not use her first name and refer to her as Ms Clarke only, throughout the chapter in respect to cultural protocols. There were 14 witnesses on the street that primarily included young Aboriginal children who were deeply affected by witnessing this event. According to news media, Ms Clarke was surrounded by eight police officers and fatally shot in the stomach after her family called emergency services for help due to a mental health breakdown – seeking support to get her to a hospital. She was carrying a knife in her hands, had recently been released from jail, and had sought help from a hospital for mental health problems shortly before she died. We must rely on news stories as a point of reference due to a dearth of legal case studies on individuals with FASD. It is critical to note that in her short life Ms Clarke experienced the child protection system when placed in care at five months of age (7news.com.au, 2020), the mental health system, the criminal justice system as a youth and as an adult. According to court records, Justice Lindy Jenkins indicated in the court record, that she accepted the results of a clinical psychiatric report stating that Ms Clarke had FASD. Further the magistrate requested that prison authorities arrange for assessment and diagnosis for FASD as Ms Clarke was deemed to be at high risk in the community.

Ms Clarke was described as having intellectual impairment and developmental disabilities which were compounded by being victimised and bullied at school. Burd & Edwards (2019) indicate that physical, emotional, and sexual abuse are experienced by about 75% of youth with FASD and this becomes more complex over time. Without proper assessment and diagnosis, systems such as child welfare and youth justice are responding ineffectively. Further, the risk of mortality is much higher for individuals with FASD (Burd & Edwards, 2019). Early substance use and involvement with the law were both critical factors in Ms Clarke's history. Early, cumulative risky behaviour is not uncommon in the life trajectory of individuals with FASD and their life histories are often filled with trauma and victimisation. Australia is currently undertaking a National Senate Inquiry into FASD that will be completed in 2020. Ms Clarke case is being closely monitored by the Aboriginal Health Council of Western Australia.

Who needs to have training on FASD? The clear answer is anyone who is connected to the lives of individuals with FASD including families; kinship care providers; caregivers such as foster carers, group home staff and other facilities providing child and youth services, kinship care providers, child protection workers, legal and justice system staff including police, lawyers, judges, those working in probation and in institutions that house prisoners. FASD training is delivered in three main ways – in face to face workshops, through conferences aimed at professional development and through online learning. For example, the Canada FASD Research Network offers basic FASD training online as well as discipline specific professional training for school staff, judicial and legal professions, solicitor general (justice system staff), the Prevention Conversation, Towards Improved Practice and Multidisciplinary Team Training. These courses have been taken up in Canada and internationally. Badry has offered a course on FASD and Child Welfare Practice to BSW students in the Prairie Provinces in Canada on an annual basis for the past ten years. However, training on FASD is generally absent from university curriculum. While research has not yet been undertaken on the efficacy of online FASD training, it does provide an important venue for training, particularly when other forms of training are not available. As we write this chapter the 2020 9th International Conference on Adolescents and Adults with FASD, focussed on integrating research, policy, and practice around the world, at the University of British Columbia was cancelled due to the COVID-19 pandemic, highlighting the critical need for access to online learning.

From a culturally secure and culturally informed perspective, face to face training is critical in grounding the work of learning in the space of community. It is challenging for families to access FASD training. Many families struggling with poverty would likely find it a challenge to access training through online platforms, as this requires access to resources such as a computer and the internet. From a cultural lens, Indigenous people in Western Australia have identified their preferred delivery for FASD information is in small groups and community forums (Williams, 2018). This allows for Aboriginal people to engage, yarn, and debrief about the content and materials in respect of local traditions and context. Yarning for Aboriginal people is a culturally safe approach in engaging on sensitive topics (Bessarab & Ng'andu, 2010).

Community-based workshops held on FASD should incorporate a trauma-informed approach as this supports and allows the facilitator to debrief with participants, and also, to follow up with Aboriginal and non-Aboriginal agencies for debriefing if required. In the study by Stewart & Glowatski, 2014) police indicated their training preference was workshop training, including review of case studies and role-play scenarios. In research on the FASD Community of Practice in Alberta, Canada, Pelech, Badry, & Daoust (2013) noted that a minimal 12 hours of training should be provided to foster carers prior to placement of a child and that caseworkers and foster parents benefit from cross training. The benefits of face to face training include the opportunity for sharing of multiple experiences in relation to FASD and this approach provides the opportunity to hear more than one voice, contributing to a much deeper exchange of knowledge. The authors of this chapter endorse both modes of training, however, best practice in communities would be FASD training delivered in workshop settings incorporating a trauma and culturally informed approach and where possible, delivered by Aboriginal trainers. It is essential that any FASD training delivered online or in workshops stay current and up to date on emerging FASD evidence. In summary, Ms Clarke never benefitted from a diagnosis, but it was clearly stated and noted by the Magistrate that she accepted a clinical psychiatric report in the courts that she had FASD. Ms Clarke experienced marginalisation, oppression, and her death within a system in which she was completely misunderstood. When FASD is an unrecognized disability, individuals are at higher risk of adverse outcomes and mortality. The life story of Ms Clarke serves to underscore the critical need and national acceptance that people with FASD deserve and have a right to assessment, diagnosis, and clinical interventions from service providers who understand their disability and can provide services to effectively meet their needs. Communities have a right to expect competency amongst professionals working with individuals who have prenatal substance exposure and FASD. While children and youth with FASD experience adverse outcomes, the plethora of adverse outcomes in child protection, youth, and adult justice systems needs to stop. Training on FASD and developing community capacity to respond to FASD is one step in the right direction. To our knowledge, we believe this is the first time that Ms Clarke is referenced in academic literature rather than news media, and her short life highlights the need to acknowledge how the stacking of systemic failures contributed to a tragic outcome for this family.

Moving forward

There is a significant risk that FASD is discounted as a valid medical condition in the justice and health systems which simply should not be the case in 2020 in Australia and globally. The ever-increasing rates of alcohol use are a significant health problem that is too great to ignore. However, effective responses to FASD require consistent policy and practice regulations in child protection, health, and the justice system. When FASD goes unrecognised, the needs of human beings with this disability who require professional help are ignored and this contributes to marginalisation and oppression. From an anti-oppressive lens, it is critical to acknowledge that individuals with FASD are complex and have high care needs that should be effectively supported.

The Mental Health Carers NSW (2017, p. 4) published a statement on *Recognizing Fetal Alcohol Spectrum Disorder as a Disability in Australia for Access to Support under the NDIS,* noting concerns such as poor mental health, depression, risk of suicide, and lack of diagnostic resources:

> Nationwide recognition of FASD as a disability will undoubtedly improve the quality of life for individuals with FASD, and further support the ability for their families and carers to continue in their caring roles without compromise to their own mental health outcomes...MHCN believes this will greatly improve the chances that people with FASD receive the necessary levels of support they require... to continue their caring responsibilities without detriment to their own social, economic, and mental health outcomes...it would be beneficial to establish more support groups for people living with FASD and their families and carers throughout Australia.

Previous involvement with the child welfare system implies that children and families have experienced multiple disadvantages over their lifespan. Corrado et al. (2011) state there is a well-established linkage between placement in child welfare care and later involvement with the youth and adult criminal justice systems. While difficult to disentangle, it is hypothesised that the intersection of interpersonal challenges and system experiences in out of home care, intertwine and contribute to greater involvement with the justice system. Youth with unrecognised FASD who are in the child welfare system are particularly disadvantaged, as their disability is wrongly perceived as a behaviour problem and these children are ineffectively served. This disadvantage continues when youth with FASD become criminally involved and system responses become increasingly punitive. Cunneen & White (2006) suggest that the term 'juvenile offender' is seen as a code reflecting youth who are poor and marginalised and suggest that the risks for engagement in criminal activity are strongly tied to adverse childhood experiences and social structures.

It is imperative that correctional workers, care staff, and health workers become FASD aware and are able to create regimes that do not inflict further damage on already traumatised children. Blagg, Tulich, Mutch, Williams, & May (2018) have identified the need for screening and recognition of neurodevelopmental disorders in the criminal justice system, as individuals with FASD are highly vulnerable to victimisation and adverse outcomes while incarcerated. A belief and recognition that FASD is relevant to every stage of involvement with the justice system, from the criminal act, arrest, court proceedings, and sentencing outcomes, needs to be adopted. The challenge, however, is that national FASD policy does not exist in Australia and access to diagnostic services, particularly for adults, is limited. Further, many adults who have FASD have not had their disability recognised in either the child welfare or youth justice system, contributing to the pathway of incarceration as adults. It is imperative to recognise that a diagnosis makes a difference.

Baldry, Dowse, and Trollor (2013, p. 227) note that experiences such as early contact with police as children and youth experiences, child protection involvement and out of home care, contribute to early entry into incarceration for those with a cognitive disability and mental disorder.

It is clear that the ultimate destination of incarceration and reincarceration is the result of a trajectory that has multiple causative factors, which feed back into each other in negatively synergistic and compounding ways…characterized by dislocation, discontinuity, poverty, deprivation, ill health and violence.

Individuals with FASD have borne unparalleled levels of stigma at every intersection of their lives and are often born into intergenerational chaos and trauma – a direct result of colonisation. These individuals experience extreme disadvantage early in life. Long before youth become involved with the justice system, interventions that interrupt cycles of disparity related to poverty, food insecurity, homelessness, trauma, abuse – physical, emotional, sexual and neglect, exclusion, bullying, punishment for behaviours that are a result of an unrecognised cognitive disability, are required. Eventually, the stacking of these experiences leads to involvement with increasingly risky behaviour. Individuals with FASD are highly susceptible to peer influence and given the experiences noted above, it is not surprising that they would do anything to gain acceptance from their peers, including engagement in criminal activity. Life course theory (Elder, 1998) has a critical role to play in responding to FASD in Australia, as this theoretical framework recognises a holistic circle of life and acknowledges that events across the lifespan are connected. Decisions made about the care of children living on the margins in child protection, including assessment and diagnosis of disability, decisions about child protection interventions such as kinship care or removal to out of home care, all influence outcomes for adult life.

FASD has gone unrecognised for decades within the criminal justice system, and outcomes for individuals are often poor due to multiple disadvantages over their lifespan. Envisioning a makeover for the way in which the criminal justice system responds to individuals with FASD is essential from a human rights perspective. The linkage between FASD and colonisation cannot be ignored as alcohol rates soar and a leading cause of disability goes unrecognised. Screening and assessment of FASD must be prioritised for the population of children in the care and criminal justice settings. In order to provide early intervention and FASD informed case management planning across the lifespan, FASD training of case managers and custodial staff that includes FASD case studies should be mandatory. Pei et al. (2016) in a study in the Yukon Territory in Canada noted that ongoing, consistent training is critical, as a lack of education on FASD is a barrier to effective service provision. Training across the sector needs to include judges, lawyers, police, corrections workers, and victim services. Pei et al. (2016) recognise that the lack of training on FASD in any comprehensive way, services as a barrier to FASD informed case management. All carers including respite providers should also have access to training on FASD.

For the Aboriginal community, decolonisation of FASD interventions are imperative and require resourcing of local Aboriginal agencies, along with decolonising of the criminal justice system (Blagg, Tulich, & Bush, 2015). The current approach contributes to risk and harm, necessitating the remodelling of traditional punitive responses. Common threads in recommendations for youth with FASD in care and custody include the need for FASD and trauma-informed care. Sound case management includes the need for structure and routine, recognition of FASD as a disability requiring lifelong supports and the inclusion of the voice of youth in care plans. The construct of cultural security is particularly important for Aboriginal offenders with FASD as culture can provide an important foundation for rehabilitation. Without FASD informed support, housing is reported as being an ongoing issue. The need exists to prepare for managed release of offenders into the community and the need for 'community navigators' who can help youth and families negotiate access to support services.

Critical discourse has been unfolding for decades on FASD and there are generations of young people who have struggled with intergenerational trauma, victimisation, substance use, incarceration, violence, and systemic disparity in child protection and youth justice. The life of Ms Clarke offers the justification for FASD training from a human rights lens, in recognition of the worth and dignity of every life, and as a matter of social justice. We have to ask the question: How is it possible for the child protection system and the youth and adult criminal justice systems to ignore FASD? Moving forward in a meaningful way implies that justice sector training on FASD will be implemented for the children, the youth, the adults, and their families who enter this system with the expectation that the professionals providing care to them will understand their disability.

References

American Psychiatric Association. (2013). *Diagnostic and statistical manual of mental disorders (DSM-5®)*. Arlington, VA: American Psychiatric Pub.

Australian Institute of Health and Welfare. (2019). *Young people in child protection and under youth justice supervision: 1 July 2014 to 30 June 2018*. Canberra, Australia: AIHW.

Australian Institute of Health and Welfare. (2020). *Child protection Australia: Children in the child protection system*. Retrieved from https://www.aihw.gov.au/reports/child-protection/child-protection-australia-children-in-the-child-protection-system

Badry, D., & Pelech, W., & Milne, D. (2014). The FASD community of practice project: Promising practices for children in care with fetal alcohol spectrum disorder: A model for casework practice. In D. Badry, D. Fuchs, H. M. Montgomery & S. McKay (Eds.), *Reinvesting in families: Strengthening child welfare practice for a brighter future: Voices from the prairies* (pp. 21–43). Regina, Saskatchewan: University of Regina Press.

Badry, D., & Wight Felske, A. (2013). Policy development in fetal alcohol spectrum disorder for individuals and families across the lifespan. Living with FASD. In E. P. Riley, S. Clarren, J. Weinberg & E. Jonsson (Eds.), *Fetal alcohol spectrum disorder: Management and policy perspectives of FASD*. Weinheim, Germany: John Wiley & Sons.

Bagley, K., & Badry, D. (2019). How personal perspectives shape health professionals' perceptions of fetal alcohol spectrum disorder and risk. *International Journal of Environmental Research and Public Health, 16*(11), 1936.

Baldry, E., Briggs, D. B., Goldson, B., & Russell, S. (2018). "Cruel and unusual punishment": An inter-jurisdictional study of the criminalisation of young people with complex support needs. *Journal of Youth Studies, 21*(5), 636–652.

Baldry, E., Clarence, M., Dowse, L., & Trollor, J. (2013). Reducing vulnerability to harm in adults with cognitive disabilities in the Australian criminal justice system. *Journal of Policy and Practice in Intellectual Disabilities, 10*(3), 222–229.

Baldry, E., McCausland, R., Dowse, L., & McEntyre, E. (2015). *A predictable and preventable path: Aboriginal people with mental and cognitive disabilities in the criminal justice system.* Sydney, Australia: UNSW Australia.

Barker, B., Goodman, A., & DeBeck, K. (2017). Reclaiming Indigenous identities: Culture as strength against suicide among Indigenous youth in Canada. *Canadian Journal of Public Health, 108*(2), e208–e210.

Blagg, H., Tulich, T., & May, S. (2019). Aboriginal youth with foetal alcohol spectrum disorder and enmeshment in the Australian justice system: Can an intercultural form of restorative justice make a difference? *Contemporary Justice Review, 22*(2), 105–121.

Blagg, H., Tulich, T., & Bush, Z. (2015). Diversionary pathways for Indigenous youth with FASD in Western Australia. Decolonising alternatives. *Alternative Legal Journal, 40*(4) 257–260.

Blagg, H., Tulich, T., Mutch, R., Williams, R., & May, S. (2018). *FASD and the criminal justice system: Report to the Australian National Advisory Council on Alcohol and Drugs* (ANACAD) Secretariat (Reference ID: 6000078020).

Bower, C., Watkins, R. E., Mutch, R. C., Marriott, R., Freeman, J., Kippin, N. R., Safe, B., Pestell, C., Cheung, C. S., Shield, H., & Tarratt, L. (2018). Fetal alcohol spectrum disorder and youth justice: A prevalence study among young people sentenced to detention in Western Australia. *BMJ open, 8*(2), e019605.

Brown., J. Harr., D., Morgan, S., Varga, S., & Fenrich, A. (2017). Fetal alcohol spectrum disorder (FASD): A call on mental health professionals to become informed. *Journal of Psychology and Psychiatry, 1*, 2–3.

Brownell, M., Enns, J. E., Hanlon-Dearman, A., Chateau, D., Phillips-Beck, W., Singal, D., MacWilliam, L., Longstaffe, S., Chudley, A., Elias, B., & Roos, N. (2019). Health, social, education, and justice outcomes of Manitoba First Nations children diagnosed with fetal alcohol spectrum disorder: A population-based cohort study of linked administrative data. *The Canadian Journal of Psychiatry, 64*(9), 611–620.

Chasnoff, I., Wells, A., & King, L. (2015). Misdiagnosis and missed diagnoses in foster and adopted children with prenatal alcohol exposure. *Pediatrics, 135*(2), 264–270.

Choate, P., & Badry, D. (2019). Stigma as a dominant discourse in fetal alcohol spectrum disorder. *Advances in Dual Diagnosis, 12*(1/2), 36–52.

Chudley, A. E., Conry, J., Cook, J. L., Loock, C., Rosales, T., & LeBlanc, N.; Public Health Agency of Canada's National Advisory Committee on Fetal Alcohol Spectrum Disorder. (2005). Fetal alcohol spectrum disorder:

Canadian guidelines for diagnosis. *Canadian Medical Association Journal, 172*(5), S1–S21.

Comparative Youth Penalty Project. Retrieved from https://www.cypp.unsw.edu.au/node/128

Corrado, R., & Freedman, L. (2011). Risk profiles, trajectories, and intervention points for serious and chronic young offenders. *International Journal of Child, Youth and Family Studies, 2*(2.1), 197–232.

Cunneen, C., & White, R. (2006). Australia: Control, containment or empowerment. In J. Muncie & B. Goldson (Eds.), *Comparative youth justice: Critical issues* (pp. 96–110). London, UK: Sage Publications.

Domeij, H., Fahlström, G., Bertilsson, G., Hultcrantz, M., Munthe-Kaas, H., Gordh, C. N., & Helgesson, G. (2018). Experiences of living with fetal alcohol spectrum disorders: A systematic review and synthesis of qualitative data. *Developmental Medicine & Child Neurology, 60*(8), 741–752.

Eades, A., Hackett, M., Liu, H., Brown, J., Coffin., J., & Cass, A. (2020). Qualitative study of psychosocial factors impacting on Aboriginal women's management of chronic disease. *International Journal for Equity in Health, 19*(8), 1–8. doi:10.1186/s12939-019-1110-3.

Elder, G. H. (1998). The life course as developmental theory. *Child Development, 69*(1), 1–12.

Elliot, E., & Bower, C. (2004). FAS in Australia: Fact or fiction? *Journal of Paediatrics and Child Health, 40*(1–2), 8–10.

Fitts, M. S., & Soldatic, K. (2020). Who's caring for whom? Disabled Indigenous carers experiences of Australia's infrastructures of social protection. *Journal of Family Studies*, 1–16. doi:10.1080/13229400.2020.1734478.

Flannigan, K., Pei, J., Rasmussen, C., Potts, S., & O'Riordan, T. (2018). A Unique Response to Offenders with Fetal Alcohol Spectrum Disorder: Perceptions of the Alexis FASD Justice Program. Canadian Journal of *Criminology and Criminal Justice, 60*(1), 1–33.

Freckelton, I. (2017). Assessment and evaluation of fetal alcohol spectrum disorder (FASD) and its potential relevance for sentencing: A clarion call from Western Australia *Psychiatry, Psychology, and Law, 24*(4), 485–495.

Fuchs, D., Burnside L., Reinink, A., & Marchenski, S. (2010). *Bound by the clock: The voices of Manitoba youth with FASD leaving Care.* Public Health Agency Canada. Retrieved from https://cwrp.ca/sites/default/files/publications/MB-Youth_with_FASD_Leaving_Care.pdf

Gatwiri, K., McPherson, L., Parmenter, N., Cameron, N., & Rotumah, D. (2019). Indigenous children and young people in residential care: A systematic scoping review. *Trauma, Violence, & Abuse*, 1524838019881707.

Green, A., Abbott, P., Davidson, P. M., Delaney, P., Delaney, J., Patradoon-Ho, P., & DiGiacomo, M. (2018). Interacting with providers: An intersectional exploration of the experiences of carers of Aboriginal children with a disability. *Qualitative Health Research, 28*(12), 1923–1932.

Hamilton, S., Reibel, T., Maslen, S., Watkins, R., Jacinta, F., Passmore, H., Mutch, R., O'Donnell, M., Braithwaite, V., Bower, C., & Bower, C. (2020).

Disability "In-Justice": The benefits and challenges of "Yarning" with young people undergoing diagnostic assessment for fetal alcohol spectrum disorder in a youth detention center. *Qualitative Health Research, 30*(2), 314–327.

Hill, T., Cass, B., Newton, B. J., & Valentine, K. (2012). *Indigenous carers.* Department of Social Services. Australia.

Lange, S., Probst, C., Gmel, G., Rehm, J., Burd, L., & Popova, S. (2017). Global prevalence of fetal alcohol spectrum disorder among children and Youth. A systematic review and Meta-analysis. *JAMA Pediatrics, 171*(10), 948–956.

Libesman, T. (2014). *Decolonising Indigenous child welfare: Comparative perspectives.* Milton Park, UK: Routledge.

Mann-Johnson, J., & Kikulwe, D. (2018). Exploring decolonization through kinship care assessments. In D. E. Badry, D. Kikulwe, M. Bennett, D. Fuchs & H. M. Montgomery (Eds.), *Imagining child welfare in the spirit of reconciliation: Voices from the prairies* (pp. 45–68). Regina, Saskatchewan: University of Regina Press.

McCausland, R., Baldry, E., Segrave, M., Spivakovsky, C., & Eriksson, A. (2017). "I feel like I failed him by ringing the police": Criminalising disability in Australia. *Punishment & Society, 19*(3), 290–309.

McCreary Centre Society. (2012). *PLEA evaluation report: PLEA programs for youth in conflict with the law with illicit substance abuse issues and other challenges.* Retrieved from https://www.mcs.bc.ca/pdf/PLEA_Evaluation_Report.pdf

Mela, M., Coons-Harding, K. D., & Anderson, T. (2019). Recent advances in fetal alcohol spectrum disorder for mental health professionals. *Current Opinion Psychiatry, 32*(4), 328–335.

Mental Health Carers Network. (2017). *Recognising fetal alcohol spectrum disorder as a disability in Australia for access to support under the NDIS.* Position Statement. Retrieved from https://www.mentalhealthcarersnsw.org/wp-content/uploads/2019/01/MHCN-Position-Statement-on-Recognising-Fetal-Alcohol-Spectrum-Disorder-as-a-Disability-in-Australia-for-Access-to-Support-under-the-NDIS-1.pdf

Mukherjee, R., Wray, E., Curfs, L., & Hollins, S. (2015). Knowledge and opinions of professional groups concerning FASD in the UK. *Adoption & Fostering, 39*(3), 212–224.

Mutch, R. C., Jones, H. M., Bower, C., & Watkins, R. E. (2016). Fetal alcohol Spectrum disorders: Using knowledge, attitudes and practice of justice professionals to support their educational needs. *Journal of Population Therapeutics and Clinical Pharmacology, 23*(1), e77–e89.

O'Connor, M. J., Portnoff, L. C., Lebsack-Coleman, M., & Dipple, K. M. (2019). Suicide risk in adolescents with fetal alcohol spectrum disorders. *Birth Defects Research, 111*(12), 822–828.

Payne, J., Elliot, E., D'Antoine, H., O'Leary, C., Mahony, A., Haan, E., & Bower, C. (2005). Health professionals' knowledge, practice, and opinions about fetal alcohol syndrome and alcohol consumption in pregnancy. *Australian and New Zealand Journal of Public Health, 29*(6), 558–564.

Peled, M., Smith., A., & McCreary Centre Society. (2014). *Breaking through the Barriers: Supporting Youth with FASD who have substance use challenges.* Vancouver, BC: McCreary Centre. Society.

Petrenko, C. L., Alto, M. E., Hart, A. R., Freeze, S. M., & Cole, L. L. (2019). "I'm doing my part, I just need help from the community": Intervention implications of foster and adoptive parents' experiences raising children and young adults with FASD. *Journal of Family Nursing, 25,* 314–347.

Poole, N., Schmidt, R. A., Green, C., & Hemsing, N. (2016). Prevention of fetal alcohol spectrum disorder: Current Canadian efforts and analysis of gaps. *Substance Abuse: Research and Treatment, 10,* SART-S34545.

Proven, S., Ens, C., & Beaudin, P. G. (2014). The language profile of school-aged children with fetal alcohol spectrum disorder (FASD). *Canadian Journal of Speech-Language Pathology & Audiology, 37*(4), 268–279.

Reid, N., Moritz, K. M., & Akison, L. K. (2019). Adverse health outcomes associated with fetal alcohol exposure: A systematic review focused on immune-related outcomes. *Pediatric Allergy and Immunology, 30*(7), 698–707.

Riches, V., Parmenter, T., Wiese, M., & Stancliffe, R. (2006). Intellectual disability and mental illness in the NSW criminal justice system. *International Journal of Law and Psychiatry, 29*(5), 386–396.

Royal Commission into the Protection and Detention of Children in the Northern Territory. (2017). Retrieved from https://www.royalcommission. gov.au/sites/default/files/2019-01/rcnt-royal-commission-nt-final-report-volume-1.pdf

Samaroden, M. (2018). Challenges and resiliency in Aboriginal adults with fetal alcohol spectrum disorder. *First Peoples Child & Family Review, 13*(1), 8–19. Retrieved from https://fpcfr.com/index.php/FPCFR/article/view/335

Smith, A., Cox, K., Poon, C., Stewart, D., & McCreary Centre Society. (2013). *Time Out III: A profile of BC youth in custody.* Vancouver, BC: McCreary Centre Society. Retrieved from https://www.mcs.bc.ca/pdf/Time_Out_III.pdf

Sotiri, M., McGee, P., & Baldry, E. (2012). No end in sight. *The imprisonment, and indefinite detention of Indigenous Australians with a cognitive impairment: Aboriginal Disability Justice Campaign.*

Stewart, M. (2016). FASD & justice: The ethical case for effective training and knowledge mobilization practices for frontline justice professionals in Canada. In M. Nelson & M. Trussler (Eds.), *Fetal alcohol spectrum disorders in adults: Ethical and legal perspectives* (pp. 191–206). Switzerland: Springer International Publishing.

Stewart, M., Lawley, L., Tambour, R., & Johnson, A. (2018). Listening in a settler state: (Birth) mothers as paraprofessionals in response to FASD. In D. E. Badry, D. Kikulwe, M. Bennett, D. Fuchs & H. M. Montgomery (Eds.), *Imagining child welfare in the spirit of reconciliation: Voices from the Prairies* (pp. 45–68). Regina, Saskatchewan: University of Regina Press.

Tait, C. L. (2003). *Fetal alcohol syndrome among Aboriginal people in Canada: Review and analysis of the intergenerational links to residential schools.* Ottawa, Canada: Aboriginal Healing Foundation.

Watson, S. L., Coons, K. D., & Hayes, S. A. (2013). Autism spectrum disorder and fetal alcohol spectrum disorder. Part 1: A comparison of parenting stress. *Journal of Intellectual & Developmental Disability, 38*(2), 95–104.

Williams, R. (2018). *Understanding fetal alcohol spectrum disorder through the stories of Nyoongar families and how may this inform policy and service delivery*. Health Sciences. Curtin University. Unpublished thesis.

Wyper, K., & Pei, J. (2016). Neurocognitive difficulties underlying high risk and criminal behaviour in FASD: Clinical implications. In M. Nelson & M. Trussler (Eds.), *Fetal alcohol spectrum disorders in adults: Ethical and legal perspectives* (pp. 101–120). Cham, Switzerland: Springer.

7news.com.au (2020, May 26). WA cop enters plea after being charged over murder of Joyce Clarke in Geraldton. Retrieved from https://7news.com.au/news/wa/wa-cop-pleads-not-guilty-to-womans-murder-c-1062836

7 FASD, the criminal justice system, and Indigenous people

Diversionary pathways and decolonising strategies

Harry Blagg

Introduction

High rates of FASD in Aboriginal communities are the consequence of unhealed intergenerational trauma linked to colonial violence and dispossession (Blagg & Tulich, 2018; Blagg, Tulich & Bush, 2015, 2016, 2017). It is not simply the result of bad choices by mothers. Research confirms the importance of triage, early screening, and assessment, and opportunities for diversion at every point of contact with the justice system into community owned and managed structures (Blagg & Tulich, 2018; Blagg et al., 2015, 2016, 2017). It is not enough to develop multidisciplinary approaches and multidisciplinary teamwork if Indigenous knowledge is excluded from the process. Initiatives on a local level must be initiated from the bottom up, not the top down, and centre Indigenous law and culture. While clinical interventions may be important, they risk perpetuating colonial relationships of domination and subordination if they operate in isolation from community-driven endeavours. Given that, as we stress at several points in this book, FASD is not 'curable', then there is no reason why medical knowledge, and medical professionals, should take the lead role in determining the scope of interventions. Indeed, there are sound reasons to *decentre* the medical model, in favour of an approach more centred in Indigenous knowledge that nests intervention in Indigenous cultural practices of healing and reintegration. The evidence base for this chapter is culled from research in Australia, mainly in the state of Western Australia, but it has relevance across jurisdictions and globally.

There is a dearth of comprehensive and reliable data on rates of FASD within criminal justice systems (but see the discussion of prevalence in Chapter 3). Research in the United States suggests that over half of persons with FASD will interact with the criminal justice system: around 60% will be arrested, charged, or convicted of a criminal offence, and about half will have spent time in juvenile detention, prison, inpatient treatment, or mental health detention (Streissguth et al., 2004, pp. 230–231). Canadian research also indicates that young people with FASD are 19 times more likely to be arrested than their peers (Brown et al., 2015, p. 144). The cycle is particularly concerning in the context of the worsening over-incarceration of Aboriginal youth in Western Australia (Amnesty International, 2015; Loh & Ferrante, 2005; Parliament of Australia, 2011). Despite constituting only 6.4% of youth in Western Australia (Australian Institute of Health and Welfare, 2014), Aboriginal youth account for 77% of youth in juvenile detention, and are 53 times more likely to be detained than their non-Indigenous peers (Amnesty International, 2015; Department of Corrective Service, 2015a, b). In the Northern Territory, Indigenous youths count for roughly 27% of the youth population yet all the youths in detention are Indigenous. A recent inquiry (*Royal Commission into the Detention and Protection of Children in the Northern Territory*, 2017, Vol 2A, p. 356) suggested that FASD was a major, but ignored, problem and recommended that screening for FASD for youths entering custody become standard practice.

Punitive justice

Enough is known about FASD from the existing knowledge base for us to map out with some confidence the kinds of practices required to improve outcomes for people with FASD and build preventive strategies to reduce the incidence of FASD in the long term. In the context of the criminal justice system, this requires us to move beyond the punitive logic currently underpinning interventions with young people and explore alternative strategies. Indigenous peoples across the Anglophone societies of Australia, Canada, Aotearoa/New Zealand, and the United States of America (collectively known as 'CANZUS' countries) have been particularly badly impacted by the 'punitive turn' in criminal justice policy, which placed the emphasis on zero tolerance policing of public spaces, mass incapacitation, reduced access to parole, and bail (Anthony, 2013).

Imprisonment rates of Indigenous people accelerated from the late twentieth century onwards: although Australian Indigenous peoples have the unenviable record of being the most incarcerated across CANZUS jurisdictions (Anthony, 2013; Australian Law Reform Commission, 2018; Johnson, 1991; Lakota People's Law Project (USA); Office of the Correctional Investigator, 2020 (Canada); Waitangi

Tribunal, 2017 (NZ)). The rate of over-representation of Aboriginal peoples in correctional systems in Australia, even out strips rates of over-representation experienced by African Americans in the United States (Walmsley, 2017). This is not surprising since CANZUS countries all followed a similar trajectory in relation to the 'management' of Indigenous populations, which has relied heavily on various forms of incarceration. Enforced confinement in a variety of sites (locked hospitals, islands, missions, orphanages, residential schools, reformatories, police cells, leper colonies, cattle stations, the pearling industry) typified settler colonial management of Indigenous peoples. Prison is simply the latest site for managing the dispossessed.

Today, Indigenous peoples remain over-represented at every stage of contact with the criminal justice system, but particularly at the 'sharp end' of incarceration. Anthony and Blagg (2020) following work by Loic Wacquant in the USA, describe this high rate of incarceration as a form of 'hyperincarceration', meaning an historically extreme rate of imprisonment concentrated in a massively disadvantaged community. While it has been employed mainly in the context of the 'crumbling black ghetto' in the USA (Wacquant, 2001) it has also been employed in the context of Indigenous youth incarceration (White, 2014). Indigenous youths are less likely than the mainstream settler population to be diverted from the system, to get bail, to be granted parole, or benefit from community-based orders.

Settlers deliberately set out to undermine Indigenous notions of law and justice. Australia, for example, was deemed to be *terra nullius*, no man's land, and the Indigenous population was deemed to be incapable of possessing law. In the other CANZUS societies, treaties between settlers the Indigenous population were constantly broken by settlers. Indigenous populations were assumed, by their very natures, to be *a priori* criminal. Indigenous men were labelled as brutal savages in need of discipline, while women were deemed to be helpless creatures in need of domestication and control (Sturm, 2017). This kind of thinking instantiated a pattern of brutal destruction of Indigenous communities and their habitat.

For writers such as Patrick Wolfe (2006), settler colonialism involves not simply the exploitation but the wholesale appropriation of land. Settler colonialism is a 'form of colonialism in which "outsiders" come to make a new home on the land that is already inhabited by other humans', Tuck and Mckenzie (2015, p. 635) maintain. In the process, settlers become the natives and the natives become outcasts. The necessity of violence runs through settler colonisation. As Dunbar-Ortiz (2014, p. 9) notes in relation to the United States of America, settler colonialism, 'requires violence or the threat of violence to attain its goals.' People do not freely give up their lands, their children, the cultures they have practiced for centuries, without the use of force.

The 'founding violence' of colonisation has cascaded through time leaving destruction in its wake. The notion of 'inter-generational trauma', which we consider to play a pivotal role in FASD, conveys the extent to which the pain and trauma associated with colonial dispossession are transmitted on to the next generation through parenting practices modelled on neglectful institutional regimes (which replaced family for many of so-called 'half caste' children removed from their homes). They are also present in self and other destructive coping mechanisms, such as alcohol, that became normalised when Indigenous people were moved off their lands and crowded into town camps and reserves, where the 'right to drink' became the only tangible right the white mainstream bestowed with any consistency on Indigenous people (see for example Dodson, 1991).

Can't not won't

The mainstream justice system is founded on the belief that offenders *won't,* rather than *can't* obey the law, whereas for people with FASD its more a case of *can't* not *won't*. 'Just deserts' theories for example assume offenders to be reasoning beings, able to predict the likely consequences of their actions and amenable to general and specific modes of deterrence. Similarly, 'rational choice theories' hold that people freely choose their actions and behaviours, and are motivated by the avoidance of pain and the pursuit of pleasure. Individuals evaluate their choice of actions in accordance with each option's ability to produce advantage, pleasure, and happiness (Siegel & McCormick, 2006). A person with FASD, however, may not correspond to the normative, pleasure seeking, rational individual assumed by these theories. As we have pointed out, people with FASD, and other cognitive impairments, simply do not make rational choices. Even strategies designed as an alternative to mainstream systems can set people with FASD up for failure and further enmesh them in the criminal justice system: often because they assume an impossible degree of 'agency' from people with FASD and other cognitive impairments in terms of life and time management skills, while expecting them to undertake tasks requiring a capacity to plan, turn up for appointments and retain information.

Increasingly, Indigenous peoples in Anglo origin, settler colonial societies maintain that meaningful change requires a process of *decolonisation,* rather than the reform, of the criminal justice process (Agozino, 2004; Blagg & Anthony, 2019; Cunneen & Tauri, 2016; Jackson, 2017). Decolonising justice processes can take a myriad of forms: truth and reconciliation commissions; transitional justice processes; the Indigenisation of justice procedures and laws; the repeal of racist/ apartheid legislation; the search for reparations; the reintroduction of traditional justice mechanisms; or some hybridised model, combining elements of colonial and Indigenous justice. For many commentators and advocates, restorative justice offers this kind of hybridity.

Restorative justice?

Restorative justice appears, at least facially, to be an obvious vehicle for exploring, and facilitating, a decolonising process that affords respect to traditional Indigenous justice mechanisms. Restorative justice's record in this regard, however, inclines us towards caution rather than unrestrained optimism (Blagg, 2016) and we maintain that there are elements of restorative justice practice that also require decolonising if they are to be relevant to the needs of Aboriginal people with FASD. Restorative justice processes can replicate some of the worst features of the mainstream system if not tempered with FASD awareness and led by Aboriginal people themselves (Goulding & Steels, 2006, 2013; Blagg, Tulich & May, 2019).

A number of researchers have argued that restorative justice and Indigenous justice are different, but not necessarily irreconcilable, projects (Braithwaite, 2002; Daly, 2002; Daly & Marchetti, 2012). However, there are also suggestions that restorative justice is simply another mechanism for binding Indigenous communities to a system of justice that is fundamentally incapable of meeting their needs, while offering a superficial gloss of cultural appropriateness (Blagg, 2016; Cunneen & Tauri, 2016).

Restorative justice, contrary to myth, is not an organic Indigenous justice practice, but is freighted into Indigenous communities in a pre-assembled format by justice agencies. In its 'globalised' form, Cunneen and Tauri (2016, p. 140) caution, it represents a *'purposeful and significant commodification of Indigenous life-worlds by policy workers, restorative justice advocates and justice entrepreneurs'* (emphasis in the original). We suggest, however, that restorative justice principles can build bridges between mainstream and Indigenous philosophies of justice, provided that restorative justice does not attempt to colonise Indigenous justice (Blagg, 2016; Blagg & Anthony, 2019) and instead assists in the decolonisation of justice systems (Park, 2015, p. 273), as we discuss in more detail later.

Telling their story

The impairments associated with FASD can create some insurmountable problems for accused people and offenders in the mainstream justice system. Restorative justice shares a number of the mainstream system's shortcomings in relation to people with cognitive impairments. Advocates for restorative justice argue that youth conferencing, in which offenders meet their victims and an attempt is made to find alternative sanctions, such as an apology, and an undertaking to do community work, is far from being a 'soft option' for young people. Indeed, conferencing has been sold to a sceptical public, the police, and judiciary on the basis that it is, in its own way, more demanding than the court system, due to the weight of expectations placed on young people to be other than just passive spectators to their judicial proceedings. It lays heavy stress on direct accountability of offenders, a feature shared with other areas of contemporary penalty (Richards, 2017). It is also promoted on the grounds that it is more likely to make parents accept responsibility, as Richards observes, 'restorative justice measures are championed on the grounds that they would responsibilise parents and families in a way that existing criminal justice measures had failed to' (Richards, 2017, pp. 102–103).

Hayes (2017, p. 410) describes how 'young offenders are invited to tell their side of the 'story', demonstrate empathy, articulate how they were 'feeling, before, during and after the offending.' Conferences can be highly charged encounters, requiring emotional maturity and oral competencies. Hayes goes on (p. 410): 'for these emotional states to be expressed and observed, young offenders must effectively engage in conversations about their wrongdoing and about ways of repairing harms they have caused.' As we outlined in Chapters 2, 3 and 4, people with FASD often experience difficulties with higher-level language skills, which mean that they are unable to adequately understand and participate in justice processes even where they appear, superficially, to have verbal capacity (Hand et al., 2019; Kippin et al., 2018; Reid et al., 2020). What possible role can there be for a method that relies so heavily on language, comprehension and communication, and the capacity for empathy and self-reflection on the part of participants, in the identification of pathways out of the justice system for young people with FASD? How can restorative justice offer a 'learning experience' for children who are involved in the justice system precisely because they are unable to learn? Restorative justice cannot achieve good outcomes for offenders with FASD if it holds on to notions of best practice that assumes a 'good' conference to be one in which young people 'engage' in this way. It is time we looked at alternative processes and measures of success.

Family conferencing

The difficulties experienced by young people with FASD do not stop when the conference ends: they may be exacerbated at the next stage of the diversionary process. Family group conferences place heavy emphasis on good conference 'outcomes'; these include commitments to do community work, write letters of apology, work to make restitutions, and so on. Conferences are in many respects mini judicial proceedings, which is why, under the New Zealand *Oranga Tamariki Act 1989* (NZ), children have the right to legal representation at family group conferences (s 251(1)(g)). As we have outlined in Chapter 2, people with FASD are often compromised in the areas of intellectual functioning, verbal learning, and memory; they lack inhibition, impulse control, and are poor decision-makers; their reasoning and judgement are impaired and they are highly suggestible. These impairments not only render key principles like deterrence, denunciation, and personal responsibility, as we suggested earlier, completely unattainable, but they also problematise face-to-face truth-telling, atonement, and 'epiphany', and other cherished aspects of an ideal restorative conferencing.

Furthermore, it is likely that parents of children with FASD will have the condition, and/or be carriers of inter-generational trauma. Berating, cajoling and 'responsibilising' family in conferences may be a futile and unnecessarily punitive practice. This may mean that young people with FASD lose out on opportunities to be diverted from the court system altogether. If diversionary conferencing and other features of restorative youth justice are not fit for purpose in relation to FASD, what role can restorative justice play? Our view is that rather than focus on conferencing, as presently understood, we need to focus instead on strengthening, repairing, and reinforcing the fabric of Aboriginal community life by nurturing what we call, place-based and community-owned initiatives managed by Aboriginal entities. A critical element in this paradigm shift involves a collaborative approach to working with communities; not assuming, for example, that an immersion in the Western canon of restorative justice equips us with the capacity to understand and relate to Aboriginal worldviews, which have been shaped by the experience of deep colonisation, inter-generational trauma, and violence. We suggest that a form of 'intercultural' approach to restorative justice is required that does not assume a priori that 'we' have the answers: these need to be arrived at through processes of dialogue and engagement.

A relevant restorative justice

To be of any relevance to this group, who are the most likely to be families affected by FASD, restorative justice should modify its stance; and instead of focussing on individual offenders, work thera-peutically with the families in partnership with Elders and kin. Rather than an excessive focus on face-to-face negotiation and the acceptance of personal responsibility ('telling the truth'), conferences would in-stead focus on 'truth-telling' about the structural and historical fac-tors that have created the family's situation. Circles would adopt a FASD aware and trauma-informed perspective. A 'trauma-informed approach' (Atkinson, 2002, 2013) recognises that families affected by FASD often carry multiple forms of trauma that can be re-ignited by contact with the justice system. Attention would need to be given to ensuring meeting places are culturally secure environments. For Ab-original and Torres Strait Islander peoples, a culturally safe environ-ment is one where they feel safe and secure in identity, culture, and community. This makes a careful choice of venues essential. In New Zealand, Māori conferencing processes often take place on the Marea, a traditional meeting and cultural centre.

Aside from the important issue of creating culturally secure environments, people with FASD require a complete wrap around service. Conferencing must focus on creating the structures needed to support people with FASD, what is sometimes referred to as 'scaffold-ing.' There should be a preference, for example, for resourcing family and community to provide full-time mentorship. A strengths-based approach would inform strategies, recognising that the 'solution' resides not with mainstream or restorative justice process, but with the Aboriginal community.

Culturally secure and on-country

For Aboriginal people, being 'on-country' and 'in place' are functional prerequisites for healing (Mackean, 2009). This is being reflected in the emergence of what are known in Australia as 'on-country' programmes that provide a total cultural immersion for youths and families. The Yirriman Project run out of Fitzroy Crossing in the re-mote Kimberley region of Western Australia, by local Elders, known locally as 'cultural bosses', has been offering diversionary 'camps' on remote traditional lands for a number of years. Evaluations of the pro-gramme suggest that it is particularly good at stabilising children and family members who carry trauma and are in danger of enmeshment in the justice system (Blagg, 2016; Palmer, 2010, 2013). The 'relational scaffolding' provided by this kind of initiative may also prevent the contributory outcomes produced by the negative impact of the system itself (see Chapter 2). Circles held on-country, led by Elders, where Indigenous culture provides the framework within which communities, families, and agencies reach decisions about the future care of children and families with FASD, instantiates a decolonising process. Restorative justice practitioners would participate in, rather than script, lead, and control these meetings. Where mainstream agencies become especially important is in ensuring that the system they work in create partnerships with Indigenous organisations and, in particular, create diversionary pathways out of the justice system and into community controlled services.

Diversion

The 1991 Royal Commission into Aboriginal Deaths in Custody in Australia (Johnson, 1991) mounted a powerful case for developing strategies that would divert young people from unnecessary contact with the criminal justice system. The need to divert Indigenous youth with FASD from contact with the justice system has been acknowledged by a number of official sources. The Australian Parliament's House of Representatives Standing Committee on Indigenous Affairs (2015, para. 5.84) recently reported that '[t]here is…a great need for diversion programmes which redirect individuals [with FASD] who come in contact with the criminal justice system.' The Western Australian Inspector of Custodial Services (2014, p. 10) has recommended 'community-based alternatives to custody orders for people who are found unfit to stand trial but require some degree of supervision.' Diversionary alternatives are sorely needed. However, research raises questions about the relevance of mainstream diversionary mechanisms to this task: particularly given the failure of existing community-based sanctions to stem the floodtide of Indigenous over-incarceration in Australia. FASD amplifies the chances of Indigenous youth being caught up in the justice system, including indefinite detention in prison if found unfit to stand trial (see Chapter 4). A fresh diversionary paradigm is required.

Diversion can take place at any point of contact between an accused person and the justice system. Pre-trial diversion is now a feature of the justice landscape in Australia and most societies operating on the British common law model. This model grants discretion to law enforcement agencies to deal with certain matters informally. All CANZUS jurisdictions have some form of diversionary programmes in place, managed in most instances by the police at the 'front end', or point of first contact, with the justice system. In Australia and Canada the police are the key decision-makers where diversion is concerned. Only New Zealand – under the *Oranga Tamariki Act 1989* (NZ) – reduces police discretion. The police cannot prosecute a young person in most instances but must refer cases for family group conferencing run by a youth justice agency. Even courts, in most instances cannot hear cases involving young people until a Family Group Conference has been convened. Not only does this method reduce the impact of systemic bias against Māori youth; it also enhances the role of family ('whanau') in decision-making.

Diversionary practices favour the least intrusive option at any point of interaction between an accused person and the justice system: the 'parsimony' principle. With a presumption towards non-intervention where possible. When employed imaginatively, diversion may offer opportunities for channelling youths with disabilities into therapeutic programmes and spare them exposure to the potentially criminogenic and disabling impacts of the justice system.

Facilitating diversion at the first point of contact

The police are the 'gatekeepers' of the criminal justice system and its key decision-makers where most youth offending is concerned, because they have the discretion to deal with many cases informally or formally (Blagg & Wilkie, 1997; Cunneen & White, 2007). Australian states and territories have followed an international trend by adopting diversion as the preferred way of dealing with most juvenile crime, most of the time. Yet, doubt remains as to whether current diversionary practices are fit for purpose in relation to Indigenous youth and their families (Cunneen, 1999). Currently, Indigenous youth are over-represented in custody and under-represented in police diversion. How do we encourage the police to employ discretionary authority to deal informally with matters where there is some indication that a young person has FASD or other cognitive impairment? The solution may lie in having a wider network of agencies engaged in pre-court diversion and easier referral pathways to treatment and support to assist police decision-making. It might also be improved by following the New Zealand option of having clear legislation that *reduces* police discretion to prosecute while making diversion mandatory in most instances *Oranga Tamariki Act 1989* (NZ), s254(1)). The latter option may reduce the tendency for decision-making to be influenced by systemic racism or unconscious cultural bias, where negative assumptions about Indigenous peoples inform police decision-making, a factor blamed for the over-representation of Indigenous people in the justice system (Blagg et al., 2005). Research in Western Australia (Blagg & Tulich, 2016) suggests that diversion for young people with FASD should not simply involve shepherding them out of the justice system, it must involve channelling them into community options that offer wrap around care and support; to families as whole, not just children.

Recalibrating diversionary pathways

A simple way of enhancing diversion at the first point of contact with the justice system is to train police officers to be FASD aware sufficient for them to recognise when a young person *may* have FASD. There should be protocols in place to refer a case, as part of a caution or warning, to youth justice and family and children's services, who should liaise with the school, family and an Indigenous service provider. This may encourage greater use of cautioning by the police, if they feel a young person's behaviour is being addressed.

This process is captured in Figure 7.1. This sets out a pathway for a brief intervention that would trigger a response from local agencies commensurate with the degree of perceived disability.

Secondary Diversion (Figure 7.2) is a more intensive process and reserved for cases that would usually be destined for court. A family group conference (a model borrowed from New Zealand under its *Oranga Tamariki Act 1989* (NZ)) may be convened which brings together family and others of significance to the child, a victim (where appropriate), and justice agencies.[1] This may be the route to a more intensive intervention, but one focussed on the welfare needs of the child, and family, rather than on adjudication of guilt. One of the admirable

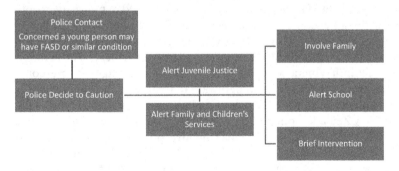

Figure 7.1 Primary Diversion – Police Cautioning or Warning.

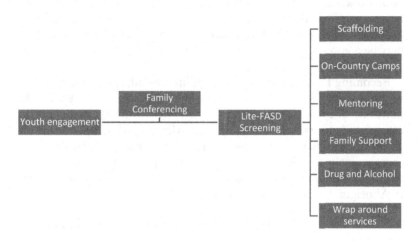

Figure 7.2 Secondary Diversion: Family Conferencing.

qualities of the family group conference is its flexibility. It can be convened in any setting, including on-country, and it can include Elders and extended family, teachers, and carers. A light screening tool could be employed, under the philosophy employed by the Russell Family Fetal Alcohol Disorders Association (2015), 'for the purpose of implementing interventions and strategies - if it looks like FASD and sounds like FASD treat it like FASD.'

Family group conferences develop plans that may focus on offending behaviour, but they can also be a catalyst for linking the child and family with support services.

Developing strategies at the front end of the system will necessitate a lowered threshold for identifying potential FASD cases. It offers an opportunity for a pathway to support more intensive engagement than in Figure 7.1 but avoiding the stigma of the formal justice system. Aboriginal involvement in the diversion process may be a critical factor in ensuring that interventions are culturally competent. This approach may require that *decisions to prosecute children must be rigorously vetted both internally by a senior officer, and/or at a later stage by prosecution services, to decide if it's in the child's or the public's best interests.* The possibility of FASD would place the onus on diversion into community-based networks of care and support, rather than prosecution. For example, under Western Australia's *Young Offenders Act 1994* (WA), the Children's Court can refer a matter to a *Juvenile Justice Team* - multi-agency team which may involve the young person, their family and the victim – instead of hearing the matters, where it believes an informal approach is merited. Diversion 'on-country' and deeper involvement with Elders and others of significance to the child, may be a good way of constructing supportive 'relational scaffolding' or circle of care around the child.

Becoming FASD aware and developing a mindset capable of working in a diversionary space, poses a challenge for police. Research, however, does demonstrate that, adequately trained, many police officers are more than capable of acknowledging the impact of FASD on Indigenous youth. For some, greater awareness of FASD made them re-evaluate previous cases they had dealt with. One senior officer working in remote Western Australia, with a long history of working in Aboriginal communities, told researchers:

> Learning about FASD...made me remember a kid in Beagle Bay (on the Dampier Peninsula). He kept getting in trouble, his family could not control him, but he was the nicest kid you could meet ....I used to keep asking 'why did you do that?' (break into the school, steal from the store, etc.). I used to say 'when will you ever learn?'. And that's the thing, he couldn't learn could he?
>
> (Blagg, Tulich & Bush, 2017, p. 337)

Justice reinvestment

A successful diversionary approach would necessitate investment in community structures. Currently, criminal justice budgets are consumed by prisons and detention centres: it is estimated that taxpayers pay $3.8 billion a year to keep people in prison (The Australian, December 2016): over $300 per night, while it costs around $30 per day for community supervision. This has increased demands for an alternative strategy where there would be investment in community alternatives. *Justice Reinvestment* is an evidence led strategy in which money currently spent on incarcerating people will be diverted into building community supports. Research in a locality would identify clusters of vulnerability and there would be local strategic planning involving all relevant agencies and community organisations. Over time there would be a transfer of resources away from building prisons to building communities. Evidence-based FASD programmes run by community organisations would be an obvious focus for investment. The model is being trialled in Bourke New South Wales (see https:// www.justreinvest.org.au/justice-reinvestment-in-bourke/; also Brown et al., 2016).

Moving forward

A diversionary approach to FASD in the justice system should be both multidisciplinary *and* community-focussed, maximising therapeutic outcomes while responding to the needs, including cultural needs, of Indigenous people with FASD who come into contact with the justice system. There would be a focus on multidisciplinary training for judicial and legal professionals, correctional staff, police, health, schools, and other professions that intersect with the justice system, about FASD and its medical, social, and legal implications. This training should also, as outlined in Chapter 5, be trauma-informed and decolonised. Rather than medicalised. It is not necessary to conduct costly and time-consuming diagnostic tests before providing supports and children, adults, and families.

We need a greater focus on diversion from the criminal justice system by the police, supported by local communities. Greater investment in diversionary multi-agency teams and capacity building/resourcing for local Aboriginal agencies to provide services. There needs to be an urgent review of bail and remand alternatives for accused persons with FASD, reducing the likelihood of repeated offending, which could be achieved by using 'on country' facilities instead of mainstream bail facilities. The decolonisation of FASD interventions would see greater use of on-country programmes, designed by Aboriginal people with the backing of Elders, and a greater emphasis on culture-based activities.

'Cultural reports' in New Zealand and, more recently, in some Australian states such as Queensland, provide courts with more than a simple at-risk assessment, instead exploring the impact of cultural dislocation and family history on the actions of the accused. In Canada, *Gladue Reports* have been in existence for some years. The reports provide a history of the accused person, with a focus on the negative impact of state policies of assimilation and segregation on them and their communities, and offer sentencing options to best meet the needs of the individual. As we mentioned earlier, diversionary conferencing should move towards this kind of 'truth telling' rather than fixating on just the actions of young offenders.

Contributory outcomes

The experience of prison and youth detention can be an extremely debilitating experience. For young people with FASD it can be particularly harmful. They may have trouble complying with prison rules and may be victimised due to their suggestibility (Douglas, 2010, p. 228). A failure to identify FASD increases the risk of multiple and ongoing contact with the criminal justice system (Roach & Bailey, 2009, p. 4). Even if prisoners are identified as having FASD, challenges exist to the effective management of people with FASD in the correctional system, including a lack of appropriate treatment programmes (see Chapter 6). There is also the likelihood of people with FASD developing what are known as *contributory outcomes*, such as substance abuse, anxiety disorders, or mental illness, which increases their susceptibility to further contact with the criminal justice system on release (Douglas, 2010, p. 225; Koren, 2004, p. 4). Contributory outcomes are a cluster of social and psychological problems that develop as a result of FASD's primary effects being exacerbated by repeated negative contact with the criminal justice and related systems; inadequate support and misdiagnosis; existence on the margins of society; racism; and institutionalisation (Streissguth & Kanter, 1997).

Importantly, however, contributory outcomes can be prevented or the impact reduced by appropriate interventions: by improving the responsiveness of the justice system and support services to young people with FASD. It is crucial that the identification of FASD does not itself, however, become the source of greater harm (Roach & Bailey, 2009, p. 5). Criminological research warns that even well-intended intervention can have the unintended consequence of widening the carceral net by drawing young people deeper into judicial and correctional systems in order for them to receive treatment and support (see e.g., Cunneen & White, 2007). Indigenous organisations should be funded to provide mentoring and family support services, interlaced with 'on-country' camps that help to stabilise young people and heal families, thereby reducing the likelihood of further generations being lost to FASD. The potential game changer then, that could provide the basis for a new FASD aware, Indigenous youth justice paradigm, emerges not from Western epistemology alone but at the point of intersection between Indigenous and non-Indigenous knowledge. Indigenous 'place' (or 'country') should be at the heart (in both a figurative and metaphorical sense) of this nascent sphere. Indigenous place can become a fulcrum upon which a new decolonised justice system can be leveraged into being. We suggested earlier that the weakness of criminological theories lies in their tendency to assume law breakers have 'agency' in terms of their behaviour (it is deliberate and planned, and its likely consequences, for self and others, recognised). FASD, and other cognitive impairments, pose a considerable challenge to this orthodoxy, and urge us to radically recalibrate diversion.

Note

1 For a discussion of the historical and theoretical framework see: New Zealand Parliamentary Debates (NZPD) Vol. 497, *Children and Young Persons Bill - Report of the Social Services Committee,* (20 April 1989), pp. 10105 ff; G. Maxwell et al., *Achieving effective outcomes in youth justice.* Final report, Ministry of Social Development, February 2004, pp. 7–15, and 238; and J. Tolmie and W. Brookbanks, *Criminal Justice in New Zealand,* LexisNexis, 2007, pp. 359–363.

References

Agozino, B. (2004). Imperialism, crime and criminology: Towards the decolonisation of criminology. *Crime Law and Social Change, 41*(4), 343–358.

Amnesty International Australia. (2015, May). *A brighter tomorrow: Keeping indigenous kids in the community and out of detention in Australia.* Report, Broadway, Australia.

Anthony, T. (2013). *Indigenous people, crime and punishment.* Abingdon, Oxford, UK: Routledge.

Anthony, T., & Blagg, H. (2020). "Hhyperincarceration and Indigeneity." *Oxford Research Encyclopedia of Criminology.* doi:10.1093/acrefore/9780190264079.013.656. Retrieved 22 Septemeber 2020 from https://oxfordre.com/criminology/view/10.1093/acrefore/9780190264079.001.0001/acrefore-9780190264079-e-656.

Atkinson, J. (2002). *Trauma trails, recreating song lines: The transgenerational effects of trauma in Indigenous Australia.* North Melbourne, Australia: Spinifex Press.

Atkinson, J. (2013). Trauma-informed services and trauma-specific care for Indigenous Australian children. *Closing the Gap Clearinghouse*, Resource sheet no. 21. July.

Australian Institute of Health and Welfare. (2014). *Youth detention population in Australia 2014.* Report, Australian Government, Australia, November.

Australian Law Reform Commission. (2018). *Pathways to justice – Inquiry into the incarceration rate of Aboriginal and Torres Strait Islander Peoples.* Report, Australian Government, Australia, March.

Blagg, H. (2016). *Crime, aboriginality and the decolonisation of justice* (2nd ed.). Sydney, Australia: Federation Press.

Blagg, H., & Anthony, T. (2019). *Decolonising criminology: Imagining justice in a post-colonial world.* Palgrave, UK: Critical Criminological Perspectives Series.

Blagg, H., Morgan, N., Cunneen, C., & Ferrante, A. (2005). *Systemic racism as a factor in the overrepresentation of Aboriginal people in the criminal justice system.* Report to the Equal Opportunity Commission and Aboriginal Justice Forum, Melbourne, Australia.

Blagg, H., & Tulich, T. (2018). *Developing diversionary pathways for indigenous youth with foetal alcohol spectrum disorders (FASD): A three community*

150   *Harry Blagg*

study in Western Australia. Report to the Australian Institute of Criminology, Australia.

Blagg, H., Tulich, T., & Bush, Z. (2015). Diversionary pathways for indigenous youth with FASD in Western Australia: Decolonising alternatives. *Alternative Law Journal, 40*(4), 257–260.

Blagg, H., Tulich, T., & Bush, Z. (2015/2016). Placing country at the centre: Decolonising justice for indigenous young people with foetal alcohol spectrum disorders (FASD). *Australian Indigenous Law Review, 19*(2), 4–16.

Blagg, H., Tulich, T., & Bush, Z. (2017). Indefinite detention meets colonial dispossession: Indigenous youths with foetal alcohol spectrum disorders in a white settler justice system. *Social and Legal Studies, 26*(3), 333–358.

Blagg, H., Tulich, T., & May, S. (2019). Aboriginal youth with foetal alcohol spectrum disorder and enmeshment in the Australian justice system: Can an intercultural form of restorative justice make a difference? *Contemporary Justice Review, 22*(2), 105–121.

Blagg, H., & Wilkie. M. (1997). Young people & policing in Australia: The relevance of the UN convention on the rights of the child. *Australian Journal of Human Rights, 3*(2), 134–156.

Braithwaite, J. (2002). Restorative justice. In P. Bean (Ed.), *Crime: Critical concepts in sociology*. London, UK: Routledge.

Brown, D., Cunneen, C., Schwart, M., Stubbs, J., & Young, K. (2016). *Justice reinvestment winding back imprisonment*. London, UK: Palgrave Macmillan.

Brown, N. N., Burd, L., Grant, T., Edwards, W., Adler, R., & Streissguth, A. (2015). Prenatal alcohol exposure: An assessment strategy for the legal context. *International Journal of Law and Psychiatry, 42*, 144–148.

Cunneen, C. (1999). *Diversion and best practice for Indigenous people: A nonIndigenous view*. Conference Paper, Australian Institute of Criminology and Department for Corrections, Adelaide, Australia.

Cunneen, C., & Tauri, J. M. (2016). *Indigenous criminology*. Bristol, UK: Policy Press.

Cunneen, C., & White, R. (2007). *Juvenile justice: Youth and crime in Australia* (3rd ed.). South Melbourne, Australia: Oxford University Press.

Daly, K. (2002). Restorative justice – The real story. *Punishment and Society, 4*, 55–79.

Daly, K., & Marchetti, E. (2012). *Innovative justice processes: Restorative justice, indigenous justice, and therapuetic jurisprudence*. Indigenous justice clearinghouse, Published by Griffith University. Retrieved from https://www.indigenousjustice.gov.au/resources/innovative-justice-processes-restorative-justice-indigenous-justice-and-therapuetic-jurisprudence/

Department of Corrective Services. (2015a). *Young people in detention quick reference statistics*. Perth, Australia: Department of Corrective Services.

Department of Corrective Services. (2015b). *Young people managed in the community quick reference statistics*. Perth, Australia: Department of Corrective Services.

Dodson, P. (1991). *Regional report of inquiry into underlying issues in Western Australia,* Canberra, Australia: AGPS.

Douglas, H. (2010). The sentencing response to defendants with foetal alcohol spectrum disorder. *Criminal Law Journal, 34*(4), 221–239.

Dunbar-Ortiz, R. (2014). *An Indigenous peoples' history of the United States.* Boston, MA: Beacon Press.

Goulding, D., & Steels, B. (2006). Developing, implementing & researching a communitarian model of restorative & transformative justice for adult offenders in magistrates' courts' (M. King & K. Auty Eds), *eLaw Journal (Special Series), 1,* 27.

Goulding, D., & Steels, B. (2013). Ten years on, the 'three circle' model of restorative & transformative justice: A tool to combat victimization and recidivism. *Asian Criminology, 8*(4), 321–333.

Hand, L., Pickering, M., Kedge, S., & McCann, C. (2019). Oral language and communication factors to consider when supporting people with FASD involved with the legal system. In M. Nelson & M. Trussle (Eds.), *Fetal Alcohol Spectrum Disorders in Adults: Ethical and Legal Perspectives* (pp. 139–147). Switzerland: Springer.

Hayes, H. (2017). Emotion and language in restorative youth justice. In A. Deckert & R. Sarre (Eds.), *The Palgrave handbook of Australian and New Zealand criminology, crime and justice* (pp. 407–419). Cham, Switzerland: Palgrave Macmillan.

Jackson, M. (2017, 14 October). *Prison should never be the only answer. E-Tangata.* Retrieved from https://e-tangata.co.nz/comment-and-analysis/moana-jackson-prison-should-never-be-the-only-answer/

Johnson, E. (1991). *Royal commission into aboriginal deaths in custody.* National Report. Canberra, Australia: Australian Government Publishing Service.

Kippin, N. R., Leitão, S., Watkins, R., Finlay-Jones, A., Condon, C., Marriott, R., … Bower, C (2018). Language diversity, language disorder, and fetal alcohol spectrum disorder among youth sentenced to detention in Western Australia. *International Journal of Law Psychiatry, 61,* 40–49.

Koren, G. (2004). Hypothetical framework: FASD and criminality – Causation or association? The limits of evidence based knowledge. *Journal of FAS International, 2*(2), 1–5.

Lakota People's Law Project (USA). Retrieved from https://www.lakotalaw.org/

Loh, N., & Ferrante, A. (2005). *Aboriginal involvement in the Western Australian criminal justice system: A statistical review.* Perth, Australia: Crime Research Centre.

Mackean, T. (2009). A healed and healthy country: Understanding healing for Indigenous Australians, *Medical Journal of Australia, 190*(10), 522–523.

Office of the Correctional Investigator. (2020). News release: *Indigenous people in federal custody surpasses 30% correctional investigator issues statement and challenge.* Retrieved from https://www.oci-bec.gc.ca/cnt/comm/press/press20200121-eng.aspx

Oranga Tamariki Act 1989 or *Children's and Young People's Well-being Act 1989, New Zealand,* known as *The Children, Young Persons, and Their Families Act 1989* prior to 14 July 2017.

Palmer, D. (2010). *Opening up to be kings and queens of country: An evaluation of the yiriman project.* Report, Kimberley Aboriginal Law and Culture Centre, Fitzroy Crossing, Australia, November.

Palmer, D. (2013). *We know they healthy cos they on country with old people: Demonstrating the value of the Yiriman Project 2010–2013.* Report, Yiriman Project, Australia.

Park, A. S. J. (2015). Settler colonialism and the politics of grief: Theorising a decolonising transitional justice for Indian residential schools. *Human Rights Review, 16*(3), 273–293.

Parliament of Australia House of Representatives Standing Committee on Aboriginal and Torres Strait Islander Affairs. (2011, June). *Doing time - Time for doing indigenous youth in the criminal justice system.* Report, Parliament of Australia, Australia.

Parliament of Australia House of Representatives Standing Committee on Indigenous Affairs. (2015). *Inquiry into the harmful use of alcohol in Aboriginal and Torres Strait Islander communities: Alcohol, hurting people and harming communities.* Report, Parliament of Australia, Australia, June.

Reid, N., Kippin, N., Passmore, H., & Finlay-Jones, A. (2020). Fetal alcohol spectrum disorder: The importance of assessment, diagnosis and support in the Australian justice context. *Psychiatry, Psychology and Law, 27*(2), 265–274.

Richards, K. (2017). Responsibilising the parents of young offenders through restorative justice: A genealogical account. *Restorative Justice, 5*(1), 93–115.

Roach, K., & Bailey, A. (2009). The relevance of fetal alcohol spectrum disorder in Canadian criminal law from investigation to sentencing. *University of British Colombia Law Review, 42,* 1–68.

Royal Commission into the Detention and Protection of Children in the Northern Territory. (2017). Retrieved from https://www.royalcommission.gov.au/sites/default/files/2019-01/rcnt-royal-commission-nt-final-report-volume-1.pdf

Russell Family Fetal Alcohol Disorders Association. (2015). Rffada FASD screening tool. Retrieved from https://rffada.org/

Siegel, L. J., & McCormick, C. R. (2006). *Criminology in Canada* (3rd ed.). Australia: Thomas Nelson.

Streissguth, A. P., Bookstein, F., Barr, H., Sampson, P. D., O'Malley, K., & Young, J. K. (2004). Risk factors for adverse life outcomes in fetal alcohol syndrome and fetal alcohol effects. *Journal of Developmental and Behavioural Pediatrics, 25*(4), 228–238.

Streissguth, A. P., & Kanter, J. (Eds.). (1997). *The challenge of fetal alcohol syndrome: Overcoming secondary disabilities.* Seattle: University of Washington Press.

Sturm, Circe. (2017). Reflections on the anthropology of sovereignty and settler colonialism: Lessons from Native North America. *Cultural Anthropology, 32*(3), 340–348.

The Australian. (2016). *Jump in prisoner numbers costs $3.8 billion a year.* December.

Tuck, E., & McKenzie, M. (2015). Relational validity and the "where" of inquiry: Place and land in qualitative research. *Qualitative Inquiry, 21*(7), 633–638.

Wacquant, L. (2001). Deadly symbiosis: When ghetto and prison meet and mesh. *Punishment & Society, 3*(1), 95–134.

Waitangi Tribunal. (2017). *Report on the crown and disproportionate reoffending rates.* Retrieved from https://waitangitribunal.govt.nz/news/disproportionate-reoffending-rate/

Walmsley, R. (2017). World prison brief. *World Pre-trial/Remand Imprisonment List* (3rd ed.). Retrieved from https://www.prisonstudies.org/sites/default/files/resources/downloads/wptril_3rd_edition.pdf

Western Australian Inspector of Custodial Services. (2014). *Mentally impaired accused on 'custody orders': Not guilty, but incarcerated indefinitely.* Report, Western Australia, April.

White, R. (2014). Indigenous young people and hyperincarceration in Australia. *Youth Justice,*15(3), 256–227.

Wolfe, P. (2006). Settler colonialism and the elimination of the native. *Journal of Genocide Research, 8*(4), 387–409.

8 FASD, justice, decolonisation, and the dis-ease of settler colonialism

Contemporary justice issues in Canada

Michelle Stewart

Introduction

This chapter will focus on the role of settler colonialism when thinking about FASD. My contribution is grounded in my own experiences as someone involved in applied research and evaluation, development of frontline interventions, as well as policy analysis and policy development. The information presented here will focus empirically on Canada but with connections to broader questions about settler colonialism that are applicable in Canada, Australia, and New Zealand. The chapter assumes the reader to have a working knowledge of FASD based on the content presented thus far about prevalence, training, FASD in the courts and best practices to address client needs. Building on the work of previous chapters, the reader will be invited to blend their own understandings about FASD, alongside considerations of settler-colonialism presented in this chapter, and then draw conclusions about what it looks like to decolonise practices within the context in which the reader lives/researches/works. As researchers/ workers we must *position ourselves* in the work we do – and, I would argue, *take a position* in the work we do. The ultimate goal of this chapter, and my work more broadly, is to decolonise justice practices and in so doing to decolonise FASD. But as has been pointed out to me by close collaborators and editors alike, to decolonise a practice or a policy requires one to establish clarity about what type of colonisation is being addressed and, from that, *what* exactly is colonial about the practice or policy.[1] Ultimately, the process of identifying colonial structures can help to denaturalise that which appears logical, and to then challenge and dismantle that which is unjust. However, this is a path that is fraught with discomfort and dis-ease as it challenges many to think differently about their own practices as well as the ongoing impacts of settler colonialism. Accordingly, this chapter will position the author, offer a conceptual framework for settler colonialism, deliver a short summary of FASD and justice in a Canadian context, and offer a few preliminary examples about what it might look like to decolonise practices and policies therein.

Positioning author

I am a professor at a mid-size university in the prairies of Canada. I have lived and worked here, on Treaty 4 Territory, for approximately nine years. I am originally from the unceded Coast Salish Territory in British Columbia, Canada. I was raised as a settler and afforded all the privilege that comes with presenting as a white cis woman. That said, my family has a complex history as it relates to colonial policies in Canada including an infamous piece of federal legislation, the Indian Act, that stripped Indigenous women of their legal status when they married non-Indigenous men. My grandmother on my father's side was likely Indigenous and had status before marrying my grandfather who was a settler. She then had children who also did not have status because she had married a settler. This is the state-making project of assimilation. Like so many other families, we did not talk about her history in much the same way that she did not talk about her own history with us. A complete articulation of assimilation – but more specifically it is an articulation of settler colonialism as I will discuss shortly.

Reframing FASD

My initial concerns with FASD came about tangentially. Prior to arriving in Treaty 4 Territory, I completed my PhD on police training practices in Canada including the need to reckon with colonialism (Stewart, 2011). FASD presented itself to me unexpectedly. While attending community trainings or workshops, people working for and with police would talk about someone 'looking' like they had FASD and how that would make them 'at risk' of being involved in criminal activities. When I started my position at the University of Regina, I decided to take my background in Science and Technology Studies, as well as legal/political and medical anthropology and focus my attention on *how* FASD was understood by frontline police. I wanted to reframe discussions about FASD. Knowing very little about FASD, I wanted to explore how it was that police appeared to be creating a causal relationship between a disability and criminality.

In the years that followed, I came to frame an investigation about FASD and justice through three lenses. First, police appeared to be focussed on FASD when they were working with Indigenous peoples which raised a clear set of questions about systemic racism and racialised policing practices (Comack, 2012; Razack, 2015). Second, police appeared to be blending causal understandings of crime and criminality with what they understood to be the physical characteristics of a disability. This raised a number of concerns about ableism and seemed to harken a group of dated theorists who drew on biological determinism and physical traits to make links between disability, criminality, and/ or deviance which I found troubling (for analysis see Beckman, 2017; for original text see for example Lombroso, 2004). Third, the research *about FASD* demonstrated FASD was over-represented in the justice system and that individuals *with FASD* were at high risk for justice involvement (Fast & Conry, 1999; Streissguth et al., 1996, 1999).[2] My first intervention, at that time, was to research how police and other justice professionals understood FASD. I conducted research with police as well as all branches of frontline justice professionals (from judges to prosecutors, legal aid, and court advocates). In this work, I speculated that increased awareness of the disability (via training and outreach) might increase the use of discretionary powers (to not lay a charge for example) and diversion (including the use of restorative justice) – and that increased awareness could drive down the over-representation of Indigenous peoples in the courts. While I have been involved in the training of hundreds of justice professionals over the years, I can say that more education is not the solution to the situation.[3] At least not as it had been framed in my mind. Reframing the discussion is critical if we are going to bring about transformational change and start to decolonise these systems. Part of changing systems is changing the language we use and this is where I have run into challenges. The conversation requires we use specific language; language that has been bracketed off and fortified. I am speaking here of settler colonialism.

Settler colonialism

To talk about FASD and the justice system is complex. FASD is a complex disability. For example, some of that complexity arises when we consider that it is often described as an 'invisible disability', which means people might be able to 'pass' as not having the disability which can create incredible challenges when their cognitive disability goes unrecognised and, therefore, unaccommodated. In another example of complexity, the context(s) surrounding drinking during pregnancy can be multifaceted. For example, a woman might not know she is pregnant as more than 50% of pregnancies are unplanned; however we must consider the role of trauma as it relates to drinking as a coping mechanism. A cluster of researchers have drawn attention to the social construction of the disability and what constitutes good mothering/ parenting therein (Salmon, 2011; Tait, 2001). And if one thinks from the lens of critical disability studies, there are many intersecting factors that we must attend to when thinking about disability including but not limited to: race, class, gender, and colonialism. Some have taken on elements of this complexity: for example the interlocking impacts of colonialism and neoliberalism (Blagg et al., 2019; Liebel, 2017; Salmon, 2011). That said, a wide swath of research and reporting on FASD often flattens these nuances and complexities. Instead, the literature can appear to speak in short-hand and absolutes that can render a social issue into a causal one if we simply state people with FASD have disproportionate contact with social services, justice, and youth and child welfare systems (Brintnell, 2009; Burnside & Fuchs, 2013; Douglas et al., 2012; Fast & Conry, 2009; Flannigan, Pei, Stewart & Johnson, 2018; Sinclair, 2004). As each of these authors knows, the stories are more complex but often we don't take time with that complexity.

For quite some time, I used to think that this complexity required that I have different language and strategies to speak to different audiences. For example, when speaking to settlers and those that are often driving outcomes in the justice system, I would speak very generally about structural inequality surrounding the over-representation of Indigenous peoples and those with FASD and then turn my attention to discussing the disability itself. When speaking about FASD to community members, those who have FASD, and those who have friends/ family with FASD, I would speak tangibly about the elements of the disability as well as the pain that surrounds this striking social injustice and name colonialism a bit louder and for a bit longer. It was not that I avoided discussions about colonialism with justice workers, but my frame was different and the points of emphasis were changed. In trying to bring about different justice outcomes for people with FASD, I tried to make the content a bit more palatable to frontline justice workers. In some cases, I would use the language of reconciliation. Very infrequently would I use the language of decolonisation. I didn't realise that what I was more broadly coming up against was that bracketing that I discussed earlier. In different settings a group of people (largely settlers) were fine to talk about FASD in very general terms. What they were not fine with was discussing the broader contexts – and that if we are talking about individuals with FASD that are Indigenous, we must be willing to talk about trauma and colonialism. Here the work of Paulette Regan (2010, p. 11) outlines the challenge:

> Canadians are still on a misguided, obsessive, and mythical quest to assuage colonizer guilt by solving the Indian problem. In this way, we avoid looking too closely at ourselves and the collective responsibility we bear for the colonial status quo. The significant challenge that lies before us is to turn the mirror back upon ourselves and to answer the provocative question posed by historian Roger Epp regarding reconciliation in Canada: How do we solve the settler problem?

The 'settler problem' that Regan discusses here is a key challenge when thinking about FASD and the justice system. To have a frank and open discussion about FASD, a complex cognitive disability, in the Canadian context, requires an equally complex discussion about settler colonialism. Wolfe points out that settler colonialism means 'invasion is a structure not an event' (Wolfe, 1999, p. 165). Razack (2015) alongside Woroniak and Camfield argue (2013) that settler colonialism has a primary aim: to displace Indigenous bodies (to make room for the ongoing settlement). If we take these different perspectives on settler colonialism and apply the analysis to the justice system (and child welfare system) we see what has been described by some as a child welfare to prison pipeline (see for example Smandych & Corrado, 2018; Stewart & La Berge, 2019). A pipeline that is fuelled by risk narratives and assessment tools that strip Indigenous children out of their homes, and have limited willingness to account for the impacts of trauma or structural inequality; a pipeline that can *translate* trauma or disability into risk – seeking first to punish rather than to adjust and to accommodate. Seen this way, the justice system (child welfare and criminal justice) is the most recent in a long line of state tactics used to displace Indigenous bodies and to further the aims of settler colonialism.

Canada, Australia, the United States, and New Zealand are all settler states with ongoing impacts through dispossession (e.g., Nielson & Robyn, 2003; Scholtz, 2006). Each of these states has an overrepresentation of Indigenous peoples in their justice system (Cunneen & Tauri, 2019). Williams (2018, p. vi) notes that 'FASD exists against the backdrop of colonisation, stolen generations, and systemic racism' such that it results in a multi-fold form of dispossession that moves from child welfare to justice settings with compounding effects on individuals, families, and communities (Badry & Felske, 2013; Blagg et al., 2017; Salmon, 2011; Rudin, 2016). For Canada and Australia in particular, there is a shared history of settler colonialism including policies that stripped children from their family homes, practices that included residential and boarding schools, as well as placing children with foster or adoptive parents. Processes of violent assimilation have included starvation and disease as a mechanism to clear the plains during early settlement (Daschuk, 2013). These processes have continued, the act of settling is ongoing, as is violent dispossession that continues to this day through justice and child welfare policies that remove children and adults from communities and place them in facilities (group homes, foster homes, youth detention, jails, and prisons). Dollars flow to child welfare and justice government agencies (and the workers therein) and not to communities such that the trauma that surrounds settler colonialism serves as the basis for removal – whole sectors focussed on the management and displacement of Indigenous bodies from cradle to grave.

As discussed in the introduction, there is a need to outline what settler colonialism is as well as put forth examples of colonial structures – through the framework of settler colonialism – to better understand how structures function *and* how they might be dismantled if we are seeking to decolonise. Alternatively, these systems will continue to thrive on the subjection of Indigenous peoples and further intensify the displacement of Indigenous children, youth, and adults. One need only look to Canada, Australia, and New Zealand to see the ways in which each of these settler states are articulating settler colonialism through the over-representation of Indigenous peoples in child welfare and justice systems. Complacency with these statistics serves as tacit agreement with the violent aspirations of settler colonialism. But if discussion about settler colonialism can make a group of settler people uncomfortable then a discussion about decolonising practices is that much more likely to produce dis-ease. Not just discomfort but outright dis-ease.

And so, this is what I have come to understand in recent years. Settler colonialism causes dis-ease. I say this thinking about the training spaces as well as policy work; I say this also when thinking about so many conversations I have had with fellow researchers. While there might be agreement to a passing comment about historic trauma, there is often resistance when I try to sustain a discussion about the tangible impacts of settler colonialism as it relates to FASD. I have come to recognise this dis-ease, how it presents with different audiences, and the need to still push to try and sustain the discussion.

To do otherwise, is to agree that we should be able to speak about FASD with a particular *ease*. There should not be any *ease* when speaking about FASD. One look at the justice statistics in Canada, Australia and New Zealand should affirm that we simply cannot avoid the question of settler colonialism – and that we should feel incredible dis-ease with the current state of affairs in the justice system. Again, anyone exposed to alcohol in utero can develop FASD. My point here is that a conversation about FASD in settler states must account for the role of alcohol and trauma in the lives of Indigenous women, children, and families. I say this because the so-called over-representation of FASD in the justice system in settler states is about intersecting forms of oppression grounded in the foundations of settler colonialism. The preliminary space that has opened to discuss some of these issues has come through the framework of reconciliation. In the following section I will speak briefly about the Canadian state's relationship to reconciliation, how this national discussion about reconciliation opened a tangible space to discuss FASD and colonialism, and the ever-growing need to keep our focus on decolonisation.

FASD and justice in the Canadian context – A summary of 25 years of reconciliation

In June 2008, the Prime Minister of Canada delivered a National Apology 'to former students of Indian residential schools. The treatment of children in these schools is a sad chapter in our history.' Framed from the start as 'a sad chapter', and therefore a discrete, and historical, segment of time, the Prime Minister sat on the floor of Parliament surrounded by dignitaries and apologised for the impacts of the Indian Residential School programme. This programme, funded by the Government of Canada, found over 150,000 First Nations, Inuit, and Métis children taken from their homes and brought to residential schools that were run primarily by churches and were the sites of violent assimilation policies as well as sexual, physical, and emotional abuse and trauma (Truth and Reconciliation Commission, 2015). The apology was hailed by many as a new era that held the promise of transformative change.

Harper's apology was delivered just months after Australia's Prime Minister Kevin Rudd also delivered a National Apology to the Stolen Generations. Both Rudd and Harper were conservative leaders placed in a position to offer a profound act: recognise settler colonialism in all of its violent articulations. However, if one dives a bit deeper it becomes clear that both leaders were, in fact, compelled to deliver these Apologies. Rudd was responding to the National Inquiry into the Separation of Aboriginal and Torres Strait Islander Children from their Families, Bringing Them Home Report (sections 5a and 5b); Harper was complying with the settlement of a class action lawsuit. The depth of the Canadian Apology is easily measured if we fast-forward to September 2019, when the Prime Minister was speaking about the successes of the Canadian economy during the world economic crisis. Harper noted to the media that 'we [Canada] also have no history of colonialism. So we have all of the things that many people admire about the great powers but none of the things that threaten or bother them (Ljunggren, 2009).' Indeed, Canada has nothing that will threaten or bother. In the years that followed, the Canadian government would place roadblocks up as the Truth and Reconciliation Commission (TRC) launched a multi-year investigation into the ongoing impacts of the Residential School programme in Canada (2015).

The TRC collected stories and generated reports and findings between 2008 and 2015. During this time there were a number of gatherings in which the Commission heard testimony from over 6,000 witnesses. In June 2015, the TRC released 94 Calls to Action that were meant to facilitate reconciliation. It included 17 action items in the area of justice reform including TRC Call to Action #33 and #34 that spoke about FASD prevention and justice reform. The Commission used the language of 'cultural genocide' to characterise the impact of the residential schools. While Prime Minister Harper attended the events associated with the release of the Calls to Action, his government remained silent at the time and the regime was replaced in October of that same year. Once again there appeared to be a watershed moment during the change in leadership.

Prime Minister Trudeau took leadership in the Fall of 2015 and spoke directly about the TRC and reconciliation. His appointment letters to his cabinet of Ministers reminded each Minister of their role in reconciliation. However, in the years that have followed, there has been little progress made to improving 'nation-to-nation' relations. The Canadian state continues to boast the over-representation of Indigenous children in state care (dubbed the millennial scoop in Canada); cross-Canada resistance has highlighted opposition to natural resource extraction and the lack of consultation with Indigenous communities and leadership about resource management; there is an ongoing lack of equitable access to drinkable water, healthcare, and education on reserves; as well as the ever-increasing rates of over-incarceration of Indigenous peoples. This is to say that the issue of reconciliation is not simply about *who* is in power. But rather it is to render transparent that these gestures to reconciliation, when they are not accompanied by structural change, serve to affirm, and reinforce settler colonialism. And, if we return to the settler guilt that Regan spoke of, the appearance of reconciliation (speaking about it) without the commitment to decolonise and actually change systems and practices, serves to fortify the inequalities and violence that are the critical bedrock of settler colonialism.

So what does this have to do with FASD?

We need to be able to speak truthfully about FASD. If we are going to speak about FASD and the justice system we need to be able to point to the broad-scale social injustices that surround the justice system. Perhaps most critically we need to be able to look at the 'outcomes' in the justice system and rather than saying the system is broken, instead recognise it as configured to bring about the aspirations of settler colonialism: displacement. When I say 'we' I am speaking to the settlers as they read this chapter – this is a process of recognition. But I also say 'we' more broadly because after that recognition comes a collective obligation to decolonise these systems if we want to bring about real change in the lives of individuals. We must first decolonise before we can think about reconciliation. In the absence of taking steps to decolonise we will only see a further 'Indigenisation of the justice system' in Canada and other settler states.

Decolonising practices in action: step one, name it

In January 2020, Ivan Zinger, the Federal Correctional Investigator of Canada (watchdog for federal prisons) called attention to the fact that the rates of incarceration of Indigenous peoples have only *increased* over the past four years, which means the rates have actually gone up following the release of the 94 Calls to Action. To be clear, in the years most focussed on the need to engage in reconciliation, the Canadian state has incarcerated *more* Indigenous peoples. This is coupled with an adjacent reality: there are currently more children in state care than at the height of the Residential School programme – 'by a factor of three', notes Cindy Blackstock, as she argues that child welfare has replaced residential schools (Blackstock, 2007). In other words, reconciliation is dead. Ivan Zinger was quoted as saying:

> On this trajectory, the pace is now set for Indigenous people to comprise 33% of the total federal inmate population in the next three years. Over the longer term, and for the better part of three decades

now, despite findings of Royal Commissions and National Inquiries, intervention of the courts, promises and commitments of previous and current political leaders, no government of any stripe has managed to reverse the trend of Indigenous over-representation in Canadian jails and prisons. The Indigenization of Canada's prison population is nothing short of a national travesty (2020).[4]

Zinger argued it was long-overdue for the Correctional Service to take responsibility for its role in the ongoing over-representation of Indigenous people in the justice system and that transformational change was required as 'tweaks around the edges of the system simply won't cut it.' In addition to speaking directly to the need for specialised supports and services for individuals with FASD, Zinger called for the need to 'transfer resources and responsibility to Indigenous groups and communities for the care, custody and supervision of Indigenous offenders.' In doing so, Zinger effectively called for redistribution of power and resources that would see Indigenous communities taking control over justice matters. If implemented across Canada, this would signal a substantial gain in the area of sovereignty and nation-to-nation relations. I raise this intervention by Zinger because it serves as an opportunity to think about what an act of decolonisation would look like in the justice system: power given back to communities and traditional risk and assessment tools replaced by tools and practices that are responsive to the needs of Indigenous individuals and communities and take into account the role of systemic racism.

Zinger uses the language of 'Indigenisation', which has frequently been used to speak to the need to increase representation such that the Indigenisation of the Academy would indicate better Indigenous representation. To say the 'Indigenization of Canada's prison population' further politicises Zinger's indictment of the justice system – and draws a stark contrast between the auspices of reconciliation and the realities in the justice system. While Zinger may not frame his intervention as an act of decolonisation, I would say that he is not committed to the gentle tones of reconciliation and in fact underscores that those efforts have failed.

Approximately one month after Zinger released his scathing report on Corrections, I found myself at a small conference focussed on FASD and Justice. Asked to deliver the keynote talk, I shared with the audience that they would be sampling a part of a chapter that I was preparing (for this book). I started off with a few bullet points:

- This talk is going to be frustrating at times;
- This talk is going to be challenging and personal at times;

- This talk is not going to be a talk;
- This will be a workshop talking about messy stuff.

This was going to be a talk and workshop about decolonizing FASD.

I shared a quote by Jesse Wente, an Ojibwe writer/broadcaster/curator/speaker/producer/activist from the Serpent River First Nation, who hailed the death of reconciliation in a radio interview stating that it 'deserved to die as the truth is too much for this country to bear' and another from Pam Palmater, a Mi'kmaq lawyer whose family originates from the Eel River Bar First Nation in northern New Brunswick, from a talk in which she stated 'if it feels good, it's not reconciliation.'[5] Rather than shying away from the discomfort and dis-ease the audience was going to feel, instead I named it at the front: this talk was going to be about colonialism and decolonising practices. I said they could choose Wente or Palmater's framework to think through but they needed to dig in – that it was going to be messy and that it was okay for them to feel uncomfortable. And they did. I shared information about apologies and the TRC, and I said that actions speak louder than words. I then shared the statistics slide that I have shared in presentations and trainings in Australia and Canada. The statistics get updated from time to time (the numbers only increase as illustrated by the Correctional Investigator's comments earlier). Most of these rates are captured in an article about FASD prevalence in Australia (Bower et al., 2018): My slide read:

- **Canada**: Indigenous peoples make up less than 4% of the population but over 30% of the prison population (2020).[6]
- **Australia**: Aboriginal and Torres Island people make up 27% of the prison population with children making up more than 53% of the justice population.
- Prevalence rates of FASD in these justice settings indicate: Canada estimated 11–23%; Australia recently noted upwards of 36%.

After a few more slides, and naming colonialism as a factor that must be addressed, I asked the audience to engage in discussions with people at their table and talk about what they would do to try and decolonise FASD. The room held frontline justice workers, policy-makers, and researchers including settlers and Indigenous folks. While I was attempting to pull the brackets off of settler colonialism, I can say that I was not entirely successful as I was pushed in the room to justify what this had to do with colonialism and to define colonialism. It was a learning opportunity for us all. And while I can speculate as to why the question was being asked by someone who presented as a white, male settler, it allowed for it to be stated for others in the room and for a preliminary response to be explored in public. In this space, as someone that presented as a white settler woman, I could say that we need to talk about colonialism and we need to talk about systemic racism otherwise we are having a conference about FASD and justice and bracketing out the biggest contributing factors in Canada. I was stating emphatically, to the mixed audience, that I was not going to allow us to talk about FASD and justice with ease. I was going to force us, collectively, into the dis-ease that is necessary. I can say that my definition of colonialism was not great and that I brushed the question off a bit to allow for the tabletop discussion to happen. But I can say that it gave me new language and ideas moving forward.

By the end of the workshop, participants put their ideas about how to decolonise FASD on bright post-it notes that stayed on the wall for the rest of the conference. I added a definition of colonisation around clusters of ideas so that for the next two days at a FASD conference, we were surrounded by the idea of colonisation and ideas that people had about how to change systems. As participants grabbed their coffee, waited in line for food, or wandered around the room during the breaks, they could read these ideas about decolonising FASD:

- Decarceration;
- Transfer significant funding from custodial sentences to community supports;
- Decolonise the system by: revitalising culture, restoring traditional knowledge systems, language barriers;
- Respect and acknowledgement of Indigenous Laws;
- Language barriers in court;
- Unrealistic expectations;
- Unjust;
- Some get charged for nothing;
- More resources for FASD awareness in courts; and
- Deconstructing gangs.

This cross-section of ideas that were presented by participants reflect the larger conversations that were taking place at the table tops including: how violent FASD assessments can be as they are tools that require maternal confirmation (of alcohol consumption) and reinforce blame on Indigenous parents instead of the colonial systems that continue to produce trauma within and between generations; the inaccessibility of courtrooms as some individuals do not speak English as their first or second language leaving them totally isolated and confused; and how the strengths of individuals with FASD are often forgotten and how the devaluation of those with FASD is codified into social service programmes that effectively punish adults (financially) if they don't live up to the lack of expectations (lost supports if someone is "making too much money" in a job, etc.). Ultimately, the process of identifying oppression in systems allowed for a broader conversation about the relationship between that form of oppression and particular characteristics of colonialism. It also allowed for a room of people to experiment with using the language of systemic racism and colonisation with their peers and colleagues, but also strangers. It was the first time that I did not step back from the dis-ease of speaking about FASD and settler colonialism. That is not to say it was easy or that I was proficient, but it is to say that the frame was set that day and it allowed me to practice decolonising the space of a conference.

Conclusion

FASD is a complex cognitive disability. In the context of Canada, a discussion about FASD requires an equally complex discussion about context: settler colonialism. While anyone exposed to alcohol while in utero *could* get FASD, there is a need to have a particular discussion when someone has FASD and is Indigenous in a place like Canada, Australia, and New Zealand. This is a different discussion because it must carefully and thoughtfully consider the ongoing impacts of settler colonialism, the role of intergenerational trauma, and systemic racism. In many ways this chapter might be unsatisfying for some as it discussed decolonisation but it does not offer a roadmap. But this was quite intentional; my goal here was to offer a few ideas to get the reader thinking. Decolonising ourselves and our practices is slow and steady work. It is deeply personal work and as such I positioned myself at the start. I started by sharing with the reader the ways in which colonial systems have directly impacted my family and resulted in the displacement of my own family's heritage and I positioned myself as someone that presents in a particular way and is subsequently afforded many privileges.

I can, and have, stood on the stage at large conference and training spaces. And it is in these spaces that I can choose *each time* to talk about the broader context of FASD. I can choose to speak about FASD *with ease* or bring the audience into a discussion that is fraught with dis-ease. I say this because it is a choice. I choose to engage in different research and evaluation practices to commit myself to projects of decolonisation. But these are choices. I am currently the project manager of a multi-year project that is funded under TRC Call to Action #34, focussing on justice reform and supporting individuals with FASD who are justice involved. At each corner of this project, our team works collectively to decolonise our work and to narrow in and understand the role of trauma as it would erupt in the lives of people who are engaged in the justice system. We are trying to actively undo the violence of the courts by offering sustained supports to Indigenous peoples involved in the justice system. We are saying to them that we are listening as we work with them to try and support them in new and creative ways in the community because we know the justice system has many beds waiting and ready for them—we are trying to counter the Indigenisation of the justice system one client at a time. It is slow work that requires us to be enveloped in the power of settler colonialism as we also attempt to bring about real-world changes in the lives of individuals and families. For me, on a daily basis, that means checking my privilege and being willing to listen to new ideas and think about different ways of doing things from programme design and delivery to programme evaluation. It also means pushing at the brackets each time we do a training or an outreach session, to figure out how to talk about colonialism and to take the brackets off that discussion. To talk about FASD in Canada means we must be talking about settler colonialism. I might not always do a good job in these sessions, but I force myself to raise it and to bring in new ideas about how to challenge structures as we work towards transformational change.

I now invite the reader to engage in their own thought experiment, to step into the dis-ease.

For the student, think about what you know from your studies: what could or should change in the system; what processes are colonial and what could be decolonised – what could you do to decolonise yourself and your practices? For the researcher, similarly think about what you know; what could you change in your research or practices – how could you contribute to identifying structures and decolonising them accordingly? To the frontline worker, think about the system and your role therein; what power do you hold and how can you shift power back to the individuals you work with?

For us all, what can we do individually and collectively to name the colonial practices and structures and how can we work towards transformational change? Colonial structures are massive and interlocking, and rely on compliance and complacency as much as ideology and violence. These structures are upheld by bureaucracies that are operationalised by individuals. To decolonise FASD is to decolonise systems – at all levels – and that takes a lot of work. Accordingly, this chapter serves as an invitation to reimagine and reconfigure who we are, what we do, and how we do it. This serves as an invitation to sit with the dis-ease and to find others that will do so with you. This is challenging work. It can be quiet work, it can be loud work, but most of all it is work.

Notes

1 I want to take a moment here to thank Robyn Pitawanakwat for insights not only on this chapter but projects and collaborations more broadly as the aims of decolonizing one's work and practices can often come about through the careful labor of others whose attention to our actions and language help bring about transformative change and yet often go unrecognized. Thanks also to Chris Kortright and Krystal Glowatski for comments on this chapter. Thanks also to Myles Himmelreich for pushing me to think differently. Additionally, I want to thank the editors of *Settler City Limits: Indigenous Resurgence and Colonial Violence in the Urban Prairie West* and in particular Robert Henry and David Hugill for discussion about specificity in the language we choose. Lastly I want to thank the editors and authors of this volume as our conversations in recent years have helped to shape and reshape my own conceptual frameworks and understandings. I hope this book serves to further our own discussions and helps to foster others.
2 I would note here that I did not trouble this link early in my work but rather allowed it to remain as a fact unchallenged in grant applications and early writing.
3 I would note that it was equally hard to have many researchers agree to this discussion years ago. To address the issues associated with FASD and justice in Canada requires a deep dive into a challenging topic: colonisation. And more specifically settler colonialism. It would take a number of years for me to better recognize why it was hard to bring about these conversations. But with that recognition—of the times that I tried and failed to make the conversation happen—served to mark a tacit agreement amongst many researchers to simply bracket colonialism out of the discussion for a number of years. Not all researchers, there were some that would name and engage in this discussion many years ago (Salmon, 2011; Tait, 2013).
4 For more information on this press advisory please review: https://www. oci-bec.gc.ca/cnt/comm/press/press20200121-eng.aspx
5 For full access to the Jesse Wente interview please see: https://www. cbc.ca/news/canada/toronto/jesse-wente-metro-morning-blockades-indigenous-1.5475492; for access to Pam Palmater's talk please see: https:// www.youtube.com/watch?v=89s3l2mYGWg.
6 This slide brought together a complex set of statistics. For further background on statistics in Canada please review: https://www.oci-bec. gc.ca/cnt/comm/press/press20200121-eng.aspx; *https://www150.statcan. gc.ca/n1/pub/85-002-x/2019001/article/00010-eng.htm*

References

Badry, D., & Felske, A. W. (2013). An exploratory study on the use of Photovoice as a method for approaching FASD prevention in the Northwest Territories. *First Peoples Child & Family Review, 8*(1), 143–160.

Beckman, L. (2017). Undoing ableism: Disability as a category of historical and legal analysis. *On_Culture, 3*, 2–28. https://d-nb.info/1137465999/34

Blackstock, C. (2007). Residential schools: Did they really close or just morph into child welfare. *Indigenous Law Journal, 6*, 71–78.

Blagg, H., Tulich, T., & May, S. (2019). Aboriginal youth with foetal alcohol spectrum disorder and enmeshment in the Australian justice system: Can an intercultural form of restorative justice make a difference?. *Contemporary Justice Review, 22*(2), 105–121.

Bower, C., Watkins, R. E., Mutch, R. C., Marriott, R., Freeman, J., Kippin, N. R., Safe, B., Pestell, C., Cheung, C. S., Shield, H., & Tarratt, L. (2018). Fetal alcohol spectrum disorder and youth justice: A prevalence study among young people sentenced to detention in Western Australia. *BMJ open, 8*(2), 1–10.

Brintnell, S. (2009). Social service needs of adults with FASD in the correctional system. Paper presented at the Conference on Fetal Alcohol Spectrum Disorder (FASD) – Across the Lifespan. Edmonton, AB.

Burnside, L., & Fuchs, D. (2013). Bound by the clock: The experiences of youth with FASD transitioning to adulthood from child welfare care. *First Peoples Child & Family Review, 8*(1), 41–62.

Cunneen, C., & Tauri, J. M. (2019). Indigenous peoples, criminology, and criminal justice. *Annual Review of Criminology, 2*, 359–381.

Daschuk, J. (2013). *Clearing the plains: Disease, politics of starvation, and the loss of aboriginal life.* Regina, SK: University of Regina Press.

Dorries, H., Henry, R., Hugill, D., McCreary, T., & Tomiak, J. (Eds.). (2019). *Settler city limits: Indigenous resurgence and colonial violence in the urban prairie west.* Manitoba, Canada: Univ. of Manitoba Press.

Douglas, H., Hammill, J., Russell, E., & Hall, W. (2012). Judicial views of foetal alcohol spectrum disorder in Queensland's criminal justice system. *Journal of Judicial Administration, 21*(3), 178–188.

Fast, D. K., Conry, J., & Loock, C. A. (1999). Identifying fetal alcohol syndrome among youth in the criminal justice system. *Journal of Developmental & Behavioral Pediatrics, 20*(5), 370–372.

Flannigan, K., Pei, J., Stewart, M., & Johnson, A. (2018). Fetal alcohol Spectrum disorder and the criminal justice system: A systematic literature review. *International Journal of Law Psychiatry, 57*, 42–52.

Harper, S. (2008, June 11). Prime Minister Stephen Harper's statement of apology. *CBC News.* Retrieved from https://www.cbc.ca/news/canada/prime-minister-stephen-harper-s-statement-of-apology-1.734250

Leibel, M. S. (2017). Reproductive narratives: Settler-colonialism and neoliberalism in Alberta's child welfare system. Masters dissertation, University of Alberta.

Lombroso, C., & Ferrero, G. (2004). *Criminal woman, the prostitute, and the normal woman.* Durham, NC: Duke University Press.

Ljunggren, D. (2009, September 26). Every G20 nation wants to be Canada, insists PM. *Reuters.* Retrieved from https://www.reuters.com/article/columns-us-g20-canada-advantages-idUSTRE58P05Z20090926

Nielsen, M. O., & Robyn, L. (2003). Colonialism and criminal justice for Indigenous peoples in Australia, Canada, New Zealand and the United States of America. *Indigenous Nations Journal, 4*(1), 29–45.

Razack, S. (2014). It happened more than once: Freezing deaths in Saskatchewan. *Canadian Journal of Women and the Law, 26*(1), 51–80.

Razack, S. (2015). *Dying from improvement: Inquests and inquiries into Indigenous deaths in custody.* Toronto, Canada: University of Toronto Press.

Regan, P. (2010). *Unsettling the settler within: Indian residential schools, truth telling, and reconciliation in Canada.* Vancouver: UBC Press.

Rudin, J. (2016). Aboriginal peoples and the criminal justice system. Research Paper delivered to the Attorney General of Canada. Retrieved from https://www.attorneygeneral.jus.gov.on.ca/inquiries/ipperwash/policy_part/research/pdf/Rudin.pdf

Salmon, A. (2011). Aboriginal mothering, FASD prevention, and the contestation of neoliberal citizenship. *Critical Public Health, 21*(2), 165–178.

Scholtz, C. (2006). *Negotiating claims: The emergence of indigenous land claim negotiation policies in Australia, Canada, New Zealand, and the United States.* New York: Routledge.

Simpson, A. (2011). Settlement's secret. *Cultural Anthropology, 26*(2), 205–217.

Sinclair, B. (2004). Commentary on the challenge of fetal alcohol syndrome in the criminal legal system. *Addiction Biology, 9*(2) 167–168.

Smandych, R., & Corrado, R. (2018). "Too Bad, So Sad": Observations on key outstanding policy challenges of twenty years of youth justice reform in Canada, 1995–201. *Manitoba Law Journal (Robson Crim), 4335.*

Stewart, M. (2011). The space between the steps: Reckoning in an era of reconciliation. *Contemporary Justice Review, 14*(1), 43–63.

Streissguth, A. P., Barr, H. M., Kogan, J., & Bookstein, F. L. (1996). *Understanding the occurrence of secondary disabilities in clients with fetal alcohol syndrome (FAS) and fetal alcohol effects (FAE).* Final report to the Centers for Disease Control and Prevention (CDC). Seattle: University of Washington.

Streissguth, A. P., Bookstein, F. L., Barr, H. M., Press, S., & Sampson, P. D. (1998). A fetal alcohol behavior scale. *Alcoholism, Clinical and Experimental Research, 22*(2), 325–333.

Tait, C. L. (2013). Resituating the ethical gaze: Government morality and the local worlds of impoverished Indigenous women. *International Journal of Circumpolar Health, 72*(1), 1–6.

Truth and Reconciliation Commission of Canada. (2015). *Honouring the truth, reconciling for the future: Summary of the final report of the truth and reconciliation commission of Canada.* Retrieved from http://www.trc.ca/websites/trcinstitution/File/2015/Exec_Summary_2015_06_25_web_o. pdf

Williams, R. D. (2018). *Understanding fetal alcohol spectrum disorder (FASD) through the stories of nyoongar families and how can this inform policy and service delivery.* Doctoral dissertation, Curtin University.

Wolfe, P. (2006). Settler colonialism and the elimination of the native. *Journal of Genocide Research, 8*(4), 387–409.

Woroniak, M., & Camfield, D. (2013). First nations' rights: Confronting colonialism in Canada. *Global Research: Centre for Research on Globalization.* Retrieved from http://www.globalresearch.ca/first-nations-rights-confronting-colonialism-in-canada/5321197

9 Conclusion

Harry Blagg

Introduction

Our intention in writing this book has been to encourage debate about FASD that shifts attention from the condition as solely an individual disability, towards the structural forces that have created and which perpetuate the phenomenon. In the context of Indigenous peoples in the 'CANZUS' societies, these structural forces were the consequence of a global process which involved the deliberate mass extinguishment of Indigenous sovereignty in what we now call the 'Global South'. It involved mass dispossession, and, in some instances, genocide. This global process of settler colonisation was intended to replace Indigenous people in the soil with a white settler 'stock', as part of an imperialist project undergirded by spurious theories of racial hierarchy and white superiority. A key narrative of this book is that FASD in Indigenous communities needs to be understood within a postcolonial framework. The 'post' prefix does not mean *after* colonialism has ended (it continues in multiple forms), rather it refers to the way colonisation instantiated new global hierarchies and established relationships of domination and subordination between north and south. New perspectives, of which this book forms a part, stress the extent to which the traumas and 'lived adversities' associated with colonisation are passed on to succeeding generations, not just through socialisation but through changes to the methylation and characteristics of DNA, as discussed in Chapter 3. These traumas were then amplified and exacerbated by deliberate government policy, such as forced assimilation of so-called 'half cast' children, and the contemporary 'hyperincarceration' of Indigenous people in prison. We, therefore, argue that we should move beyond the kinds of binary logic that assumes that conditions such as FASD are *either* social *or* genetic; rather we see a complex interplay of factors where the two are mutually constructed

and constructing. There is a need to break down some of the boundaries between disciplines to create not just *multi*-disciplinary approaches but also consider *post*-disciplinary approaches, where
Western sciences (both social and clinical) have to be considered as
just one world view amongst many.

Indigenous social and emotional
well-being is grounded in place and views good health as a product
of harmonious relations within a network of relationships of connections, including individuals, family, kin, land, and community.

Patrick Wolfe (2006) argues that settler colonisation is a process of
ongoing dispossession, not an event. Its impact on Indigenous peoples
has been intense, multi-dimensional, and continuing. Critics claim
that there still exists a 'colonial matrix of power' (Quijano, 2007) that
continues to structurally dispossess parts of the Global South – such as
Indigenous peoples – through the imposition of norms and values that
operate to undermine Indigenous relationality. Splitting up families
by welfare authorities, as discussed in previous chapters, demonstrate
a growing problem in Canada and Australia, reproducing the trauma
of the 'stolen generations' and residential schools eras.

Throughout the book, therefore, we have placed considerable
emphasis on the need for a decolonising practice which encourages
practitioners, researchers, clinicians, and policy-makers to interro-
gate their work, and how they do it, from a decolonising perspective.
This requires, amongst other things, that we challenge the belief that
only Eurocentric knowledge systems hold the answers to complex
human conditions in modern society. In their work on a decolonised
psychology, Dudgeon and Walker (2015, p. 276) maintain that mainstream psychology has contributed to the maintenance of colonial relationships, arguing that:

> The discipline of psychology in Australia has a history of
> domination over Indigenous Australians that is still evident today...
> Psychology colonises both directly through the imposition of uni-
> versalising, individualistic constructions of human behaviour and
> indirectly through the negation of Aboriginal knowledges and
> practices.

This double turn of imposing knowledge systems from above while
negating Aboriginal knowledge as folklore or superstition is a form
of what de Souza Santos (2007) calls 'cognitive injustice', and Spivak
(1996) calls 'epistemic violence.' The outcome, if not always the intent,
of this kind of colonial denialism, is to further damage the fabric

of Indigenous societies and undermine faith in their structures and processes. A decolonising approach acknowledges that Indigenous people's knowledge systems provide a necessary and productive counterweight to Western ways of knowing and being. Indigenous knowledge systems favour collective over individual rights and place emphasis on the importance of maintaining a holistic relationship between people and land.

Decolonising practice supports Indigenous peoples as bearers of sovereignty and recognises their claims to land or country, as the bedrock of their laws and cultures. Decolonising relationships between Indigenous and non-Indigenous people involves accepting Indigenous peoples' rights to practice their own laws and ceremonies, look after traditional lands and determine their own needs and requirements. Indigenous Elders often state that they want a 'seat at the table' when decisions are made about the governance of Indigenous communities (Law Reform Commission of Western Australia, 2006). They also want to see their own law and culture given a role in resolving problems such as family violence, alcohol use, youth crime, and community disorder. Throughout the book, we make reference to a number of innovations in courts that are creating 'hybrid' justice models that, while they remain grounded in Western notions of law, nonetheless engage with Indigenous culture in a respectful and positive manner. These new mechanisms reflect a growing awareness that the colonial system of justice fails to meet the needs of Indigenous offenders. Our adversarial criminal justice system is premised on the belief that offenders enjoy free will and are capable of making choices, understanding the consequences of their actions, and taking individual responsibility. This is patently untrue in relation to people with FASD and other cognitive disorders. A 'just desserts' model that stresses specific and general deterrence, denunciation, incapacitation, and rehabilitation is incompatible with the impairments associated with FASD. A number of innovations are discussed, such as *Gladue* reports in Canada which acknowledge the different circumstances of Indigenous people which flow from colonisation. Specialist courts can play a major role in changing the way the justice system responds to FASD. A non-adversarial approach focussed on identifying the factors that bring vulnerable people into (often repeated) contact with the justice system, and providing a range of supports, are a particularly helpful innovation: ensuring a timely diagnosis at the point of contact with the court – rather than waiting until sentencing – is especially welcome. The lack of screening for FASD in correctional and youth justice systems generally has been highlighted in Chapter 3. It is of great concern that no jurisdiction provides routine comprehensive neurodevelopmental assessments for FASD. This should be a priority. A range of disciplines have acknowledged the need to redress the harms created by colonisation, and the roles their own values, beliefs, and methodologies have played in perpetuating colonial relationships of domination and subordination. Research is not a value free or neutral practice. It is conditioned and actualised on the basis of worldviews and beliefs. Western sciences (social and clinical) have historically claimed universal status as neutral and objective methods, belying inherent bias towards Western ways of living and being as the norm. For many white researchers and practitioners, naming FASD as a legacy of colonisation can cause discomfort and unease – and even anger. It unsettles deeply rooted and taken for granted assumptions about white professionals as having an essentially benevolent and progressive role to play in the lives of Indigenous people.

Demystifying the colonial structures that underpin what we consider to be neutral, scientific procedures is a necessary step in decolonising relationships with Indigenous peoples. As argued in Chapter 8, this is a path 'fraught with discomfort and dis-ease as it challenges many to think differently about their own practices as well as the ongoing impacts of settler colonialism.' As a number of commentators suggest: white people can be fragile when their inherited privileges and their degree of individual and institutional power viz-a-viz non-white people, are brought to their attention.

Stereotypes of Indigenous people inform how white agencies react in micro-encounters with Indigenous people: on the street, in courts and police stations, in clinical settings, in prisons and youth detention centres. As we have suggested at several stages, falling under youth justice legislation does not automatically safeguard Indigenous children's' rights. The increasing criminalisation of Indigenous youth and the correctionalisation of the youth justice system has led to some egregious practices in detention facilities. The 2017 *Royal Commission into the Detention and Protection of Children in the Northern Territory* for example, uncovered widespread torture and abuse of children by guards: video footage of children being chemically gassed, restrained in mechanical chairs and hooded, bashed, and forcibly stripped naked by guards, was shown on national TV. The Royal Commission, found widespread, systemic harm in Northern Territory youth detention centres, inflicted by guards on the children, including girls being forcibly stripped naked, children having their heads smashed against concrete walls and floors and guards displaying sexualised behaviours. It should be born in mind that all the children in the Don Dale Youth

Detention Centre (one of the four youth detention centres visited by the Commission during their inquiry) were of Indigenous descent.

As we have argued throughout this book, correctional workers, care staff and health workers must become FASD aware and able to create regimes that do not inflict further damage on already traumatised children. The Royal Commission recommended (Recommendation 19.1 1) that '[a] case management system be implemented in all youth detention centres: to manage behaviours in a therapeutic non-punitive, non-adversarial, trauma-informed and culturally competent way.' An unknown, but probably high, number of youths in the facility would have FASD, yet there was no consistent screening of detainees for FASD or other cognitive disabilities. The regime at the Don Dale Youth Detention Centre was only possible with the tacit consent of correctional management and government ministers. Indeed, when questioned about the regime, the then, Chief Minister for the Northern Territory, Adam Giles (2017, p. 3280 cited in Blagg & Anthony, 2019) said publicly that if he were Prisons Minister he would dig:

> a big concrete whole and put all the bad criminals in there. Right, you're in the hole, you're not coming out, start learning about it. I might break every United Nations Convention on the rights of the prisoner, but get in the hole.

In opposition to this kind of thinking, we consider it essential that young people in custody are provided with FASD- and trauma-informed care. As outlined in Chapter 6, there needs to be 'structure and routine' and a recognition that FASD is a 'disability requiring life-long supports and the inclusion of the voice of youth in their care plans.' This raises the issue about high quality throughcare, where planning for return to community begins on entry. Families and communities must be partners in this process. The throughcare plan should achieve the mobilisation of key agencies, such as disability services, education, housing, and health, as well as Indigenous community-owned social and emotional health services – who would, ideally, be the lead agency. There is a need for the creation of transitional spaces, such as homes run by Indigenous communities, in between custody and family, catering for young people with weaker family ties, or where family lack the resources to manage them. Funding needs to be found to employ family to provide the 'scaffolding' that will ensure young people with FASD are able to meet commitments (such as parole, bail conditions, achievable community-based orders, undertakings from family conferences, etc.) and ensure they access social and health services. Indigenous 'community navigators' could play an essential role in guiding individuals and families through the complex maze of government organisations responsible for providing social security, pensions, and unemployment benefits. Family and community are best placed to provide culturally secure support which is the cornerstone for rehabilitation and healing from Indigenous trauma.

Stereotyping of Indigenous people as dangerous, inherently criminal, druggies, and alcoholics has led to a number of preventable deaths in police custody in Australia where police have failed to adequately check on the health of Indigenous detainees. This reflects a long-term process of criminalising Indigenous people that began with colonisation, viewing Indigenous men as criminals and Indigenous women as damaged souls in need of discipline and control, and helped legitimise and normalise the European takeover of Indigenous lands.

Too heavy a focus on the weaknesses and limitations of individuals and families with FASD perpetuates the deficit model of intervention and ignores the important role of Indigenous knowledge in creating alternative pathways. This is why we argue for an approach that goes beyond the multi-disciplinary approach and embraces Indigenous communities as partners, indeed *leading* partners, in FASD initiatives and solutions. Having Indigenous people in a leadership role can counter the kinds of collusion that often takes place between white professionals who, while having numerous professional differences, share in the same assumptions and unconscious biases about Indigenous people as dysfunctional, hopeless, and helpless. It also helps achieve a balance between clinical and social pathways to stabilisation. The former can dwell on the habits and deficiencies of individuals and can constitute a form of 'victim blaming' when restricted to questioning Indigenous women on their drinking habits and sexual relationships, without taking account of intergenerational trauma and their personal histories of institutional and family violence. This is not intended to deny the importance of diagnosis and assessment which remain critically important.

FASD is often referred to as an 'invisible' disorder. It has gone unrecognised and unaddressed for decades within the criminal justice system. Throughout the book, we underscored the need for better and more accessible diagnostic services at key points of contact with the criminal justice system, citing a number of cases where judicial officers have criticised children and youth services for not screening children brought before the court for disabilities, including FASD. Early diagnosis is essential and might prevent long term enmeshment in the justice system.

In Chapter 7, we argue that diversion from the criminal justice system at the point of first contact, the police, may help to head off future tragedies if police are trained to recognise possible FASD, or if decisions to prosecute are made by justice workers trained in recognising possible disabilities such as FASD. This would ensure that children were diverted into family conferences tasked with identifying the factors in the child's life that have brought them into contact with the justice system. This is the case in New Zealand under the *Oranga Tamariki Act 1989* (NZ) (also known as the *Children's and Young People's Well-being Act 1989* (NZ) and, we suggest, this could act as a model for youth justice conferencing across CANZUS societies. An assessment for FASD and other disabilities should be an option in youth conferencing. The New Zealand approach is to view Māori culture as a strength rather than a weakness and attempt to promote and nurture family support for children and young people.

Access to diagnostic services, particularly for adults is limited. Further, many adults who have FASD have not had their disability recognised in either the child welfare or youth justice systems and this contributes to the pathway of incarceration as adults. We deem it impossible that young people with FASD are miraculously cured when they reach adult status. We urgently need some initiatives in the adult correctional system to identify the scale of the problem and to then build appropriate diagnostic processes.

Reforms to domestic laws and policies that impact Aboriginal peoples with FASD should be centred around Indigenous 'place' (or 'country'), and support Aboriginal-led knowledge and solutions, community-based services, and provide what we describe as culturally appropriate 'external scaffolding' around Aboriginal youth with FASD and his/her family. As we outline in Chapter 5, 'scaffolding' would include extended family, community, and Aboriginal organisations, all embedded in Aboriginal country.

Where a person who has been found unfit to stand trial is to be held in detention, it must be demonstrated that all reasonable steps have been taken to avoid this outcome, and the person must be held in a place of therapeutic service delivery. In line with Australia's international obligations and the Noble decision, legislative reform is needed in Australian states and territories to abolish indefinite detention for accused persons found unfit to stand trial. Funding is needed to establish places of therapeutic service delivery for those found unfit to stand trial with cognitive impairment; to ensure interventions are needs and strengths based; to support participation in court proceedings so that unfit accused can exercise legal capacity.

As asserted in Chapter 6, mass levels of incarceration do not mean that the settler justice system is somehow 'broken'. The 'hyperincarceration' of Indigenous peoples is no abnormality or unintended consequence (Anthony & Blagg, 2020; Cunneen, Baldry, Brown, Schwartzand, & Steel, 2013), it is the logical outcome of several centuries of policies, laws and practices designed to complete the dispossession of Indigenous people and render Indigenous families dysfunctional. Canadian Yellowknives Dene scholar Coulthard (2014) describes the settler-colonial relationship in terms of 'structured dispossession' intended to secure: 'ongoing state access to the land and resources' (2014, pp. 6–7, italics within). From this perspective, hyperincarceration does not insinuate a 'malfunctioning' system. It suggests that the system in optimally fulfilling its function as a dumping ground for Indigenous people. A decolonising approach would reverse the process of dispossession on a number of levels. As researchers, clinicians, and advocates, we should be arguing for structural change and supporting Indigenous strategies of place-based healing. We need also to be demanding more resources. Funding is needed for programmes with expertise to facilitate expedited assessments and reports of offenders suspected of having FASD, including recommendations for effective management, for courts to consider at unfitness to stand trial determinations. Funding is needed for programmes to enable timely identification, assessment, and diagnosis of offenders with FASD in court. Standardised screening, diagnosis, and individualised support is needed for young people and adults coming into contact with police, legal practitioners, courts, and the justice system with suspected or diagnosed FASD.

References

Anthony, T., & Blagg, H. (2020). "Indigenous hyperincarceration." *Oxford Research Encyclopedia: Criminology and Criminal Justice.*

Blagg, H., & Anthony, T. (2019). *Decolonising criminology: Imagining justice in a post-colonial world.* Palgrave, UK: Critical Criminological Perspectives Series.

Coulthard, G. (2014). *Red skin, white masks: Rejecting the colonial politics of recognition.* Minneapolis, MN: University of Minnesota Press.

Cunneen, C., Baldry, E., Brown, D., Schwartzand, M., & Steel, A. (2013). *Penal culture and hyperincarceration: The revival of the prison.* Farnham, UK: Ashgate.

Dudgeon, P., & Walker, R. (2015). Decolonising Australian psychology: Discourses, strategies, and practice. *Journal of Social and Political Psychology, 3*(1), 276–297.

Law Reform Commission of Western Australia. (2006). *Aboriginal customary laws* (Project 94). Retrieved from https://www.lrc.justice.wa.gov.au/_files/P94_FR.pdf

Northern Territory Royal Commission. (2017). *Report of the royal commission and board of inquiry into the protection and detention of children in the Northern Territory.* Retrieved from https://www.royalcommission.gov.au/royal-commission-detention-and-protection-children-northern-territory

Oranga Tamariki Act 1989 (NZ) or *Children's and Young People's Well-being Act 1989* (NZ), known as *The Children, Young Persons, and Their Families Act 1989* (NZ) prior to 14 July 2017.

Quijano, A. (2007). Coloniality and modernity/rationality. *Cultural Studies, 21*(2–3), 168–178.

Santos, de Sousa, B. (Ed.). (2007). *Cognitive justice in a global world.* London, UK: Oxford University Press.

Spivak, G. C. (1996). *The Spivak reader: Selected works of Gayatri Chakravorty Spivak.* Edited by Landry, D. & MacLean, G. London, UK: Routledge.

Wolfe, P. (2006). Settler Colonialism and the elimination of the native. *Journal of Genocide Research, 8*(4), 387–409.

Index

Note: Page numbers followed by "n" refer to notes.

Northwest Central Alberta FASD
Services Network Clinical
Network 116

O'Connor, M. J. 119
Odds Ratio 64n1
oppression 2, 9, 124, 125, 160, 166
Oranga Tamariki Act 1989 143,
144, 178

PAE *see* prenatal alcohol exposure
(PAE)
Palmater, P. 164
Parmenter, N. 112
Parmenter, T. 119
'parsimony' principle 143
Payne, J. 24
Pei, J. R. 127
Pelech, W. 124
Peled, M. 25, 121
person-to-person support 30
Poole, N. 26–27
post-traumatic stress disorder
(PTSD) 25, 63; *see also* trauma
prenatal alcohol exposure (PAE)
19, 31, 118; diagnosis of 55, 56;
dysmorphic facial features of 20;
memory impairment and 60–61
prevalence 1, 3, 11, 21, 33, 43–51,
112, 113, 115, 164
Prevention Conversation 123
A profile of BC youth in custody 119
prospective memory 60
PTSD *see* post-traumatic stress
disorder (PTSD)
punishment 26, 28, 32, 50, 55, 98, 99
punitive justice 135–137

rational choice theories 137
Razack, S. 158
recidivism 29, 46
reconciliation 160–162
Regan, P. 158
rehabilitation 29, 48, 88, 89, 99, 103,
108, 128, 174, 177
Reid, N. 117
relational scaffolding 142, 146
Residential School programme
161, 162
restorative justice 103, 138–142, 156

resurgent authoritarianism 2
retrospective memory 60
Richards, K. 139
Riches, V. 119
Roquette, J. 18
Rotumah, D. 112
Royal Commission into Aboriginal
Deaths in Custody in Australia
(1991) 142
Royal Commission into the
Detention and Protection of
Children in the Northern Territory
111, 175, 176
Rudd, K. 160–161
Russell, S. 23
Russell Family Fetal Alcohol
Disorders Association 145

Said, E. 5
Salmon, A. 121
Samaroden, M. 121
Santos, B. de Sousa 173
scaffolding 102, 141, 176;
community-based 107–108;
external 5, 101, 178; relational 142,
146; *see also* circle of care
Schmidt, R. A. 26–27
selective attention 61
self-harm 25, 44, 46
Senate Standing Committees on
Community Affairs 86
sentencing 2, 10, 11, 21, 27, 81, 87,
92, 97–108, 126, 174; challenges
of 97–99; community-based
100–103; dispositions 88;
innovative courtroom policy and
practice 105–106; judicial and legal
practitioner education 103–105;
necessary community-based
scaffolding 107–108; responses
22; specialist courts 106–107;
therapeutic options 100–103
service delivery 120–121
settler colonialism 2, 4–8, 11, 113, 136,
137, 154–168, 172, 173, 175, 179
Smith, D. 19
Smith, L. T. 6
social communication 56, 63–64
social skills 63–64
societal lack of knowledge 116–117

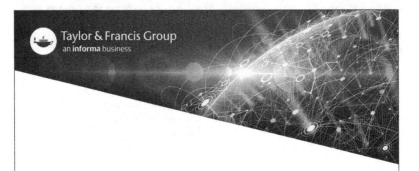

Printed in the United States
by Baker & Taylor Publisher Services